Building Resilience

Praise for this book

'The Global WASH Cluster welcomes this handbook as a critical and timely resource that strengthens coordinated action across WASH, health, and nutrition actors in humanitarian crises. Its clear guidance and operational tool provides invaluable support for the humanitarian practitioners, government officials, and development partners to deliver more integrated, accountable, and resilience focused services to communities facing increasingly complex emergencies and humanitarian crises.'

Monica Ramos, Global WASH Cluster Coordinator, UNICEF

Building Resilience

Coordination guidelines for integrated WASH, health, and nutrition programming in crisis settings

Nikolas Sorensen
Mariëlle Snel
James Ray III
Syed Yasir Ahmad Khan

Practical Action Publishing Ltd
25 Albert Street, Rugby,
Warwickshire, CV21 2SD, UK
www.practicalactionpublishing.com

A catalogue record for this book is available from the British Library & Library of Congress

ISBN 978-1-78853-470-3 Paperback
ISBN 978-1-78853-471-0 Digital book

Citation: Sorensen, N., Snel, M., Ray III, J., and Khan, S.Y.A. (2026) *Building Resilience: Coordination Briefs for Integrated WASH, Health, and Nutrition Programming in Crisis Settings*, Rugby, UK: Practical Action Publishing https://doi.org/10.3362/9781788534710

Since 1974, Practical Action Publishing has published and disseminated books and information in support of international development work throughout the world. All print editions are produced and distributed via ethical and sustainable print on demand global facilities.

Practical Action Publishing is a trading name of Practical Action Publishing Ltd (Company Reg. No. 01159018 | VAT 880 9924 76). All profits are covenanted back to its parent group, Practical Action (Charity Reg. No. 247257).

Cover design by: Katarzyna Markowska, Practical Action Publishing
Typesetting by: vPrompt eServices, India

The manufacturer's authorised representative in the EU for product safety is Lightning Source France, 1 Av. Johannes Gutenberg, 78310 Maurepas, France. compliance@lightningsource.fr

Contents

Case studies vii
List of figures ix
Acknowledgements xi
Acronyms xiii
Glossary xv
Foundational principles for integrated WASH programming xix
Executive summary xxiii
Quick start guide for emergency actors xxix

1. Integration by design: Coordination guidelines for resilient WASH programming in humanitarian contexts 1
    Introduction 1
    Understanding CCP pressures 4
    Barriers to intersectoral collaboration 10
    Enablers for intersectoral collaboration 13
    Measurement and indicators 14
    Conclusion 18
    Notes 20
    Bibliography 21

2. Integration in emergencies: Guideline for coordinating WASH with health at the national level 27
    2.1 Summary 27
    2.2 Stakeholder coordination 30
    2.3 Emergency WASH actions 39
    2.4 Monitoring 50

3. Integration in emergencies: Guideline for coordinating WASH with nutrition at the national level 57
    3.1 Summary 57
    3.2 Stakeholder coordination 60
    3.3 Emergency WASH actions 68
    3.4 Monitoring 76

4. Integration in emergencies: Guideline for coordinating WASH with health at the community level 81
   - 4.1 Summary 81
   - 4.2 Stakeholder coordination 84
   - 4.3 Emergency WASH actions 95
   - 4.4 Monitoring 107

5. Integration in emergencies: Guideline for coordinating WASH with nutrition at the community level 113
   - 5.1 Summary 113
   - 5.2 Stakeholder coordination 116
   - 5.3 Emergency WASH actions 126
   - 5.4 Monitoring 139

6. Transforming WASH response: Toward integration, localization, and sustainability 145
   - Current WASH trends and future directions 146
   - Building local resilience and ownership 147
   - Financing innovation and governance reform 150
   - Leveraging artificial intelligence to reduce dependency 151
   - Diverse role of WASH professionals moving forward 152
   - Conclusion: From crisis response to sustainable transformation 153
   - Bibliography 153

Annex 1: Practitioners' Toolkit for Integrated WASH in Emergencies 157
   - Summary 157
   - Sections 159

Annex 2: Addressing conflict, COVID-19, and climate change: A multisectoral approach to integrated WASH programming 223

Annex 3: Sources consulted in the creation of the guidelines 225

Annex 4: Case study references 229

Index 231

Case studies

Chapter 1

1.1 Myanmar: WASH and nutrition-health integration in IDP camps 8
1.2 Nigeria: Cross-sectoral WASH integration in conflict zones 12
1.3 Bangladesh: User-centred WASH monitoring in refugee Settlements 17

Chapter 2

2.1 Afghanistan: Integrating emergency response with groundwater sustainability 42
2.2 Yemen: Evidence-based water management in conflict zones 52

Chapter 3

3.1 Nigeria: Integrating WASH with maternal and child nutrition 71
3.2 Yemen: Solar-powered water infrastructure for nutrition security 75

Chapter 4

4.1 Syria: Child-centred hygiene promotion during COVID-19 86
4.2 Nigeria: Community-led WASH management in nutrition centres 100
4.3 West Bank: Portable wastewater treatment for healthcare settings 104
4.4 Iraq: Solar-powered WASH solutions in critical public facilities 107

Chapter 5

5.1 Syria: Integrating WASH with shelter for nutritional well-being 130
5.2 Iraq: Community-driven WASH in conflict-affected schools 132
5.3 Jordan: Refugee-led environmental health for nutrition security 137

List of figures

Figure I.1	Four key domains of WASH guidelines. These interconnected domains provide a comprehensive framework for designing, implementing, and evaluating integrated WASH responses.	xxiv
Figure 1.1	Deficit vs. strengths-based approaches to WASH programming. A strengths-based approach recognizes and builds upon local capabilities, creating sustainable WASH solutions that foster community resilience and ownership in CCP contexts.	6
Figure 1.2	Humanitarian–development–peace nexus flow. Effective guidelines create pathways to navigate the challenging transitions between immediate humanitarian response and sustainable development while building peace and resilience to future CCP shocks.	7
Figure 1.3	Traditional vs. integrated WASH response across crisis phases. Integrated WASH programming creates continuous pathways from crisis to development by leveraging multisectoral approaches and local strengths at each phase.	10
Figure 1.4	Overcoming barriers to effective WASH coordination. Effective guidelines transform barriers into enablers by providing clear pathways for intersectoral collaboration in complex humanitarian contexts.	11
Figure 1.5	Guidelines for integrated WASH with health and nutrition.	19
Figure 2.1	Guideline for coordinating WASH with health at the national level: Multi-stakeholder coordination wheel with seven segments.	31
Figure 3.1	Guideline for coordinating WASH with health at the national level: Multi-stakeholder coordination wheel with seven segments.	61
Figure 4.1	Guideline for coordinating WASH with health at the national level: Multi-stakeholder coordination wheel with seven segments.	86
Figure 5.1	Guideline for coordinating WASH with health at the national level: Multi-stakeholder coordination wheel with seven segments.	118

Acknowledgements

We extend our sincere thanks to the incredible team at The WASH Road Map for making this work possible. We are also deeply grateful to the generous reviewers whose timely and thoughtful feedback significantly strengthened the final draft, including Bruce Gordon, Linda Doull, and Margaret Montgomery (WHO); Omar El Hattab, Sacha Greenberg, and Jamel Shah (UNICEF); Farah Al-Basha (IFRC); Jill John-Kall and Suzanne Brinkmann, with the International Medical Corps (IMC); and Nasr Mustafa with Save the Children International.

Acronyms

AAR	after action review
ACF	Action Against Hunger
AI	artificial intelligence
CCP	climate, conflict, and pandemics
CQI	collaborative quality improvement
GWC	Global WASH Cluster
IDP	internally displaced person
IFRC	International Federation of Red Cross and Red Crescent Societies
IOM	International Organization for Migration
IPC	infection prevention and control
IPC	integrated phase classification
ISC	intersectoral collaboration
IYCF	infant and young child feeding
JMP	Joint Monitoring Programme
M&E	monitoring and evaluation
MEAL	monitoring, evaluation, accountability, and learning
MHM	menstrual hygiene management
MIRA	multi-sector initial rapid assessment
MOH	Ministry of Health
MOU	memorandum of understanding
MUAC	mid-upper arm circumference
NGO	non-governmental organization
OECD	Organisation for Economic Co-operation and Development
OFDA	Office of U.S. Foreign Disaster Assistance
ORT	oral rehydration therapy
PDSA	plan-do-study-act
PHAST	participatory hygiene and sanitation transformation
PLW	pregnant and lactating women
PSEAH	protection from sexual exploitation, abuse, and harassment
PWDs	persons with disabilities
SAG	Strategic Advisory Group
SDG	Sustainable Development Goal

SMART	Standardized Monitoring and Assessment of Relief and Transitions
TOR	terms of reference
UN	United Nations
UNHCR	United Nations High Commissioner for Refugees
UNICEF	United Nations Children's Fund
WASH	water, sanitation, and hygiene
WASH FIT	water and sanitation for health facility improvement tool
WASH-IPC	WASH infection prevention and control
WHO	World Health Organization

Glossary

Accountability The obligation of WASH actors to take responsibility for their actions, be transparent about their decisions and performance, and be answerable to affected communities and other stakeholders.

After action review (AAR) A structured debrief process used to reflect on completed project phases or critical events to identify strengths, weaknesses, and lessons learned for future improvement.

Behaviour change The process of influencing individuals, households, and communities to adopt and sustain positive practices related to water, sanitation, and hygiene.

Capacity building The process of strengthening the skills, knowledge, and resources of individuals, organizations, and systems to enhance their ability to plan, implement, and maintain WASH services.

Climate, conflict, and pandemics (CCP) The three major pressures that exacerbate humanitarian crises and strain WASH services.

Collaborative quality improvement (CQI) A team-based problem-solving methodology that uses systematic testing and scaling of service delivery changes through Plan-Do-Study-Act (PDSA) cycles to improve WASH programme effectiveness.

Community engagement The process of involving affected communities in the design, implementation, and monitoring of WASH interventions to ensure that they are relevant, acceptable, and sustainable.

Community-led total sanitation (CLTS) A participatory approach that mobilizes communities to eliminate open defecation and promote the construction and use of latrines, without relying on external subsidies or hardware support.

Community level The coordination and implementation sphere involving local community members, community-based organizations, village committees, traditional leaders, local health workers, community volunteers, and beneficiary representatives who participate directly in the design, implementation, and monitoring of WASH interventions at the grassroots level.

Conflict-sensitive programming An approach that analyses and addresses the impact of conflict on WASH interventions while ensuring that programming does not inadvertently contribute to or exacerbate tensions.

Coordination guideline(s) A set of practical, step-by-step recommendations designed to support integrated WASH coordination across sectors and levels during emergency response. Refer specifically to the coordination steps outlined in Chapters 2–5 in this book (also referred to as guideline(s)).

Coordination mechanisms The structures, processes, and tools used to facilitate communication, information sharing, and joint decision-making among different actors involved in WASH response.

Emergency actions The immediate life-saving WASH interventions implemented during the first 0–14 days of a humanitarian response to address critical public health risks and prevent disease outbreaks.

Environmental enteropathy A chronic inflammatory condition of the small intestine associated with poor sanitation and hygiene conditions that impairs nutrient absorption and contributes to malnutrition and stunting.

Humanitarian-development-peace nexus The conceptual link between short-term emergency relief and longer-term development goals, emphasizing sustainability and resilience.

Humanitarian response The immediate actions taken to save lives, alleviate suffering, and maintain human dignity in the aftermath of a crisis or emergency.

Integrated programming An approach that seeks to address multiple interconnected needs and challenges by bringing together different sectors, disciplines, and stakeholders to design and implement coordinated interventions.

Intersectoral coordination (ISC) The process of facilitating collaboration, communication, and joint planning between different sectors, such as WASH, health, and nutrition, to address complex challenges more effectively.

Localization The process of shifting decision-making power, resources, and responsibility to local actors, with the aim of creating more context-specific, sustainable, and locally owned solutions.

Monitoring and evaluation (M&E) The systematic process of collecting, analysing, and using data to track progress, assess impact, and inform decision-making in WASH programmes.

Multi-stakeholder platform A forum or space that brings together diverse stakeholders, such as government agencies, NGOs, community representatives, and private sector actors, to discuss, plan, and collaborate on WASH issues.

National level The coordination and implementation sphere involving central government ministries, national humanitarian agencies, UN organizations, international NGOs, and other national-level stakeholders responsible for strategic planning, policy development, resource allocation, and oversight of integrated WASH programming across subnational jurisdictions.

Nutrition-sensitive WASH An approach that seeks to maximize the impact of WASH interventions on nutritional outcomes by addressing the underlying causes of malnutrition, such as poor hygiene practices and environmental enteropathy.

Participatory hygiene and sanitation transformation (PHAST) A participatory methodology that engages communities in analysing their sanitation and hygiene situation and developing appropriate solutions through interactive learning approaches.

Private sector partnerships Collaborative arrangements between humanitarian and development organizations and private sector actors, including for-profit businesses, corporations, philanthropic foundations, and private donors, to leverage resources, expertise, and innovation for improved WASH service delivery. These partnerships may involve financial contributions, technical expertise, supply chain support, infrastructure development, or capacity building to enhance the reach, quality, and sustainability of WASH interventions.

Quality improvement Systematic efforts to enhance the effectiveness, safety, and reliability of WASH services through data-driven analysis, testing of improvements, and standardization of effective practices.

Resilience The capacity of communities and systems to anticipate, absorb, adapt to, and recover from shocks and stresses, such as those caused by climate change, conflict, and pandemics.

Resilience actions The medium-term interventions implemented during days 14–90 of a humanitarian response that focus on strengthening systems, building local capacity, and creating sustainable solutions for long-term resilience.

Social accountability Mechanisms and processes that enable communities to hold service providers and implementing organizations accountable for the quality, equity, and sustainability of WASH interventions.

Strengths-based approach A methodology that prioritizes identifying and building upon existing community assets, capabilities, and leadership rather than focusing primarily on deficits. This approach empowers local stakeholders to determine their priorities and mobilize both internal and external resources accordingly, fostering sustainable solutions through local agency and ownership, particularly in contexts of reduced international assistance.

Sustainability The ability of WASH services and systems to continue functioning and providing benefits over the long term, without compromising the needs of future generations.

Water, sanitation, and hygiene (WASH) The collective term for interventions, services, and facilities that improve access to safe water, adequate sanitation, and good hygiene practices.

Foundational principles for integrated WASH programming

The following guiding principles translate the understanding of climate, conflict, and pandemics (CCP) pressures and the integrated approach outlined in Chapter 1 into actionable standards for implementation. These principles apply across all four coordination guidelines and should guide decision-making throughout the emergency response cycle. They represent the essential commitments that underpin effective WASH programming in humanitarian contexts.

1. Humanitarian imperative and do no harm

Prioritize life-saving WASH interventions that prevent disease outbreaks, reduce mortality, and address malnutrition while aligning with national humanitarian priorities. Ensure assistance is impartial, reaches the most vulnerable populations (including women, children, elderly, people with disabilities, and marginalized communities), and promotes dignity without causing unintended harm. Analyse and mitigate potential negative consequences while maintaining clear accountability mechanisms.

2. Integrated multisectoral coordination

Establish and lead coordination platforms that bring together WASH, health, nutrition, education, food security, and other relevant sectors for collaborative planning and implementation. Adopt a 'Health in All Policies' approach that systematically addresses social, economic, and environmental determinants. Promote policy coherence, joint planning, and resource optimization while ensuring regular communication and information sharing among all stakeholders at both national and community levels.

3. Community engagement, inclusivity, and empowerment

Position communities as co-developers and key partners across all aspects of WASH programming, from assessment to implementation and monitoring. Ensure participatory decision-making that actively includes women, youth, people with disabilities, and marginalized groups. Build on existing community structures, knowledge, and coping strategies while establishing accessible feedback mechanisms and promoting social accountability initiatives.

4. Capacity strengthening and sustainable resilience

Strengthen institutional capacity at all levels through ongoing mentorship, peer learning, and systems strengthening beyond one-off training. Partner with local actors to build technical, managerial, and institutional capacity for sustainable service delivery. Design climate-resilient WASH systems and invest in emergency preparedness while progressively shifting ownership and decision-making to local structures.

5. Evidence-based, adaptive programming

Establish robust systems for collecting, analysing, and using disaggregated data to guide decision-making and enable adaptive management. Develop context-specific strategies that adapt global standards (including Sphere standards) to local realities. Create participatory monitoring systems that track integrated outcomes across sectors and foster continuous learning and improvement.

6. Systems strengthening and service integration

Implement WASH interventions within broader health and nutrition systems strengthening frameworks. Ensure WASH activities align with public health priorities, surveillance systems, and nutrition objectives. Focus on comprehensive packages of interventions that address multiple determinants of health and well-being, using simple, low-cost solutions that leverage existing resources.

7. Political commitment and sustainable financing

Secure high-level political commitment for integrated WASH programming across government ministries and donor agencies. Advocate for prioritization of WASH in health, nutrition, and development policies, strategies, and budgets. Establish clear institutional roles, responsibilities, and accountability mechanisms while mobilizing resources for infrastructure, services, and personnel at all levels.

8. Disaster preparedness and climate adaptation

Integrate disaster risk reduction, emergency preparedness, and climate resilience into all WASH planning and implementation. Develop multi-hazard contingency plans, strengthen early warning systems, and promote climate-adaptive technologies. Build local capacity to anticipate, mitigate, and respond to future shocks while maintaining agile coordination mechanisms that can adapt to evolving needs.

Executive summary

This comprehensive guide provides practical resources for integrating water, sanitation, and hygiene (WASH) interventions with health and nutrition actions during humanitarian emergencies. It offers a structured framework for coordinated, multisectoral response at both national and community levels faced by the compounding pressures of climate, conflict, and pandemic.

The guide addresses a critical need for greater coordination and integration in humanitarian contexts, particularly in light of shifting global funding landscapes, including significant reductions in international assistance. It serves as an actionable resource prioritizing government leadership at all levels, supporting national and local government officials, ministry staff, and public sector institutions alongside international, regional, and community WASH, health, and nutrition professionals. The guidelines specifically emphasize strengthening government systems and capacities as the foundation for sustainable emergency response in the context of reduced international assistance. These guidelines are particularly effective in resource-constrained environments, offering practical pathways for coordination and integration even when international funding is limited.

Components and structure

This book comprises five interconnected components built around the four coordination guidelines (Chapters 2–5) and the Practitioners' Toolkit (Annex 1):

- Chapter 1: Integration by design: Coordination guidelines for resilient WASH programming in humanitarian contexts
- Chapter 2: Integration in emergencies: Guideline for coordinating WASH with health at the national level
- Chapter 3: Integration in emergencies: Guideline for coordinating WASH with nutrition at the national level
- Chapter 4: Integration in emergencies: Guideline for coordinating WASH with health at the community level
- Chapter 5: Integration in emergencies: Guideline for coordinating WASH with nutrition at the community level
- Chapter 6: Transforming WASH response: Toward integration, localization, and sustainability
- Annex 1: Practitioners' Toolkit for Integrated WASH in Emergencies

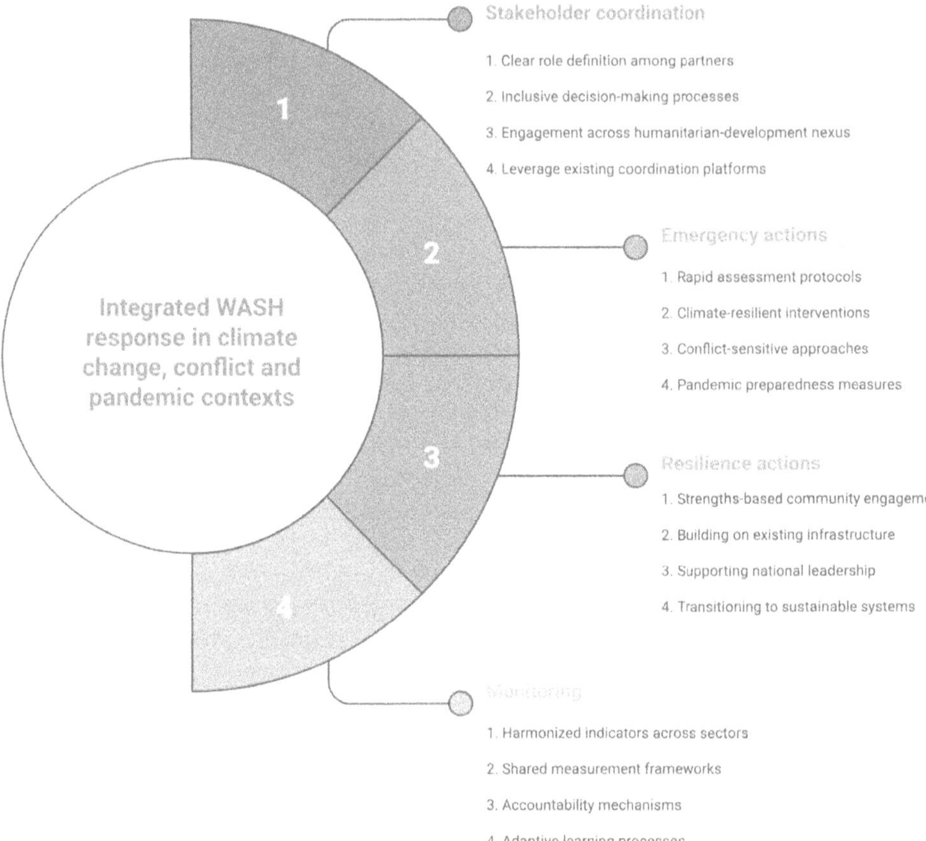

Figure I.1 Four key domains of WASH guidelines. These interconnected domains provide a comprehensive framework for designing, implementing, and evaluating integrated WASH responses.
Note: CCP, climate, conflict, and pandemics

The content is structured around four interdependent domains as illustrated in Figure I.1:

- Stakeholder coordination
- Emergency WASH actions
- Resilience actions
- Monitoring and evaluation

Each section combines strategic framing with operational tools to guide assessment, planning, and implementation of WASH interventions responsive to complex crisis dynamics.

Purpose and value

These coordination guidelines aim to optimize the effectiveness, coverage, and sustainability of emergency WASH services by strategically linking them with health and nutrition outcomes. The guidelines provide a common platform for humanitarian actors to jointly plan, implement, and monitor interventions that bolster public health, reduce malnutrition, and build resilient systems.

Shifts in global aid architecture, including the retreat of major donors and a sharp decline in international funding, have ushered in a new reality that demands careful consideration in the formulation of revised coordination guidelines. This global trend toward reduced international assistance means that humanitarian actors will increasingly focus on acute emergency responses, leaving long-term development and systems strengthening to be addressed more through domestic resources and national government leadership.

These guidelines acknowledge that sustainable WASH services ultimately depend on effective government leadership and robust systems. With the significant reduction in international humanitarian assistance, national and local governments must take the lead in coordinating and delivering WASH services. This document provides specific guidance on how to strengthen government capacities, integrate with existing public sector systems, and ensure that emergency responses build rather than bypass government institutions.

This practitioner-oriented guide fills a critical gap in the existing humanitarian coordination architecture by providing concrete protocols and tools to bridge WASH, health, and nutrition interventions. It equips decision-makers and implementers to:

- assess multi-dimensional risks and plan joint interventions
- optimize synergies between health, nutrition, and WASH programmes
- align short-term emergency activities with long-term development goals
- engage communities as central drivers of the response
- adapt global standards to local realities and capacities
- strengthen accountability for holistic, sustainable, people-centred impacts

The guidelines focus specifically on the national and community levels, recognizing that these are the key entry points for fostering local ownership, strengthening existing systems, and ensuring the relevance and sustainability of interventions. While subnational and district-level coordination are important, the guidelines prioritize direct engagement with national authorities and community structures to drive change from both the top-down and bottom-up.

This document is important for anyone involved in humanitarian WASH, health, or nutrition programming, as it provides a roadmap for delivering integrated, localized services in the face of increasing operational constraints. The guidelines are designed to be practical and modular, allowing practitioners to quickly access the specific guidance and tools they need.

The first chapter provides a comprehensive overview of the conceptual framework, evidence base, and rationale underpinning the integrated, localized approach. While this section is important for contextualizing the guidelines, practitioners may choose to skip directly to the operational guidance and tools based on their specific needs and interests.

The primary audience for this document includes WASH, health, and nutrition programme managers, coordinators, and advisers across humanitarian and development organizations, as well as national and local government officials responsible for emergency preparedness and response. Field-level practitioners, such as public health officers, community mobilizers, and frontline service providers, will also benefit from the concrete guidance and tools for operationalizing integrated approaches.

By providing a clear framework and practical resources for bridging sectoral divides, strengthening local capacities, and ensuring the continuity of essential services, these guidelines serve as a crucial tool for navigating the new humanitarian landscape and ultimately enhancing the health, dignity, and resilience of crisis-affected communities.

Framework and approach

These guidelines are grounded in a climate, conflict, and pandemics (CCP) perspective that highlights the unique and intersecting challenges that these crises pose for WASH services and the communities that depend on them.

The document identifies common barriers to effective integration, such as fragmented leadership, siloed funding streams, and inconsistent measurement approaches. Importantly, it also highlights proven enablers for overcoming these hurdles, including leveraging existing infrastructure, engaging communities as partners, nurturing multisectoral champions, and harmonizing indicators.

Audience and application

This guide is intended for a wide range of humanitarian practitioners engaged in WASH, health, and nutrition preparedness and response, including:

- government officials in relevant line ministries
- WASH, health, and nutrition cluster/sector coordinators
- UN agency emergency focal points
- NGO programme managers and technical advisers
- frontline service providers in health, nutrition, and WASH
- community-based organizations and volunteer networks

The Coordination Guidelines, and Practitioners' Toolkit provide a flexible roadmap that can be applied across the humanitarian programme cycle:

- *Preparedness*: Adapt the tools and coordination mechanisms to emergency-prone contexts as part of contingency planning and capacity building.
- *Response*: Follow the guidelines to rapidly activate and sustain coordinated WASH services from the acute emergency phase through to early recovery.
- *Recovery*: Continue applying the guidance to facilitate a smooth transition to sustainable, locally managed WASH and health-nutrition systems.

Adaptability

While grounded in global evidence and standards, the Coordination Guidelines and Practitioners' Toolkit are designed to adapt to diverse country contexts and emergency situations. The guidance can be tailored to align with existing policies, capacities, and cultural norms at national and subnational levels. The components reinforce each other but can also be applied individually based on the specific coordination needs of each context.

Call to action

This document issues a call to action for transforming WASH in the shifting humanitarian landscape. By bridging sectors, prioritizing local leadership, and innovating with approaches, we have an opportunity to reimagine business as usual and secure the foundations for a more water-secure, sanitation-served, and hygiene-healthy future for crisis-affected communities.

Unlocking the potential of integrated, localized action will require bold changes from all stakeholders. Donors and humanitarian agencies must rethink rigid funding and coordination models. Governments and service authorities must position WASH as a foundation for resilient public health and development outcomes. This requires moving beyond a transactional view of the private sector as merely a supplier of services and toward a model in which private actors are held accountable for advancing equity, ethics, and social outcomes. It means reorienting investment strategies to prioritize long-term impact over short-term returns, fostering new forms of partnerships that value community knowledge as much as technical expertise, and integrating flexibility and transparency into business models. In this moment of contraction and realignment, the private sector must evolve not only in function but in purpose, becoming part of a broader transformation that reclaims WASH as a public good grounded in dignity, justice, and shared responsibility.

This guidance aims to catalyse a paradigm shift toward a more cohesive, localized, and preventive approach to combating WASH-related disease and malnutrition in emergencies. By working collaboratively across sectors and empowering national and community actors, we can build resilience to future shocks and accelerate progress toward the Sustainable Development Goals, even in the most challenging humanitarian contexts. This means embracing integrated approaches that address root causes rather than symptoms, building upon existing community strengths rather than importing external solutions, and creating sustainable systems from day one rather than transitioning from relief to development. As the sector navigates this fundamental transformation, these coordination guidelines serve as both a practical guide and a vision for building inclusive, adaptive, and sustainable WASH solutions that are rooted in community leadership and long-term impact.

Quick start guide for emergency actors

What's different in this approach?

Key innovations for resource-constrained settings:

Strengths-based assessment: Start by mapping community assets and capacities, not just deficits.

Integrated coordination: Single platform for WASH/Health/Nutrition instead of separate clusters.

Community leadership: Local actors lead from Day 1, not after 'capacity building'.

Flexible programming: Adapt global standards to local realities rather than rigid adherence.

Sustainable from start: Build local management into emergency response, not as afterthought.

Critical actions for integrated WASH response

Immediate action (0–48 hours)	*Assessment and planning (days 1–14)*
1. **Activate coordination** a. National guidelines 2.1 b. Toolkit 1.1, 1.2 2. **Convene stakeholders** a. All guidelines 2.2 b. Toolkit 1.5, 1.6 3. **Establish structures** a. Community guidelines 2.1 b. Toolkit 4.8	1. **Conduct assessments** a. All guidelines 3.1.1 b. Toolkit 2.1, 2.2, 2.3 2. **Provide emergency services** a. National health guideline 3.1.2, 3.1.3, 3.1.4 b. Community nutrition guideline 3.1.2 3. **Integrate programmes** a. National nutrition guideline 3.1.3 b. Toolkit 4.3, 4.4
Systems establishment (days 14–30)	*Resilience building (days 30–90)*
1. **Set up monitoring** a. All guidelines section 4 b. Toolkit 5.1, 5.3 2. **Build feedback systems** a. Community guidelines 2.5 b. Toolkit 5.3 3. **Develop joint plans** a. National guidelines 2.4 b. Toolkit 3.1, 3.7	1. **Strengthen capacity** a. All guidelines 3.2.1, 3.2.2 b. Toolkit 3.4, 4,2 2. **Develop sustainability** a. Community health guideline 3.2.3 b. Community nutrition guideline 3.2.2 3. **Document learning** a. All guidelines 3.2.5, 3.2.6 b. Toolkit 5.5

Note: The section numbers provided in these tables refer to 'national guidelines' (Chapters 2 and 3), 'community guidelines' (Chapters 4 and 5), and 'all guidelines' (Chapters 2–5). Toolkit sections are found in Annex 1.

Immediate actions (0–48 hours)

Priority action	*Traditional approach*	*Integrated approach*	*Who leads*	*Details found in*
1. Activate coordination	• Separate WASH cluster • Separate health cluster • Separate nutrition cluster	• Single integrated platform • Joint WASH/Health/ Nutrition leadership • Unified decision-making	Government + WASH cluster/ health cluster	• National guidelines Section 2.1 • Toolkit 1.1, 1.2
2. Convene stakeholders	• Sector-specific meetings • International agency focus	• Multisector meeting • Community leaders as co-chairs • Local actors in leadership roles	Platform co-chairs	• All guidelines Section 2.2 • Toolkit 1.5, 1.6
3. Establish structures	• Top-down task forces • Technical focus only	• Community committees included • Technical + local knowledge • Clear accountability to communities	Local authority + Partners	• Community guidelines 2.1 • Toolkit 4.8

Assessment and planning (days 1–14)

Priority action	*Traditional approach*	*Integrated approach*	*Who leads*	*Details found in*
4. Conduct assessments	• Separate sectoral assessments • Focus on gaps/ needs • External assessment teams	• Joint WASH/Health/ Nutrition assessment • Map capacities *and* needs • Community-led data collection	Assessment teams + Communities	• All guidelines 3.1.1 • Toolkit 2.1, 2.2, 2.3
5. Provide emergency services	• Blanket distributions • Standard packages • Agency-led delivery	• Target vulnerable households • Adapt to local context • Community-managed distribution	WASH sector + Communities	• National health 3.1.2-3.1.4 • Community nutrition 3.1.2
6. Integrate programmes	• Parallel service delivery • Missed opportunities	• WASH in all health/ nutrition sites • Joint hygiene promotion • Unified messaging	All sectors	• National nutrition 3.1.3 • Toolkit 4.3, 4.4

Establishing systems (days 14–30)

Priority action	*Traditional approach*	*Integrated approach*	*Who leads*	*Details found in*
7. Set up monitoring	• Separate indicators • Agency reporting • Output focus	• Common indicators • Community scorecards • Outcome tracking	M&E teams + Communities	• All guidelines Section 4 • Toolkit 5.1, 5.3
8. Build feedback systems	• Complaints boxes • One-way communication	• Multiple channels • Two-way dialogue • Rapid response to feedback	Community committees	• Community guidelines 2.5 • Toolkit 5.3
9. Develop joint plans	• Sector-specific plans • Short-term focus	• Integrated action plans • Link emergency to development • Community priorities central	Platform + Communities	• National guidelines 2.4 • Toolkit 3.1, 3.7

Building resilience (days 30–90)

Priority action	*Traditional approach*	*Integrated approach*	*Who leads*	*Details found in*
10. Strengthen capacity	• One-off trainings • Focus on technicians • External trainers	• Continuous mentoring • Whole community approach • Peer-to-peer learning	Local institutions	• All guidelines 3.2.1-3.2.2 • Toolkit 3.4, 4.2
11. Develop sustainability	• Plan exit strategy • Handover at end • Donor dependent	• Build from Day 1 • Local market solutions • Multiple funding sources	Communities + Government	• Community health 3.2.3 • Community nutrition 3.2.2
12. Document learning	• External evaluation • Top-down lessons	• Community-led review • Continuous adaptation • Share innovations	All stakeholders	• All guidelines 3.2.5-3.2.6 • Toolkit 5.5

Decision support: What to prioritize when

With minimal resources (must do):

Action	*Target*	*Timeframe*	*Quick reference*
Integrated coordination	All levels	48 hours	All guidelines 2.1
Joint assessment	High-risk areas	Days 1–5	All guidelines 3.1.1

(*Continues*)

(Continued)

Action	*Target*	*Timeframe*	*Quick reference*
Safe water (15 L/day)	All populations	Days 1–14	All guidelines 3.1.2
Sanitation near water	Disease hotspots	Days 1–14	National guidelines 3.1.3 Community health 3.1.3 Community nutrition 3.1.2
Handwashing promotion	Vulnerable groups	Days 1–14	National health 3.1.4 Community guidelines 3.1.3
Community feedback	All sites	By Day 14	National guidelines 2.5 Community guidelines 2.8

With moderate resources (should do):

Action	*Target*	*Timeframe*	*Quick reference*
WASH in health facilities	Priority facilities	Days 7–30	National guidelines 3.1.6 Community guidelines 3.1.2, 3.1.5
Nutrition site WASH	All OTP: Outpatient Therapeutic Programme/ SFP: Supplementary Feeding Programme sites	Days 7–30	Nutrition guidelines 3.1.3
Local capacity building	WASH committees	Days 14–60	All guidelines Section 3.2.1
Market development	Urban/peri-urban	Days 30–90	Community guidelines 3.2.2
Integrated monitoring	All programmes	Day 30 onwards	All guidelines Section 4

With adequate resources (could do):

Action	*Target*	*Timeframe*	*Quick reference*
Climate-resilient infrastructure	All systems	Days 30–90	National guidelines 3.2.3 Community health 3.2.4 Community nutrition 3.2.1
Government system strengthening	National/District	Days 30–90	National health guideline 2.4, 3.2.1 National nutrition guideline 2.7, 3.2.1
Policy integration	National level	Days 45–90	National guidelines 2.5
Comprehensive M&E	All interventions	Throughout	All guidelines Section 4

Where to find detailed guidance

If you need to …	*Refer to:*
Set up coordination mechanisms	National guidelines Section 2, Toolkit Sections 1.1–1.7
Conduct integrated assessments	All guidelines Section 3.1.1, Toolkit Sections 2.1–2.6
Plan integrated responses	National guidelines Section 2.4, Toolkit Sections 3.1–3.7
Implement WASH interventions	All guidelines Section 3, Toolkit Sections 4.1–4.10
Monitor and adapt	All guidelines Section 4, Toolkit Sections 5.1–5.6
Engage communities	Community guidelines Section 2, Toolkit Section 3.3
Build sustainability	All guidelines Section 3.2, Case studies throughout

This guide provides entry points to the full Guidelines. The five key innovations above represent the fundamental shifts needed to implement integrated WASH programming successfully in resource-constrained settings.

CHAPTER 1

Integration by design

Coordination guidelines for resilient WASH programming in humanitarian contexts

Introduction

The global humanitarian landscape is increasingly characterized by protracted crises, each defined by greater complexity and scope (Guinote, 2018; Snel et al., 2024; Sorensen and Snel, 2022). The combined pressures of climate change, conflict, and pandemics are straining humanitarian systems by intensifying water scarcity, triggering displacement, undermining essential services, and exposing critical weaknesses in fragile settings. The growing impact of these interconnected challenges requires reevaluating how water, sanitation, and hygiene (WASH) services are designed and delivered. This document introduces the WASH Road Map's new Coordination Guidelines with the aim of integrating the coordination of the humanitarian and development WASH sectors with those of health and nutrition and streamlining community and national decision-making. Building upon the findings from 'Integrated WASH Narrative Literature Review: The 3Cs and Intersectoral Coordination,' this analysis incorporates the latest research to inform the development of these guidelines (Gibbons et al., 2023). This document serves as a practical decision-making model aimed at implementing recent arguments that suggest current coordination mechanisms, as they currently stand, are often too reactionary and fail to address long-term resilience effectively (Gibbons et al., 2023).

The WASH Road Map and its Initiative 6 (Multisectoral Integration of WASH, especially in public health) have been instrumental in driving the creation of this document (WASH Road Map, n.d.-b; n.d.-a). Led by key organizations across the humanitarian, health, and nutrition sectors, Initiative 6 aims to revolutionize the integration of WASH into multisectoral responses to public health emergencies. The initiative aims to break down traditional sectoral silos and promote an integrated approach that positions WASH as a critical component in addressing not only public health issues but also broader humanitarian challenges, such as nutrition, climate adaptation, and urban crises. By developing new or strengthening existing inter-cluster partnerships and coordination mechanisms, the initiative works to establish innovative operational models that will drive more effective humanitarian responses. The WASH Road Map plays a crucial role in strengthening the capacity of the WASH sector to provide high-quality, accountable responses to emergencies. The guidelines presented in this document are a direct result of its commitment to multisectoral integration and efforts to enhance the impact of WASH in global crisis responses.

The global humanitarian and development landscape is facing an unprecedented funding crisis. Long-standing sources of international assistance are contracting, with support from traditional donor countries declining sharply in recent years – global health funding alone has dropped by more than 40 per cent (Sabow et al., 2025). This broader trend represents not just a temporary setback but a fundamental shift in how international assistance will function going forward. These guidelines are specifically designed to be effective in resource-constrained environments, providing practical coordination mechanisms that maximize impact even with limited international funding. As international donors increasingly concentrate their limited resources on immediate humanitarian crises, the space for long-term development programming continues to shrink, creating a critical gap that must be filled by other actors and approaches.

This dramatic shift in humanitarian and development financing necessitates a fundamental reorientation toward government-led response mechanisms and domestic resource mobilization. As international actors shift their focus to prioritize acute humanitarian interventions, national governments must assume a greater responsibility for both emergency preparedness and long-term development. These guidelines provide concrete pathways for this transition by:

- strengthening government coordination capacity at the national and local levels to manage both emergencies and development programming
- building technical expertise within relevant ministries and departments to reduce dependence on international technical assistance
- integrating emergency response with existing government systems and structures to avoid creating parallel systems that collapse when international funding ends
- developing sustainable financing mechanisms through government budgets and domestic resource mobilization
- creating institutional memory within government agencies for future crisis response
- supporting governments to design development programmes that inherently strengthen emergency preparedness and resilience
- facilitating the transition of long-term service delivery from international to domestic management

This reorientation has profound implications for how we approach the intersection of humanitarian and development efforts. International actors must shift from being primary implementers to becoming catalysts for strengthening government capacity and systems. Emergency interventions must be designed not as stand-alone responses but as opportunities to build government preparedness for future crises. Development programming, increasingly funded through domestic resources, must prioritize resilience and emergency preparedness as core components rather than add-ons. These guidelines reflect this new reality by emphasizing government leadership, domestic capacity building, and integrating emergency preparedness into all development efforts.

Evolving humanitarian architecture and cluster integration

Parallel to shifts in the funding landscape, the humanitarian coordination architecture is facing increasing pressure to adapt. There is growing recognition that siloed sectoral approaches, particularly across WASH, health, and nutrition, are ill-suited to address the complex and interrelated nature of today's crises. As coordination systems evolve to better support integrated, people-centred responses, the implications for field-level collaboration and programming are profound. Integrated cluster approaches showcase the critical value of coordinated programming in enhancing WASH, health, and nutrition outcomes while maximizing impact on affected communities.

Potential benefits of cluster integration:

- Unified assessment and analysis frameworks that capture WASH-health-nutrition interconnections.
- Streamlined coordination, reducing the burden on government and partner participation.
- Joint resource mobilization that addresses multisectoral needs through unified proposals.
- Integrated information management systems, avoiding duplication and data gaps.
- Harmonized standards and indicators facilitating cross-sectoral programming.
- Reduced competition between sectors for limited resources.

Challenges and trade-offs:

- Risk of losing technical depth and specialized expertise within each sector.
- Potential marginalization of sectors perceived as less 'life-saving' in acute emergencies.
- Complexity of managing diverse technical competencies within unified structures.
- Need for significant capacity building to develop multisectoral expertise.
- Challenges in maintaining accountability for sector-specific standards and outcomes.

Integrating sectors such as WASH, health, and nutrition remains a critical challenge in humanitarian response. Achieving meaningful integration requires a fundamental rethinking of how assistance is conceptualized, financed, and delivered. These standard operating procedures are designed to support that shift by offering flexible frameworks that enable integrated programming regardless of the coordination structure in place. This shift will also require changes in how individual sectors approach their work. For WASH, this means placing greater emphasis on sustainable WASH activities at both the national and community levels, in alignment with the objectives and goals of integrated programming. Health actors may need to expand their focus beyond clinical service delivery to address environmental determinants of health. Nutrition programming should more explicitly incorporate WASH as a critical driver of nutritional outcomes. While these adjustments are complex, they offer a pathway to addressing the root causes of vulnerability rather than merely responding to its effects.

These guidelines are designed to provide a comprehensive guide for WASH practitioners during the critical first 90 days of an emergency response. Each guideline is organized around four key domains: stakeholder coordination, emergency WASH actions, Resilience Actions, and monitoring and evaluation. They offer step-by-step guidance, real-world examples, and adaptable tools specifically for emergency response coordination and implementation during this crucial initial period. Accompanying the guidelines is a Practitioners' Toolkit, which contains a wide range of practical resources, including assessment checklists, planning templates, coordination tools, and monitoring frameworks. While the guidelines focus specifically on the 90-day emergency window, the Toolkit's resources are designed to be easily contextualized to different settings and can be adapted to support broader humanitarian programming across all stages of the humanitarian programme cycle, from preparedness and contingency planning to post-emergency transition and recovery. By packaging focused emergency guidance with adaptable operational tools, the guidelines and Practitioners' Toolkit together aim to provide a comprehensive resource for WASH practitioners working to deliver integrated, locally driven, and sustainable responses in complex crisis settings.

Understanding CCP pressures

Climate change, conflict, and pandemics (CCP) represent three compounding pressures that fundamentally reshape how WASH practitioners must design and deliver services in humanitarian contexts, particularly as international funding becomes increasingly constrained. This lens acknowledges the distinct and overlapping challenges that climate change, violent conflict, and disease outbreaks present for WASH services and the communities that rely on them. Although the implementation of resilient WASH services faces a broad spectrum of challenges, CCP continues to represent the most critical and compounding threats (Rhodes-Dicker et al., 2022). Rather than approaching these crises through a deficit-oriented perspective, we advocate for a strengths-based approach that identifies, builds upon, and enhances existing local capacities, knowledge, and leadership. By centring community resilience and agency, the guidelines presented here offer practical pathways for local and national actors to coordinate integrated WASH responses that address immediate needs while building sustainable systems capable of withstanding future shocks.

This strengths-based approach becomes even more critical in the context of dramatically reduced international development funding. As donors concentrate their limited resources on immediate humanitarian needs, communities and governments must leverage their existing capacities to maintain essential services and build resilience. The framework recognizes that sustainable development will increasingly depend on domestic resources and locally driven solutions, making it essential to identify and build upon existing strengths rather than relying on external inputs.

As local actors and national governments increasingly shoulder the responsibility of crisis coordination and response, we must also reconsider our assessment frameworks. Traditional approaches to humanitarian needs assessment often begin by identifying deficiencies and cataloguing what communities lack, and have historically guided responses toward externally driven, gap-filling interventions. While identifying critical needs remains important, this deficit-focused model is increasingly insufficient in today's landscape of diminished international aid. A strengths-based approach offers a necessary recalibration, emphasizing the existing assets, capabilities, and leadership already present within communities, institutions, and national systems that can be leveraged for more sustainable and locally owned solutions (Grieve, 2023; Grieve et al., 2023; Snel et al., 2024; Winterford et al., 2023).

While recognizing that deficits, especially among marginalized populations, are indeed significant and pressing, strengths-based approaches empower local stakeholders to ascertain which deficits are of paramount importance and to determine how to effectively mobilize both internal and external resources accordingly. This model aligns with Amartya Sen's capabilities approach, which prioritizes freedoms and agency (Sen, 1985, 2000, 2001) and translates directly to WASH programming through community-led service design, participatory monitoring systems, and capacity building that empowers communities to make informed choices about WASH services rather than simply receiving externally provided infrastructure, and reinforces calls for greater localization and participatory development frameworks (Chambers and Conway, 1992; Chambers, 1997, 2006, 2017; World Humanitarian Summit, 2016; IASC, 2021). As Winterford et al. (2023: 19) argue, 'A strengths-based approach does not deny inequalities, injustices, and problems: it offers an alternative perspective on how these issues can be addressed … through an orientation and focus on action towards preferred futures'. This shift toward recognizing community strengths is further supported by recent findings that crisis-affected communities themselves are already shouldering an increasingly heavy burden of mutual aid and crisis response as international assistance decreases. Ground Truth Solutions in 2025 found that 'as international assistance declines in relative importance, mutual aid – always the first line of crisis response – plays a larger role,' highlighting how local actors are developing community-led solutions even in challenging contexts, while expressing

Figure 1.1 Deficit vs. strengths-based approaches to WASH programming. A strengths-based approach recognizes and builds upon local capabilities, creating sustainable WASH solutions that foster community resilience and ownership in CCP contexts.

frustration when external humanitarian assistance duplicates rather than supports these existing efforts (GTS, 2025: 5).

These guidelines are also grounded in the CCP perspective, which highlights the unique and intersecting challenges that climate change, conflict, and disease outbreaks pose for WASH services and the communities that depend on them. By understanding these complex crisis dynamics, practitioners can develop more effective, context-specific interventions that address both immediate needs and long-term resilience. When applied to these guidelines, a strengths-based lens shifts implementation from a model of substitution to one of empowerment, creating space for national and community actors to lead sustainable, long-term WASH interventions, especially in protracted and complex crisis settings. Figure 1.1 illustrates how this strengths-based approach recognizes and builds upon local capabilities to foster resilience in CCP contexts. By integrating strengths-based thinking into coordination mechanisms, guidelines can move beyond short-term fixes toward enduring, locally driven resilience (Snel et al., 2024).

The triple nexus (or humanitarian–development–peace nexus) has been identified as a critical means of addressing the growing number of protracted crises worldwide (Sorensen and Snel, 2022; Snel and Sorensen, 2023). Specifically, the triple nexus argues that integration across humanitarian, development, and peacebuilding actors significantly increases the success of crisis response. The recent creation of the Joint Operational Framework has helped clarify the importance of the triple nexus and highlighted key coordination pathways to help ensure its successful implementation (Grieve, 2023; Grieve et al., 2023). Here, we present an updated discussion of recent publications, since 2022, highlighting further support for stronger coordination mechanisms and the need for refined guidelines designed to help local and national decision-makers design, implement, and measure the immediate and long-term impacts of emergency WASH programming in a way that is cost-effective, sustainable, and resilient.

Figure 1.2 Humanitarian–development–peace nexus flow. Effective guidelines create pathways to navigate the challenging transitions between immediate humanitarian response and sustainable development while building peace and resilience to future CCP shocks.

The argument presented here emphasizes that the CCP represent the most significant challenges to integrating WASH across the humanitarian–development nexus. Each guideline has been developed to help suggest and establish standard measurements and indicators across the humanitarian–development nexus during the onset, transition, and recovery stages of a crisis. The guidelines also aim to enhance intersectoral collaboration, support affected populations, and prioritize locally led and sustainable interventions (Dickin et al., 2022; Heylen et al., 2022; Srivastava et al., 2022; Huang et al., 2023; Yasmin et al., 2023; Abbara et al., 2024).

Climate change, conflict, and pandemics place unique pressures on WASH services that require specific programmatic responses. We emphasize here that solutions must address immediate needs while building resilience to future crises. The impact of these three pressures is well-documented and thoroughly discussed. Climate change displaces populations and stresses urban systems, necessitating localized, context-specific WASH interventions (Baxter et al., 2022; Dickin et al., 2022; Kim et al., 2022; Srivastava et al., 2022; ACF, 2023; Huang et al., 2023; Yasmin et al., 2023; Abbara et al., 2024; Mansour, 2024; Snel et al., 2024). Conflict limits access to resources, as seen in areas such as Gaza, Yemen, or Myanmar, necessitating conflict-sensitive programming and local leadership (Al-Awlaqi et al., 2022; Kim et al., 2022; Maryati and Azizah, 2022). For instance, in Myanmar (Case Study 1.1), intercommunal violence since 2012 displaced hundreds of thousands, mostly women and children, into settings with inadequate WASH infrastructure, exacerbating vulnerabilities and undermining coping capacities. The COVID-19 pandemic exposed

Case Study 1.1 Myanmar: WASH and nutrition-health integration in IDP camps

In Rakhine State, Myanmar, intercommunal violence since 2012 has displaced approximately 145,000 people, 78% of whom are women and children. By 2019, 130,866 internally displaced persons (IDPs) remained in overcrowded camps with inadequate WASH infrastructure, greatly increasing health risks.

Save the Children implemented an integrated WASH, nutrition, and health response in these IDP camps. The organization maintained WASH facilities while delivering nutrition security interventions and contributing to a reduction in mortality from diarrheal diseases. Their approach ensured safe drinking water throughout camps, monitored water sources, and incorporated hygiene promotion within antenatal support and infant feeding centres.

This multisectoral strategy enabled staff from various technical areas to collaborate on achieving individual sectoral outcomes while maximizing synergies. The coordination between WASH committees and State Health Department officials created continuous pathways for service delivery that addressed both immediate needs and longer-term health outcomes. By establishing WASH committees that oversee facilities and linking them with government health structures, Save the Children created an effective governance model that balanced top-down support with bottom-up community engagement, a critical enabler for the sustainable integration of WASH and nutrition services at the point of delivery.

Attribution: Adapted from Thaw Si Htin Zaw, 2021: 47–49 (see Annex 4).

gaps in infrastructure and coordination, underscoring the need for adaptable institutional responses to mitigate future crises while maintaining essential services (Heylen et al., 2022; Kim et al., 2022; Maryati and Azizah, 2022).

While these crises present considerable challenges, they also offer a critical opportunity to rethink WASH implementation systems by strategically integrating service delivery with other sectors. Evidence demonstrates that linking WASH with health, nutrition, shelter, education, and child protection can significantly amplify outcomes for affected populations. The connections between WASH services and health outcomes, particularly in humanitarian contexts, are well established (Sorensen and Snel, 2023; Zinszer and Abuzerr, 2024). For instance, upgrading WASH in healthcare facilities through approaches such as the Clean Clinic Approach[1] can significantly improve service quality and resilience (Lopez et al., 2020). Nutrition-sensitive WASH programmes have proven highly effective in reducing childhood stunting and malnutrition in vulnerable communities (Dodos and Riems, 2023; Yasmin et al., 2023). WASH integration with shelter and food systems enhances resilience in refugee contexts (Srivastava et al., 2022; Webb, 2023). Meanwhile, school-based initiatives, such as the Three Star Approach,[2] foster long-term hygiene behaviours and have been shown to boost school attendance, particularly among girls (Corwith and Sorensen, 2023; Mansour, 2024). Finally, incorporating WASH into the design and placement of shelters, camps, and community spaces is essential to child protection efforts, and particularly for women, girls, and people living with disabilities, and is closely linked to long-term safety, education, and health outcomes (Srivastava et al., 2022; Jeffery, 2023).

The guidelines developed here aim to operationalize and scale up these multisectoral approaches by providing a clear framework for integrated action across CCP contexts. However, further innovation is needed. For instance, new financing approaches and the prioritization of integrated, interdisciplinary planning require breaking down traditional silos to facilitate better cross-sectoral funding streams that are more suited for addressing interconnected crises and fostering localized solutions (Chandratreya, 2023; Abbara et al., 2024; D'Mello-Guyett et al., 2024). Additionally, a growing emphasis is on sustainable and inclusive approaches, such as climate-resilient strategy programmes, prioritizing community-focused interventions that can significantly increase the long-term sustainability and impact of WASH programming in CCP contexts (Mansour, 2024; Snel et al., 2024). While the challenges posed by CCP are daunting, the guidelines present a roadmap for overcoming barriers to effective WASH programming and intersectoral collaboration (ISC). By leveraging proven enablers and focusing on integrating WASH with health and nutrition, the guidelines chart a course toward more holistic, localized solutions.

These new guidelines, as introduced earlier, are organized around four key domains: stakeholder coordination, emergency WASH actions, resilience actions, and monitoring and evaluation. For each domain, the guidelines

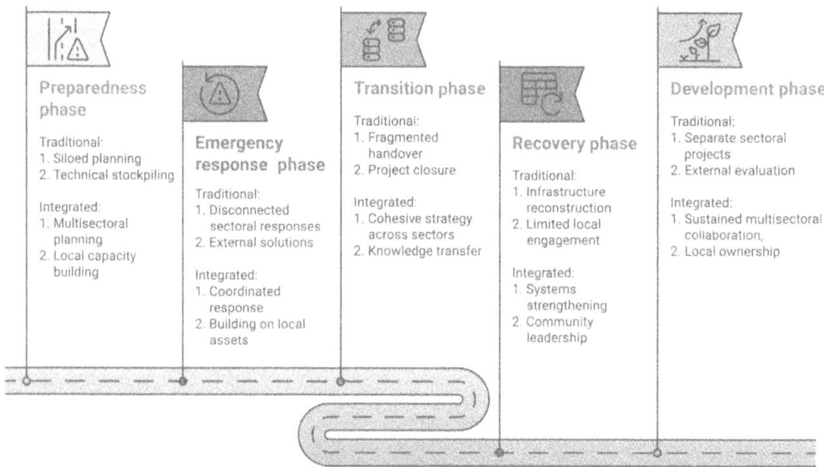

Figure 1.3 Traditional vs. integrated WASH response across crisis phases. Integrated WASH programming creates continuous pathways from crisis to development by leveraging multisectoral approaches and local strengths at each phase.

provide step-by-step guidance and tools for assessment, planning, implementation, and evaluation. Case studies furthermore demonstrate the application of guidelines in various CCP contexts throughout the humanitarian programme cycle. As shown in Figure 1.3, effective guidelines create pathways to navigate the challenging transitions between immediate humanitarian response, sustainable development, and peacebuilding while building resilience to future CCP shocks. It should be noted that the humanitarian–development–peace nexus flow is iterative, and these transitions do not occur in a linear fashion; instead, they ideally flow one after another, with multiple entry points depending on the specific context and phase of the crisis.

Each section of the guidelines combines strategic framing with operational tools, enabling practitioners to translate concepts into actionable steps. Readers can use the guidance and tools provided as a comprehensive roadmap for assessing, planning, implementing, and monitoring integrated WASH interventions. The tools and templates are designed to be adapted to specific contexts and needs, empowering practitioners to develop localized solutions in partnership with communities and stakeholders.

Barriers to intersectoral collaboration

Ultimately, current funding structures pose a significant, ongoing obstacle. Although earmarked funding is crucial for specific initiatives, its rigidity often hinders cross-sectoral collaboration (Gibbons et al., 2023). The absence of financial flexibility, as highlighted in discussions on innovative financing strategies, restricts adaptive funding mechanisms necessary for sustainability

Figure 1.4 Overcoming barriers to effective WASH coordination. Effective guidelines transform barriers into enablers by providing clear pathways for intersectoral collaboration in complex humanitarian contexts.

(Chandratreya, 2023; Yasmin et al., 2023). Resource allocation and planning challenges further impede long-term outcomes in integrated nutrition programmes (Mansour, 2024). These barriers, along with the WASH sector's reality of consistent and significant funding gaps compared to needs, greatly hinder the ability of WASH programming to shift from short-term responses to resilience building, which worsens challenges during prolonged crises (ACF, 2023; Yasmin et al., 2023).

Yet, simply having a coordination structure in place, whether diversified or not, doesn't always mean that it functions in a way that leads to better accountability (Dickin et al., 2022). As seen in Case Study 1.1 (Myanmar: WASH-nutrition-health integration in IDP camps), effective coordination requires both formalized structures (WASH committees) and meaningful connections to existing systems (state health departments). Without this dual approach, coordination mechanisms may exist on paper but fail to create the integrated pathways necessary for sustainable service delivery. This highlights the growing need for more research into WASH systems in humanitarian contexts, particularly regarding how coordination structures transform into functional accountability mechanisms (D'Mello-Guyett et al., 2024). Additionally, data sharing and communication challenges present another significant barrier that often hinders the adoption of harmonized indicators, thereby obstructing the assessment of programme efficacy. This is further exacerbated in contexts that face changing priorities and inconsistent measurement frameworks (Heylen et al., 2022; Chandratreya, 2023).

Addressing the challenges of CCP requires a robust ISC. Systemic barriers persist, hindering progress and requiring urgent attention amid reduced funding and a declining international presence. Key barriers include role ambiguity and inconsistent, fragmented leadership structures, which weaken coordination efforts and hinder effective crisis ISC (Al-Awlaqi et al., 2022; Omam and Metuge, 2023; Yates et al., 2023). Despite these obstacles, success is attainable. One example of an effective integrated approach was implemented by Save the Children. In conflict-affected regions of Nigeria (See Case Study 1.2: Nigeria: Cross-sectoral WASH integration in conflict zones), Save the Children

Case Study 1.2 Nigeria: Cross-sectoral WASH integration in conflict zones

In response to the decade-long conflict in North East Nigeria that has displaced 1.8 million people and killed over 27,000, Save the Children established operations in Borno and Yobe states in 2016. Rather than implementing stand-alone WASH programmes, Save the Children integrated WASH activities into all sectors, including child protection, education, nutrition, and food security.

This integrated approach trained WASH staff, fieldworkers, and volunteers to connect WASH programming with other priorities, providing holistic service coverage to both internally displaced persons and host communities. By strengthening evidence-based decision-making, Save the Children built trust with humanitarian donors and successfully introduced resilience activities into emergency programming. This approach enabled the organization to establish pathways across the humanitarian–development nexus based on contextual evidence of needs and opportunities.

As the crisis evolved, Save the Children implemented both short-term interventions (Food for Peace projects meeting immediate WASH needs) and long-term solutions (EU-funded rehabilitation of permanent WASH facilities in schools and communities). This dual approach encouraged IDPs to return home when safe while providing employment opportunities to people with disabilities who maintain these facilities. Even in areas where conflict continues to make development approaches challenging, Save the Children's model demonstrates how humanitarian responses can incorporate direct links to long-term development goals, creating pathways toward resilience in complex emergency settings.

Attribution: Adapted from Bishara, 2021: 27–28 (see Annex 4).

focused on their core breakthroughs (survival, learning, and protection) while embedding WASH activities within and across all programming. This integration reduced silos and created pathways that address both immediate humanitarian needs and long-term development goals. This approach is increasingly essential as financial resources for humanitarian responses dwindle.

These guidelines, as outlined in figure 1.4, address these barriers by suggesting coordination structures, assessment tools, and indicators that are easily integrated with other sector priorities. They emphasize proven enablers, such as leveraging existing infrastructure, empowering local actors, cultivating multisectoral champions, and establishing accountability mechanisms (Gooding et al., 2022; Yasmin et al., 2023). Case studies embedded throughout the guidelines demonstrate how to apply key principles in practice across various operational environments.

Enablers for intersectoral collaboration

Multisectoral champions play a crucial role in fostering collaboration and ensuring alignment among diverse stakeholders. Leaders who support ISC initiatives help close the gaps between sectors and drive collective action. Broader findings also underscore the importance of accountability mechanisms and leadership in aligning stakeholder priorities for integrated WASH programming (Dickin et al., 2022). These enablers highlight the importance of strategic action and innovative thinking in overcoming barriers to ISC. Save the Children's multisectoral WASH strategy in Myanmar IDP camps (see Case Study 1.1) provides a practical example of how coordination structures can effectively bridge humanitarian and development approaches. With the establishment of WASH committees that oversee facilities and coordinate with state health departments, they created continuous pathways for WASH, health, and nutrition services. Their integration of hygiene promotion with nutrition support at infant and young child feeding centres demonstrates how services can be aligned at the point of delivery, a critical enabler for sustainable integration. By leveraging existing infrastructure, empowering communities, and fostering cross-sectoral leadership, ISC can serve as a powerful tool for addressing the complex challenges present in CCP contexts.

Community engagement is a critical driver of ISC success, with localization serving as the cornerstone principle for effective humanitarian response. Localization – the meaningful transfer of decision-making power, resources, and implementation to local actors – is essential as international funding diminishes. Local actors play a pivotal role in designing and executing context-specific solutions that reflect the needs and realities of affected populations. In Gaza, for example, participatory action research has demonstrated how community buy-in and solidarity enhance the ownership and sustainability of WASH interventions through genuinely localized approaches (Zinszer and Abuzerr, 2024). Similarly, efforts in Cameroon have highlighted how the use of integrated community case management, like other community-driven approaches, helps build local resilience and foster localized solutions to complex problems (Omam and Metuge, 2023). There is a growing recognition that coordination structures that balance top-down and bottom-up perspectives, while prioritizing localization, can lead to more sustainable outcomes (Maryati and Azizah, 2022). Advocacy groups can lead in creating these localized coordination structures, mobilizing resources, and promoting cross-sectoral collaboration that respects and enhances local leadership.

Key enablers for enhancing ISC effectiveness in addressing CCP challenges include leveraging existing infrastructure to reduce costs and streamline programme scalability, such as the Clean Clinic Approach in healthcare facilities (Lopez et al., 2020) and climate-resilient, community-led WASH strategies in schools (Mansour, 2024). Building trust with donors and introducing resilience activities into emergency programming through evidence-based decision-making, as demonstrated by Save the Children's work in Nigeria (see Case Study 1.2: Nigeria: Cross-sectoral WASH integration in conflict zones), is another crucial factor. Training WASH staff, fieldworkers, and volunteers to connect WASH with other priorities for effective knowledge management and integration, and transitioning from short-term responses to development-focused, holistic approaches by securing local, regional, and national buy-in (Huang et al., 2023) are also key enablers.

Practical implementation of these enablers requires specific tools and frameworks. For harmonizing metrics across sectors, established frameworks such as the WHO/UNICEF Joint Monitoring Programme (JMP), WASH FIT (water and sanitation for health facility improvement tool), and SuSanA's M&E (monitoring and evaluation) toolkit provide tested approaches (see detailed discussion in the following section, 'Measurement and indicators'). Similarly, innovative financing mechanisms, including pooled funds and blended finance arrangements, are emerging to address the challenge of siloed funding, though implementation remains an evolving area of practice.

Measurement and indicators

Effective measurement and indicators are critical for evaluating and improving ISC to address CCP. Harmonized and practical evaluation frameworks ensure accountability, facilitate learning, and guide sustainable improvements. Alignment of indicators presents a central challenge in the evaluation of ISC. Harmonizing metrics across sectors is crucial for capturing nuanced impacts. For example, the Global Trachoma Mapping Project highlights the challenges in aligning data collection scales across the WASH and health sectors. Misaligned metrics can create gaps in monitoring and hinder evidence-based decision-making (Dickin et al., 2022; Gooding et al., 2022; Chandratreya, 2023; D'Mello-Guyett et al., 2024). Developing shared measurement frameworks can ensure that ISC outcomes are tracked and evaluated more accurately.

Joint measurement frameworks for integrated programming

Effective integrated WASH programming requires standardized measurement tools that capture cross-sectoral outcomes. Several established frameworks can facilitate this integration:

- *WHO/UNICEF Joint Monitoring Programme (JMP)*: Provides standardized WASH indicators that can be integrated with health and nutrition monitoring systems (https://washdata.org/). The JMP framework enables the tracking of safely managed water and sanitation services, with indicators directly linkable to health outcomes, such as reductions in diarrheal disease and improvements in nutritional status (WHO and UNICEF, n.d.).
- *Water and Sanitation for Health Facility Improvement Tool (WASH FIT)*: Offers a practical approach for measuring and improving WASH conditions in healthcare facilities. This tool integrates quality improvement methodologies with WASH standards, creating measurable links between infrastructure improvements and health service delivery outcomes (WHO and UNICEF, 2022).
- *SuSanA's Monitoring and Evaluation Toolkit*: Provides comprehensive M&E resources that span the humanitarian–development continuum. The toolkit includes indicators for sustainability, functionality, and cross-sectoral impacts, enabling programmes to track both immediate outputs and long-term systems strengthening (Okoth, 2018).
- *Integrated Phase Classification (IPC) for WASH*: When combined with IPC for food security and nutrition, this framework enables unified severity analysis across sectors, supporting prioritization and resource allocation decisions (IPC, n.d.).

These frameworks should be adapted to local contexts while maintaining core standardized indicators that enable comparison and aggregation across programmes and regions.

Enabling flexible cross-sectoral funding

The traditional, siloed funding mechanisms present significant barriers to integrated programming. Innovative financing approaches are emerging to address these constraints, though implementation remains a work in progress:

Pooled funding mechanisms: Country-based pooled funds increasingly allow for multisectoral proposals (Snel and Sorensen, 2021; Sorensen and Snel, 2022; ICVA, 2023). These mechanisms enable:

- joint proposal development across WASH, health, and nutrition sectors
- shared accountability for integrated outcomes
- reduced transaction costs for both donors and implementers
- greater flexibility in resource allocation based on evolving needs

Blended finance arrangements: Combining public and private funding sources (Dietvorst, 2018; ICVA, 2023; Aqua for All, 2024). These mechanisms create opportunities for:

- leveraging private sector investment in WASH infrastructure that supports public health outcomes
- creating sustainable financing models that blend grant funding with commercial investment
- developing innovative financing instruments such as impact bonds for integrated WASH-nutrition outcomes

Synchronized joint financing programmes: Pulling resources across sectors helps:

- aligned funding cycles across sectors to enable integrated planning
- joint donor missions that assess multisectoral outcomes
- flexible funding windows that allow reallocation between sectors based on integrated assessments
- multi-year funding commitments that span humanitarian and development phases

While these approaches show promise, significant challenges remain in their implementation. Donor policies often lag behind the needs of field-level integration, and administrative requirements can still create barriers. However, continued advocacy and demonstration of the effectiveness of integrated programming are gradually shifting donor approaches toward more flexible mechanisms.

Comprehensive planning frameworks support effective intersectoral collaboration. For instance, Burkina Faso's multisectoral nutrition planning process developed a Common Results Framework that defined roles, responsibilities, and indicators across six contributing sectors, creating a foundation for coordinated implementation and accountability. During the planning phase, they utilize scoring systems to assess the existing integration of policy and identify opportunities for strengthening nutrition across sectors (Gibbons et al., 2023; Ouedraogo et al., 2020). South Africa's experience illustrates the challenges of intersectoral collaboration when departments function in silos, highlighting the need for standardized indicators and harmonized metrics to enhance assessment of ISC efforts and improve accountability across sectors (Gibbons et al., 2023; Momberg et al., 2020).

Case Study 1.3 from Bangladesh exemplifies WASH monitoring principles, showing how refugee settlements benefited from a user-centred approach that went beyond counting facilities to understanding actual experiences. Developed through consultations involving 120 documents and 160 stakeholders, the framework established indicators for cleanliness, smell, security, privacy, and functionality of WASH facilities, as well as essential protection dimensions such as lighting, door coverage, locks, and safe pathways. By evaluating both technical and social aspects, the framework created accountability mechanisms that reflected the priorities of the beneficiaries.

Case Study 1.3 Bangladesh: User-centred WASH monitoring in refugee settlements

The WASH Sector Hygiene Promotion Strategy for Cox's Bazar refugee settlement represents a comprehensive assessment approach developed through extensive consultation. With over 740,000 Rohingya fleeing Myanmar since 2017, the Inter-Sector Coordination Group, supported by UNICEF, conducted a 10-month study to consolidate three years of lessons learned.

Over 120 documents and 160 persons (47% female) were consulted to generate a guiding framework for WASH interventions. The research established that monitoring and evaluation should move beyond basic access metrics to include the cleanliness, smell, water testing, security, and privacy dimensions of WASH facilities.

Key indicators included the ability to lock doors, sufficient door coverage, adequate lighting in latrines and pathways to facilities, and whether facilities were located within safe areas. This user-centred approach demonstrated how measurement frameworks can effectively bridge technical requirements with social and protection dimensions that drive actual WASH facility usage. The framework exemplifies how user feedback can be systematically incorporated into monitoring systems, addressing a key gap in traditional approaches that often focus solely on infrastructure existence rather than usability, safety, and acceptability to vulnerable populations.

Attribution: Adapted from D'Adamo in Corwith and Sorensen, 2023: 142 (see Annex 4).

This illustrates how measurement frameworks can evolve from tracking inputs (facilities built) to meaningful outcomes (facilities actively used).

The guidelines provide harmonized metrics to track outcomes across sectors. They recommend using geospatial tools to reveal gaps in WASH coverage and identify disease hotspots for targeted health investments. Composite indices assess community resilience in WASH, health, and nutrition. A key aspect is linking thorough monitoring with inclusive decision-making, ensuring affected communities have a voice in interventions, promoting accountability, and local ownership. Implementing these systems is vital for practical evaluation and underscores the necessity of shared responsibility among sectors.

Ultimately, these guidelines aim to catalyse a shift toward a more localized and integrated approach to WASH programming in complex crises. By bridging sectors, strengthening local capacities, and fostering innovation, we can build a more resilient future for communities affected by climate change, conflict, and pandemics. However, realizing this vision will require commitment and collaboration from all stakeholders, including governments, donors, humanitarian agencies, and local actors.

With the downsizing of the UN system, the onus is increasingly on international and national actors to proactively seek out and share data to enable effective humanitarian response. In the absence of a centralized UN-led data repository, tools like Solstice are emerging to fill the gap, with many organizations already using these platforms to exchange information (https://solstice.world/#/). It is critical that all humanitarian actors, particularly local responders who are often closest to the crisis, prioritize the timely collection and sharing of their data through such collaborative mechanisms.

This allows the broader response community to access the most current and comprehensive information available to guide evidence-based interventions. NGOs and local actors should view contributing to shared data platforms as an essential part of emergency preparedness and response, not an optional add-on. Establishing clear data sharing protocols and capacities before a crisis hits can enable a more agile, transparent, and coordinated response when it matters most.

Conclusion

Recent announcements of significant reductions in international humanitarian assistance present both substantial challenges and potential opportunities (Sabow et al., 2025). National governments and local groups must take a larger role in crisis response and building resilience. These guidelines are vital in strengthening their capacities and promoting local solutions. Effective coordination and integration across sectors will be crucial to responding efficiently to crises and building resilience for the future in this new, resource-constrained environment. By focusing on coordination, integration, and resource efficiency, the WASH sector can adapt to this new reality and effectively address the needs of affected communities.

CCP present significant challenges to delivering sustainable services during crises that aid organizations face. These contexts underscore the need for an integrated, multisectoral approach to WASH coordination as stakeholders strive to address the combined effects of climate change and pandemics. Save the Children's programming in Nigeria (see Case Study 1.2) demonstrates that humanitarian responses can align with long-term development goals, even in the midst of conflict. Their implementation of emergency Food for Peace projects alongside EU-funded WASH facility rehabilitation illustrates how humanitarian efforts can foster resilience in complex situations. This embodies the transition capabilities in our framework (Figure 1.5), where programmes link immediate needs with long-term resilience. When paired with community engagement strategies, as highlighted in Case Study 1.1, and measurement frameworks, as highlighted in Case Study 1.3, a holistic model emerges to tackle the impacts of climate change, conflict, and pandemics.

Despite ongoing barriers to ISC, these guidelines provide practical, evidence-based strategies for overcoming challenges and bridging the gap between humanitarian and development efforts. Key barriers include role ambiguity (Dickin et al., 2022; Yates et al., 2023), inconsistent measurements, data sharing difficulties (Al-Awlaqi et al., 2022; Dickin et al., 2022; Heylen et al., 2022), and limited resources due to funding fragmentation (Gooding et al., 2022; ACF, 2023; Chandratreya, 2023; Huang et al., 2023). This makes adopting an integrated, multisectoral approach to WASH coordination and resource allocation increasingly vital. Importantly, there's no need to create new systems; instead, we can utilize existing infrastructures (Dickin et al., 2022; Gooding et al., 2022; Huang et al., 2023), engage

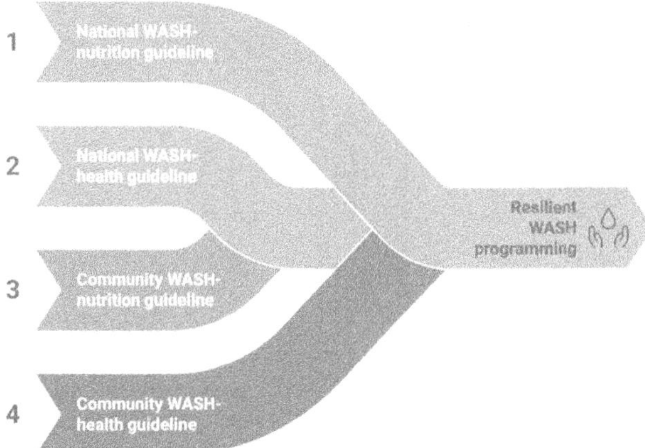

Figure 1.5 Guidelines for Integrated WASH with health and nutrition.

communities (Gooding et al., 2022; Heylen et al., 2022; Yasmin et al., 2023; Mansour, 2024), and empower multisectoral champions (Dickin et al., 2022; Heylen et al., 2022; Srivastava et al., 2022; Huang et al., 2023) as effective ways to tackle these challenges.

The global reduction in development assistance represents both a crisis and an opportunity. While the immediate impacts on vulnerable populations cannot be minimized, this shift compels us to fundamentally rethink how sustainable development and emergency preparedness are achieved. National governments, supported by strategic international partnerships, must now lead where international actors once dominated. Development programming must inherently strengthen emergency preparedness, and emergency responses must build long-term government capacity. This is not simply an adaptation to reduced funding but a more sustainable and equitable approach to global development.

By improving coordination, standardizing metrics, and supporting local solutions, these guidelines provide a vital step toward a shared roadmap for 'building forward better'. The emphasis on CCP contexts serves as an invitation to re-evaluate current systems and enhance case studies, essential indicators, decision-making frameworks, and standard operating procedures. This approach aims to better support marginalized and affected groups while enhancing WASH transitions across the humanitarian–development nexus in a manner that is both sustainable and resilient to future shocks. Governments, humanitarian organizations, and donors can ensure accountability and drive effective interventions by adopting innovative measurement systems and standardized indicators specified in the guidelines.

These guidelines are essential tools, not silver bullet solutions. They offer a significant opportunity to enhance humanitarian WASH initiatives within public health but require continual evaluation and adaptation for effective implementation. The success of these guidelines depends on the commitment of governments, donors, and implementing agencies to adopt innovative approaches that move beyond traditional silos and short-term projects. Their effectiveness will be measured by their capacity to foster collaboration and improve the lives of crisis-affected communities. In an era of escalating global challenges, it is time for audacious, barrier-breaking, and collaborative efforts. An integrated, multisectoral strategy encourages reimagining WASH programming as essential for future integration, addressing immediate needs while laying the foundation for long-term resilience.

The conceptual framework and evidence base presented in this chapter provide the foundation for the four coordination guidelines that follow. Chapters 2–5 translate the understanding of CCP pressures, barriers analysis, and enablers into actionable guidance organized around four core domains: stakeholder coordination, emergency WASH actions, resilience actions, and monitoring and evaluation. Each guideline addresses specific coordination challenges at the national and community levels while maintaining a focus on integrating WASH with health and nutrition outcomes. We acknowledge that there is some overlap among the guidelines, which was considered unavoidable due to the interconnectedness of integrated programming. As practitioners frequently operate within specific sectors or levels, we decided to develop four distinct guidelines to facilitate access and enable each guideline to serve as an individual resource when needed. The accompanying Practitioners' Toolkit in Annex 1 provides detailed tools and templates to support the implementation of the strategic guidance outlined in each guideline. Although we cannot foresee every practitioner's requirement, our goal was to provide sufficient and valuable starting points so that decision-makers wouldn't have to start from scratch in a new emergency response. Together, these components provide a comprehensive roadmap for transitioning from a theoretical understanding of integrated WASH programming to its practical implementation in complex humanitarian contexts.

Notes

1. The Clean Clinic Approach is a systematic quality improvement methodology developed by USAID's Maternal and Child Survival Program that uses a 10-step process to help healthcare facilities make incremental, effective improvements in WASH services and infection prevention and control (IPC) without relying on external investments. The approach focuses on management, motivation, and accountability as key drivers, following a Plan-Do-Study-Act model. Key steps include conducting facility assessments, establishing national minimum WASH standards, training facility staff, forming 'Clean Clinic Teams' at each facility, integrating WASH actions into annual work plans, implementing programme activities, conducting regular inspections and coaching, and providing recognition for progress.
2. The Three Star Approach is a progressive WASH in Schools framework developed by UNICEF and GIZ that uses daily supervised group activities

to promote hygiene behaviour change. Schools advance through three levels: One Star (daily supervised group hand washing with soap, clean gender-segregated toilets, and personal drinking water bottles), Two Star (expanded hygiene education including hand washing after toilet use, improved sanitation and menstrual hygiene facilities, and safe drinking water at school), and Three Star (meeting full national WASH standards). The approach emphasizes community ownership, low-cost, locally sourced solutions, and building lifelong hygiene habits through simple, scalable, and sustainable interventions that do not rely on expensive infrastructure.

Bibliography

Abbara, Aula, Reem Abu Shomar, Marwa Daoudy, Ghassan Abu Sittah, Muhammad H. Zaman, and Mark Zeitoun. 2024. 'Water, Health, and Peace: A Call for Interdisciplinary Research.' *The Lancet* 403 (10435): 1427–29. https://doi.org/10.1016/S0140-6736(24)00588-9

Action Against Hunger (ACF). 2023. 'World's Water Funding Crisis: How Donors Are Missing the Mark.' ACF. https://www.actionagainsthunger.org/publications/2023-water-funding-gap-report/

Al-Awlaqi, Sameh, Fekri Dureab, and Marzena Tambor. 2022. 'The National Health Cluster in Yemen: Assessing the Coordination of Health Response during Humanitarian Crises.' *Journal of International Humanitarian Action* 7 (1): 9. https://doi.org/10.1186/s41018-022-00117-y

Aqua for All. 2024. 'Blended Finance: Paving the Way to Climate-Smart Water and Sanitation Investments.' Aqua for All. November 21, 2024. https://aquaforall.org/news/blended-finance-paving-the-way-to-climate-smart-water-and-sanitation-investments/

Baxter, Louisa, Catherine R. McGowan, Sandra Smiley, Liliana Palacios, Carol Devine, and Cristian Casademont. 2022. 'The Relationship between Climate Change, Health, and the Humanitarian Response.' *The Lancet* 400 (10363): 1561–63. https://doi.org/10.1016/S0140-6736(22)01991-2

Bishara, Umar. 2021. 'Nigeria: Integrated WASH Programming.' In *Bridging the WASH Humanitarian–Development Divide: Building a Sustainable Reality*, edited by Mariëlle Snel and Nikolas Sorensen, 27–28. Rugby UK: Practical Action Publishing Ltd. https://practicalactionpublishing.com/book/2577/bridging-the-wash-humanitariandevelopment-divide

Chambers, Robert. 1997. *Whose Reality Counts? Putting the First Last.* London: Intermediate Technology Publications.

Chambers, Robert. 2006. 'Transforming Power: From Zero-Sum to Win-Win?' *IDS Bulletin* 37 (6): 99–110.

Chambers, Robert. 2017. *Can We Know Better? Reflections for Development.* Rugby UK: Practical Action Publishing. http://dx.doi.org/10.3362/9781780449449

Chambers, Robert, and Gordon Conway. 1992. 'Sustainable Rural Livelihoods: Practical Concepts for the 21st Century.' IDS Discussion Paper 296, Brighton: IDS.

Chandratreya, Abhijit. 2023. 'Financing Strategies for Water, Sanitation, and Hygiene (WASH) Initiatives: A Comprehensive Review.' *Community Practitioner* 20 (10).

Corwith, Anne, and Erin Sorensen. 2023. 'Integrated WASH and Education.' In *Addressing Conflict, COVID-19, and Climate Change: A Multisectoral Approach to Integrated WASH Programming*, edited by Marïelle Snel and Nikolas Sorensen. Rugby UK: Practical Action Publishing Ltd.

Dickin, Sarah, Abu Syed, Nishrin Qowamuna, George Njoroge, Carla Liera, Mohamad Mova Al'Afghani, Sidratun Chowdhury, Zoraida Sanchez, Abdulwahab Moalin Salad, Keren Winferford, Erma Uijtewaal, Virginia Roaf, John Butterworth, and Juliet Willett. 2022. 'Assessing Mutual Accountability to Strengthen National WASH Systems and Achieve the SDG Targets for Water and Sanitation.' *H2Open Journal* 5 (2): 166–79. https://doi.org/10.2166/h2oj.2022.032

Dietvorst, Cor. 2018. 'Blended Finance: Is It All in a Mix?' [blog], 14 December. IRC. https://www.ircwash.org/blog/blended-finance-it-all-mix

D'Mello-Guyett, Lauren, Camille Heylen, Elsa Rohm, Jane Falconer, Jean Lapegue, Robert Dreibelbis, Monica Ramos, Oliver Cumming, and Daniele Lantagne. 2024. 'Research Priorities for Water, Sanitation and Hygiene (WASH) in Humanitarian Crises: A Global Prioritisation Exercise.' *PLOS Water* 3 (3): e0000217. https://doi.org/10.1371/journal.pwat.0000217

Dodos, Jovana, and Bram Riems. 2023. 'WASH-Nutrition Integration: For Vulnerable Populations Affected by Conflict, Climate Change and the COVID-19 Pandemic.' In *Addressing Conflict, COVID-19, and Climate Change: A Multisectoral Approach to Integrated WASH Programming*, edited by Marïelle Snel and Nikolas Sorensen, 85–108. Rugby UK: Practical Action Publishing.

Gibbons, Marly P., Cristina Mena-Lander, and Syed Yasir Ahmad Khan. 2023. 'Integrated WASH Narrative Literature Review: The 3Cs and Intersectoral Coordination.' In *Addressing Conflict, COVID-19, and Climate Change: A Multisectoral Approach to Integrated WASH Programming*, edited by Marïelle Snel and Nikolas Sorensen, 1–32. Rugby UK: Practical Action Publishing.

Gooding, Kate, Maria Paola Bertone, Giulia Loffreda, and Sophie Witter. 2022. 'How Can We Strengthen Partnership and Coordination for Health System Emergency Preparedness and Response? Findings from a Synthesis of Experience across Countries Facing Shocks.' *BMC Health Services Research* 22 (1): 1441. https://doi.org/10.1186/s12913-022-08859-6

Grieve, Timothy. 2023. 'A WASH Framework to Address Conflict, COVID-19, and Climate Change: Leveraging the Humanitarian–Development–Peace Nexus.' In *Addressing Conflict, COVID-19, and Climate Change: A Multisectoral Approach to Integrated WASH Programming*, edited by Marïelle Snel and Nikolas Sorensen, 33–65. Rugby UK: Practical Action Publishing Ltd.

Grieve, Timothy, Thilo Panzerbieter, and Johannes Rück. 2023. *WASH Resilience, Conflict Sensitivity and Peacebuilding: Joint Operational Framework*. Triple Nexus in WASH Initiative. https://www.washnet.de/en/triple-nexus-wash/joint-operational-framework/

Ground Truth Solutions (GTS). 2025. *What Crisis Affected Communities Need from a Humanitarian Reset: A Guide Based on Two Years of Conversations with People on the Front Lines of Crisis*. GTS. https://static1.squarespace.com/static/62e895bdf6085938506cc492/t/67e16a99990a7169d380c883/1742826139841/GTS_Global+analysis+report_March+2025_EN.pdf

Guinote, Filipa Schmitz. 2018. 'A Humanitarian-Development Nexus That Works – World.' ReliefWeb [press release], 21 June 2018. https://reliefweb.int/report/world/humanitarian-development-nexus-works

Heylen, Camille, Travis Yates, Langley Topper, Franck Bouvet, Dominique Porteaud, Monica Ramos, Jean McCluskey, and Daniele Lantagne. 2022. 'Realtime Assessment of WASH Coordination in Three Humanitarian Emergencies.' *PLOS Water* 1 (11): e0000047. https://doi.org/10.1371/journal.pwat.0000047

Huang, Ai-Ju, David Githiri Njoroge, Lilian Otiego, and Alexander Danilenko. 2023. 'From a Humanitarian to Development Approach: Uganda's Ground-Breaking Journey to Achieve Sustainable Provision of Water Services to Refugees and Host Communities.' The World Bank.

ICVA. 2023. *Pooled Funding Models: Governance Systems*. ICVA. https://www.icvanetwork.org/uploads/2023/12/ICVA-Pooled-Funding-Models-Governance-Systems.pdf

Inter-Agency Standing Committee (IASC). 2021. 'The Grand Bargain (Official Website) | IASC.' March 10, 2021. https://interagencystandingcommittee.org/grand-bargain

IPC. no date. 'IPC Overview and Classification System.' IPC - Integrated Food Security Phase Classification. Accessed June 4, 2025. https://www.ipcinfo.org/ipcinfo-website/ipc-overview-and-classification-system/en/

Jeffery, Allison. 2023. 'Child Protection and WASH Integration.' In *Addressing Conflict, COVID-19, and Climate Change: A Multisectoral Approach to Integrated WASH Programming*, edited by Mariëlle Snel and Nikolas Sorensen, 153–174. Rugby UK: Practical Action Publishing.

Kim, Junghwan, Erica Hagen, Zacharia Muindi, Gaston Mbonglou, and Melinda Laituri. 2022. 'An Examination of Water, Sanitation, and Hygiene (WASH) Accessibility and Opportunity in Urban Informal Settlements during the COVID-19 Pandemic: Evidence from Nairobi, Kenya.' *Science of The Total Environment* 823 (June):153398. https://doi.org/10.1016/j.scitotenv.2022.153398

Lopez, Jason, Sergio Tumax Sierra, Ana María Rodas Cardona, and Stephen Sara. 2020. 'Implementing the Clean Clinic Approach Improves Water, Sanitation, and Hygiene Quality in Health Facilities in the Western Highlands of Guatemala.' *Global Health: Science and Practice* 8 (2): 256–69. https://doi.org/10.9745/GHSP-D-19-00413

Mansour, Luna. 2024. 'Water, Sanitation, and Hygiene in Schools: A Global Analysis of Bottlenecks and Climate Resilient Strategies.' TRITA-ABE-MBT. Master's Thesis, KTH, Sustainable development, Environmental science and Engineering.

Maryati, Sri, and Devi Martina Azizah. 2022. 'Innovation During COVID-19 Pandemic: Water, Sanitation, and Hygiene in Informal Settlements.' *Pertanika Journal of Social Sciences and Humanities*. https://api.semanticscholar.org/CorpusID:249739197

Momberg, D. J., P. Mahlangu, B. C. Ngandu, J. May, S. A. Norris, and R. Said-Mohamed. 2020. 'Intersectoral (in)Activity: Towards an Understanding of Public Sector Department Links between Water, Sanitation and Hygiene (WASH) and Childhood Undernutrition in South Africa.' *Health Policy and Planning* 35 (7): 829–41. https://doi.org/10.1093/heapol/czaa028

Okoth, Simon. 2018. 'SuSanA Monitoring and Evaluation Framework: Towards Sustainable Sanitation for All.' Sustainable Sanitation Alliance (SuSanA).

Omam, Lundi-Anne, and Alain Metuge. 2023. 'Rapid Response Mechanism in Conflict-Affected Settings of Cameroon: Lessons Learned from a Multisector Intervention for Internally Displaced Persons.' *Journal of Global Health Reports* 7 (August): e2023057. https://doi.org/10.29392/001c.85011

Ouedraogo, Ousmane, Maimouna Halidou Doudou, Koiné Maxime Drabo, Denis Garnier, Noël Marie Zagré, Dia Sanou, Kristina Reinhardt, and Philippe Donnen. 2020. 'Policy Overview of the Multisectoral Nutrition Planning Process: The Progress, Challenges, and Lessons Learned from Burkina Faso.' *The International Journal of Health Planning and Management* 35 (1): 120–39. https://doi.org/10.1002/hpm.2823

Rhodes-Dicker, Leandra, Nick J. Brown, and Matthew Currell. 2022. 'Unpacking Intersecting Complexities for WASH in Challenging Contexts: A Review.' *Water Research* 209: 117909. https://doi.org/10.1016/j.watres.2021.117909

Sabow, Adam, Matt Craven, Matt Wilson, Michael Conway, Tina Holt, Connor Rochford, and Sarah Anderson. 2025. 'The Future of Foreign Aid: A Generational Shift', 6 May. McKinsey & Company. https://www.mckinsey.com/industries/social-sector/our-insights/a-generational-shift-the-future-of-foreign-aid#/

Sen, Amartya. 1985. 'A Sociological Approach to the Measurement of Poverty: A Reply to Professor Peter Townsend.' *Oxford Economic Papers* 37 (4): 669–76.

Sen, Amartya. 2000. *Development as Freedom*. New York: First Anchor Books.

Sen, Amartya. 2001. 'Economic Development and Capability Expansion in Historical Perspective.' *Pacific Economic Review* 6 (2): 179–91. https://doi.org/10.1111/1468-0106.00126

Snel, Mariëlle, and Nikolas Sorensen. 2021. *Bridging the WASH Humanitarian-Development Divide: Building a Sustainable Reality*. Rugby UK: Practical Action Publishing Ltd. https://practicalactionpublishing.com/book/2577/bridging-the-wash-humanitariandevelopment-divide

Snel, Mariëlle, and Nikolas Sorensen, eds. 2023. *Addressing Conflict, COVID-19, and Climate Change: A Multisectoral Approach to Integrated WASH Programming*. Rugby UK: Practical Action Publishing Ltd.

Snel, Mariëlle, Nikolas Sorensen, and Reed Power. 2024. *Climate Change and Water Scarcity in the Middle East: A Transitional Approach*, 1st edn. London: Routledge. https://doi.org/10.4324/9781003436706

Sorensen, Nikolas, and Mariëlle Snel. 2022. 'The New Reality: Perspectives on Future Integrated WASH.' *Waterlines* 41 (1): 65–80. https://doi.org/10.3362/1756-3488.20-00007OA

Sorensen, Nikolas, and Mariëlle Snel. 2023. 'Integrating WASH with Health in Humanitarian Settings.' In *Addressing Conflict, COVID-19, and Climate Change: A Multisectoral Approach to Integrated WASH Programming*, edited by Mariëlle Snel and Nikolas Sorensen. Rugby UK: Practical Action Publishing Ltd.

Srivastava, Shilpi, Jeremy Allouche, Roz Price, and Tina Nelis. 2022. 'Bringing WASH into the Water–Energy–Food Nexus in Humanitarian Settings.' *IDS Working Paper 563,* Brighton: Institute of Development Studies. https://doi.org/DOI: 10.19088/IDS.2022.006

Thaw Si Htin Zaw. 2021. 'Myanmar: Multisectoral Approach to WASH in Emergencies.' In *Bridging the WASH Humanitarian–Development Divide:*

Building a Sustainable Reality, edited by Mariëlle Snel and Nikolas Sorensen, 47–49. Rugby UK: Practical Action Publishing Ltd. https://practicalactionpublishing.com/book/2577/bridging-the-wash-humanitarian development-divide

WASH Road Map. no date-a. 'Initiative 6: Multi Sectoral Integration of Wash, Especially in Public Health.' WASH Road Map. Accessed April 28, 2025. https://www.washroadmap.org/multi-sectoral-coordination.html

WASH Road Map. no date-b. 'What is the WASH Road Map.' Accessed 4 June 2025. https://www.washroadmap.org/

Webb, Susannah. 2023. 'Integrated WASH and Shelter.' In *Addressing Conflict, COVID-19, and Climate Change: A Multisectoral Approach to Integrated WASH Programming*, edited by Mariëlle Snel and Nikolas Sorensen, 109–34. Rugby UK: Practical Action Publishing.

WHO and UNICEF. 2022. *Water and Sanitation for Health Facility Improvement Tool (WASH FIT): A Practical Guide for Improving Quality of Care through Water, Sanitation and Hygiene in Health Care Facilities*. Second. Geneva: World Health Organization (WHO).

WHO and UNICEF. no date. 'About the JMP.' Accessed 23 August 2022. https://washdata.org/how-we-work/about-jmp

Winterford, Keren, Deborah Rhodes, and Christopher Dureau. 2023. *A Strengths-Based Approach for International Development: Reframing Aid*. Rugby UK: Practical Action Publishing. https://doi.org/10.1080/09614524.2023.2247582

World Humanitarian Summit. 2016. *Commitments to Action: The World Humanitarian Summit, Istanbul, 23–24 May 2016*. Agenda for Humanity. https://agendaforhumanity.org/sites/default/files/resources/2017/Jul/WHS_commitment_to_Action_8September2016.pdf

Yasmin, T., S. Dhesi, I. Kuznetsova, R. Cooper, S. Krause, and I. Lynch. 2023. 'A System Approach to Water, Sanitation, and Hygiene Resilience and Sustainability in Refugee Communities.' *International Journal of Water Resources Development* 39 (5): 691–723. https://doi.org/10.1080/07900627.2022.2131362

Yates, Travis, Andy Bastable, John Allen, Cecilie Hestbaek, Bushra Hasan, Paul Hutchings, Monica Ramos, Tula Ngasala, and Daniele Lantagne. 2023. 'Gaps in Humanitarian WASH Response: Perspectives from People Affected by Crises, Practitioners, Global Responders, and the Literature.' *Disasters* 47 (3): 830–46. https://doi.org/10.1111/disa.12571

Zinszer, Kate, and Samer Abuzerr. 2024. 'Water, Sanitation, and Hygiene Insecurity and Infectious Disease Outbreaks among Internally Displaced Populations in Gaza: Implications of Conflict-Driven Displacement on Public Health.' *Journal of Water, Sanitation and Hygiene for Development* 14 (11): 1182–92. https://doi.org/10.2166/washdev.2024.361

CHAPTER 2

Integration in emergencies

Guideline for coordinating WASH with health at the national level

2.1 Summary

This coordination guideline outlines eight critical actions that national decision-makers should take during the first 90 days of an emergency. Start with the Key actions table on the next page to see what needs to happen and when. The table also directs you to detailed guidance in this chapter and the Practitioners' Toolkit (Annex 1).

This guideline provides essential coordination guidance for national officials overseeing WASH initiatives and health initiatives respectively, during emergencies. It supports rapid response while emphasizing long-term resilience, serving as one of four complementary guidelines designed as an integrated framework for WASH coordination with health and nutrition at both national and community levels. This guideline was developed by the WASH Road Map in consultation with numerous other professionals. A list of external sources consulted in the creation of these guidelines can be found in Annex 3.

2.1.1 Purpose

This guideline helps national-level officials and humanitarian coordinators integrate WASH and health interventions during emergencies through structured, time-bound actions. It upholds the rights outlined in the Humanitarian Charter and aligns with global commitments to advance universal health coverage and primary healthcare.

Who should use this: National-level decision-makers, government ministry officials, WASH and health cluster coordinators, UN agency representatives, and technical advisers from international and national NGOs responsible for designing national emergency response strategies and coordinating multisectoral interventions.

How to use these actions: Each action in the table is connected to specific sections in this guideline (see the 'Guideline sections' column) that provide detailed coordination frameworks, and to the Practitioners' Toolkit (see the 'Practitioners' Toolkit sections' column) that offers operational tools, templates, and checklists. Begin with the action most relevant to your current emergency phase, and then refer to the corresponding sections for implementation guidance.

Key actions

Actions	*WASH*	*Health*	*Timeframe*	*Guideline sections*	*Practitioners' Toolkit sections*
Activate coordination platform and establish roles	Establish co-leadership with government and WHO; identify WASH representatives and define roles	Establish co-leadership with government and UNICEF; identify health representatives and define roles	Within 48 hours	2.1, 2.2, 2.3, 2.4	1.1, 1.2, 1.5, 1.6, 1.7
Conduct rapid integrated assessments	Lead comprehensive WASH needs, capacity, and stakeholder assessment	Lead assessments of WASH in health facilities and map health stakeholders	Days 1–14	2.3, 3.1.1	1.3, 2.1, 2.2, 2.3, 2.4, 2.6, 3.4, 3.5
Provide emergency WASH services	Provide minimum water, sanitation, and hygiene services as per minimum standards; distribute supplies; ensure WASH in health facilities meets minimum standards	Health facility managers monitor WASH infrastructure and alert appropriate staff of needs	Days 1–14	3.1.2, 3.1.3, 3.1.4, 3.1.6	2.4, 2.5, 4.4, 4.5
Establish integrated monitoring and feedback	Adapt existing community feedback systems and develop joint indicators for the local context	Adapt and utilize existing indicators and community feedback mechanisms	By day 30	2.6, 2.8, 3.2.5, 4	5.1, 5.3, 5.4, 5.6, 3.3
Implement cross-sectoral coordination	Engage in joint planning with health sector; coordinate hygiene promotion	Coordinate with WASH counterparts to integrate WASH interventions with health interventions	Days 14–45	2.7, 3.1.6	3.1, 3.6, 3.7, 4.1, 4.2, 4.7
Address specialized needs	Control vector transmission when relevant; support outbreak response	Implement activities for vector-borne disease prevention, treatment, and control including health education, disease surveillance, and utilizing national treatment protocols	Days 14–90	3.1.5, 3.1.6	2.3, 4.4, 5.2
Strengthen local capacity and transition planning	Build community and partner capacity; support transition to local management	Lead health system WASH capacity and sustainability planning	Days 30–90	3.2.1, 3.2.2, 3.2.3, 3.2.4	3.4, 3.6, 4.2, 4.8, 4.9
Review policies and document learning	Review WASH policies; capture and share lessons learned	Review health policies; document health facility improvements	Throughout response	2.5, 3.1.7, 3.2.6	1.3, 5.5, 4.3, 4.6, 4.10

The guideline sections provide the strategic frameworks for establishing coordination platforms, conducting assessments, and building sustainable systems. The Practitioners' Toolkit found in Annex 1 translates these frameworks into practical tools you can adapt and use immediately. Together, they support decision-makers in transitioning from urgent responses to resilient, locally led systems.

2.1.2 Framework pillars

These five pillars structure the detailed guidance found throughout this guideline:

1. *National coordination*: Set up inclusive national mechanisms operating through existing cluster and inter-cluster structures, with diverse ministries, agencies, and partners.
2. *Strategic assessment*: Quickly identify critical WASH and health strengths, assets, needs, risks, and existing national capacities.
3. *Integrated service delivery*: Provide services that address immediate needs while strengthening national and local systems.
4. *National capacity building*: Develop sustainable government and partner capacity for crisis preparedness and response.
5. *National monitoring*: Track performance and impacts to ensure accountability, facilitate learning, and inform future strategies.

2.1.3 Adaptability

Adapt this guideline to align with existing national policies, strategies, and systems, rather than creating parallel structures. It works in both rural and urban settings and should be used in conjunction with district and community-level guidelines for a coherent, multi-level approach. The Practitioners' Toolkit found in Annex 1 provides templates and tools that can be modified to suit your specific context.

2.1.4 Timeframe

This guideline focuses specifically on coordinated action during the first 90 days of an emergency at the national level:

- *Emergency actions (0–14 days)*: Urgent action to prevent disease outbreaks and reduce mortality.
- *Resilience actions (14–90 days)*: Establishing mechanisms for transitioning to sustainable, locally led systems.

These timeframes provide a coordination framework for establishing transition mechanisms rather than fixed deadlines for completing transitions, which remain context-dependent and may extend well beyond the initial emergency response period.

2.1.5 Cross-cutting issues

This guideline mainstreams climate resilience, protection, gender equity, and social inclusion, while clearly defining roles and responsibilities across government entities, humanitarian organizations, and community partners. It provides practical guidance to transform emergency response into sustainable progress, bridging the humanitarian–development divide at the national level.

2.2 Stakeholder coordination

The integration of WASH and health interventions requires coordinated engagement from multiple sectors and stakeholders at the national level. This guideline section outlines the approach to stakeholder coordination with a focus on establishing mechanisms for collaborative planning, implementation, and monitoring of integrated WASH and health interventions. Such coordination is particularly critical during health emergencies where waterborne diseases or sanitation-related outbreaks require swift, coordinated action across sectors.

Quick reference: Key national-level templates available in Annex 1

Purpose	*Annex 1 section*	*Use when ...*
Stakeholder mapping and coordination	1.1, 1.2, 1.5, 1.6	Establishing national coordination platforms
Joint assessments	2.1, 2.4, 2.6	Rapid situation analysis and facility assessments
Strategic planning	3.1, 3.5, 3.6	Developing integrated national response plans
Capacity building	3.4, 4.2, 4.5	Strengthening government and partner capabilities
Information management	5.1, 5.2, 5.5	Monitoring systems and performance tracking

Note: All templates in Annex 1 are designed for adaptation to different national contexts and government structures.

Further practical guidance and tools can be found in the Practitioners' Toolkit (Annex 1), including:

- Section 1.1: Stakeholder identification checklist
- Section 1.2: Coordination committee TOR template
- Section 1.3: Stakeholder analysis and mapping tools
- Section 1.5: Stakeholder roles and responsibilities matrix
- Section 1.6: Coordination performance scorecard
- Section 1.7: Coordination timeline (first 45 days)
- Section 2.4: Health facility WASH assessment checklist

- Section 2.6: WASH-IPC monitoring checklist
- Section 3.1: Integrated WASH-nutrition-health response planning template
- Section 3.3: Community engagement planning framework
- Section 3.4: Capacity assessment and building tools
- Section 3.5: Health system capacity mapping tool
- Section 3.6: Joint capacity building plan
- Section 4.1: Joint workplan and budget template
- Section 4.2: Training and staff development guides
- Section 4.5: WASH in healthcare facility improvement planning template
- Section 4.7: Integrated risk communication and community engagement plan
- Section 5.1: Integrated monitoring framework
- Section 5.2: Outbreak investigation and response checklist
- Section 5.3: Community feedback mechanism checklist
- Section 5.4: Supportive supervision checklist
- Section 5.5: Performance review and learning tools

These tools span coordination, assessment, planning, implementation, and monitoring of WASH and health integration at the national level and can be strong starting points to creating and maintaining national-level coordination systems.

2.2.1 Stakeholder identification checklist

Figure 2.1 identifies seven key stakeholder categories that should be involved in the national WASH and health multi-stakeholder coordination mechanism complementing existing sectoral clusters: government authorities, humanitarian and development organizations, community representatives, private sector, academic and research institutions, UN agencies and donors, and inter-cluster coordination. For a comprehensive stakeholder identification checklist, please refer to the Practitioners' Toolkit (Annex 1) Section 1.1.

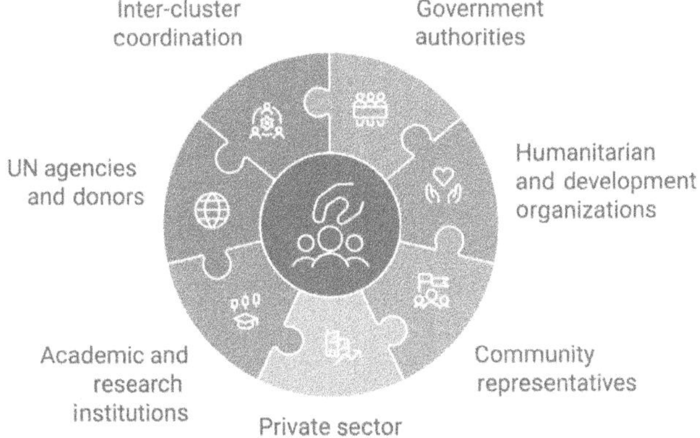

Figure 2.1 Multi-stakeholder coordination wheel with seven segments.

2.2.2 Strengthening meaningful participation

For effective national WASH and health coordination during emergencies, it is essential to allocate dedicated seats for community representatives, local civil society organizations, and academic institutions in coordination groups and decision-making bodies. Establishing formal partnership agreements or memoranda of understanding with research and training institutions will support evidence-based approaches through capacity building, data analysis, and knowledge sharing activities. The coordination platform should employ participatory approaches that actively involve community members, including vulnerable and marginalized groups, in needs assessments, solution development, and decision-making processes. This ensures their voices are heard and their specific needs are addressed in the national response strategy. Dedicating specific seats for community representatives, women's organizations, and advocates for at-risk groups in WASH and health coordination bodies will amplify their perspectives and help address the unique challenges faced by different population segments during health emergencies, ultimately strengthening the health system's resilience.

2.2.3 Coordination mechanisms

Critical action summary

Critical action	*Timeframe*	*Lead responsibility*
Activate national WASH/health coordination platform	Within 48 hours	National government with UNICEF/WHO support
Convene initial stakeholder meeting	Within 48 hours	Platform co-chairs
Create WASH Coordination Task Force	By day 5	Local authority and INGO co-chairs
Complete basic 4W mapping	First 72 hours	Information Management Team
Develop operational stakeholder map	By day 7	WASH Coordination Task Force
Establish coordination function in senior ministry	By day 14	Government leadership

Note: INGO, international non-governmental organization; 4W, who, what, where, when.

2.2.3.1 Coordination activation and structure

Establishing a robust coordination platform immediately after crisis onset creates the foundation for an effective integrated WASH and health response. This initial structure must balance rapid deployment with thoughtful design, ensuring representation from government ministries, UN agencies, NGOs, and other stakeholders. Early activation of this platform within the first 48 hours provides the operational framework for all subsequent integrated actions. It demonstrates organizational commitment to addressing public health risks through coordinated WASH interventions during emergencies.

Action: Activate the national WASH/health coordination platform within 48 hours

Key stakeholder roles summary

Stakeholder	*Coordination role*	*Implementation role*
Ministry of Health	Co-lead national platform; chair health sector meetings	WASH in health facility standards; staff training on WASH-IPC
WASH cluster/lead agency	Technical coordination; information management	Emergency WASH service delivery; capacity building
WHO	Health technical guidance; disease surveillance integration	Health system strengthening; emergency health response
Local government	Subnational coordination; resource mobilization	Service delivery oversight; community engagement
NGO partners	Field-level coordination; community liaison	Direct service implementation; community mobilization

Note: WASH-IPC: WASH infection prevention and control. *For complete roles and responsibilities, see Annex 1, Section 1.5*

Lead: National government with WASH Cluster and WHO support

Key steps:

- Establish platform co-led by national government in collaboration with UNICEF and WHO.
- Convene initial stakeholder meeting within 48 hours.
- Define terms of reference based on Inter-Agency Standing Committee (IASC) reference documents and local context (refer to Annex 1 Section 1.2).
- Ensure participation of key stakeholders (refer to Annex 1 Section 1.1).

2.2.3.2 Establishing the WASH Coordination Task Force

Creating specialized coordination structures enhances the platform's ability to address both strategic and technical dimensions of WASH and health integration. A dedicated task force provides focused leadership, technical guidance, and operational coordination across different stakeholders. By establishing clear roles and communication protocols, the task force ensures effective information flow between WASH and health actors, enabling coordinated planning, implementation, and monitoring while providing a forum for addressing challenges that emerge during the emergency response.

Action: Create a WASH Coordination Task Force with clear composition and mandate

Lead: National authority and INGO co-chairs

Task Force composition:

- Relevant government ministries and agencies
- UN agencies (UNICEF, WHO)
- International and local NGOs, including assessment specialists
- Donor agencies
- Private sector partners

Core responsibilities:

- Clearly define roles for each member (refer to Annex 1 Section 1.5).
- Ensure participatory decision-making.
- Hold regular meetings to share updates and address challenges.
- Develop information sharing protocols between WASH and health actors.
- Ensure compliance with data protection policies.

2.2.3.3 Formalizing roles and responsibilities

Comprehensive stakeholder mapping provides the intelligence foundation for the strategic coordination of integrated WASH and health interventions. This mapping evolves from a rapid initial assessment to a detailed characterization of actors' capacities, coverage, and resources. By implementing a layered approach to formalizing relationships and roles, the coordination platform can quickly establish operational partnerships while building toward more comprehensive agreements as the situation stabilizes, ensuring both immediate action and sustainable collaboration throughout the emergency lifecycle.

Action: Implement a layered approach to formalizing stakeholder roles

Lead: WASH Coordination Task Force

Rapid formalization process:

- Start with simple one-page agreements in the initial emergency phase.
- Progress to more comprehensive agreements as situation stabilizes.
- Prioritize documenting verbal agreements through meeting minutes.

Stakeholder mapping timeline:

- *First 72 hours*: Complete basic 4W mapping (who, what, where, when).
- *By day 7*: Develop an operational stakeholder map focused on:
  - geographic areas of responsibility
  - technical capacities and resource availability
  - existing services and infrastructure
- *By week 3*: Expand stakeholder map to include roles in:
  - policy and planning
  - budgeting and finance

  - regulation and enforcement
  - infrastructure development
  - service delivery
  - monitoring and evaluation

2.2.3.4 Institutional coordination mechanisms

Effective WASH and health integration requires coordination structures that span from national policy to local implementation. Establishing a dedicated coordination function within a senior ministry provides the high-level authority and cross-sectoral influence necessary for policy alignment and resource mobilization. Meanwhile, replicating coordination mechanisms at subnational levels ensures that interventions are adapted to local contexts and effectively reach affected communities. This multi-level approach bridges the gap between strategic direction and operational implementation while strengthening the integration and resilience of emergency response.

Action: Establish a dedicated coordination function within senior ministry

Lead: Government leadership with support from UN agencies

Key steps:

- Place coordination function within senior ministry (e.g. Planning or Finance) to:
  - facilitate inter-ministerial cooperation
  - align WASH and health coordination with national development plans
  - mobilize resources and track spending
  - ensure high-level oversight and accountability

Coordination team composition:

- Include dedicated staff with expertise in:
  - WASH and health
  - stakeholder engagement
  - programme management
  - monitoring and evaluation (M&E)

Subnational coordination structures:

- Replicate WASH and health coordination structures at the subnational level
- Form district/provincial teams with representatives from:
  - local government
  - service providers
  - community organizations
  - development partners

- Adapt national policies to reflect:
  - local epidemiological priorities
  - existing capacities
  - cultural factors
- Establish clear communication channels between levels to:
  - ensure vertical integration
  - facilitate bottom-up feedback loops

2.2.3.5 Policy review and updates

The emergency context offers an opportunity to identify and address policy gaps that affect integrated WASH and health programming. A thorough review of existing frameworks helps determine how these policies support or hinder effective coordination, service delivery, and sustainability. Ideally, this review and process takes place well before a crisis ever happens. By engaging diverse stakeholders in this review process, the coordination platform can develop recommendations for policy adjustments that enhance integration while ensuring alignment with national development goals, thereby laying the groundwork for both immediate response and long-term systems strengthening.

Action: Conduct comprehensive policy review to strengthen coordination framework

Lead: Senior government officials with technical support team

Key areas of policy review:

- Assess how existing frameworks:
  - define clear roles and responsibilities for WASH and health services
  - establish minimum service standards
  - enable private sector participation and partnerships
  - support progressive realization of WASH and health service goals
  - promote inclusive planning and budgeting processes

Review process:

- Engage all relevant stakeholders through consultations and public discussions.
- Document gaps, overlaps, and contradictions in existing policies.
- Identify opportunities for harmonization and integration.
- Develop actionable recommendations for policy updates.

Implementation steps:

- Form technical working group to guide policy review process.
- Develop review methodology and timeline.
- Conduct document review, stakeholder interviews, and validation workshops.

- Prepare policy briefs and recommendations for decision-makers.
- Support the development of updated policies and frameworks.

2.2.3.6 Monitoring, evaluation, and adaptive management

A unified monitoring system enables evidence-based coordination by tracking both sector-specific and integrated WASH and health outcomes. This shared information architecture connects field-level implementation with strategic decision-making, providing timely data to guide adaptive management throughout the emergency response. By establishing consistent monitoring protocols and harmonizing data collection across organizations, the coordination platform ensures that decisions are evidence-based and that resources are allocated to address the most critical needs and gaps in the integrated response.

Action: Establish robust monitoring systems for integrated WASH and health outcomes

Lead: WASH and health sector monitoring specialists

Monitoring system requirements:

- *Track key indicators*:
  - coverage and use of sanitation facilities
  - functionality and safety of WASH infrastructure
  - fecal sludge and wastewater management practices
  - household expenditure on WASH services
  - health outcomes linked to WASH interventions

Health management integration system integration requirements:

- Align all WASH-health indicators with national health management information system (HMIS) from day 1.
- Integrate data collection with existing health facility reporting systems.
- Ensure compatibility with national disease surveillance systems.
- Establish data sharing protocols with Ministry of Health information managers.
- Use national health data standards and definitions where available.
- Link WASH outcome data to health facility patient management systems.
- Coordinate with national health information officers for indicator harmonization.

Implementation steps:

- Harmonize monitoring protocols across government and non-government actors.
- Establish consistent data flow mechanisms and reporting timelines.

- Align monitoring systems with WASH response indicators.
- Ensure data quality assurance mechanisms.
- Develop feedback loops for adaptive management.

Joint analysis process:

- Schedule regular joint analysis meetings.
- Review integrated indicator data and identify trends.
- Analyse the contribution of WASH interventions to health outcomes.
- Document learning and best practices.
- Formulate evidence-based recommendations for programme adjustments.

2.2.3.7 Cross-sectoral coordination

Effective WASH and health integration requires mechanisms that bridge sectoral boundaries and create synergies between complementary interventions. Cross-sectoral coordination ensures that hygiene promotion activities are aligned with broader community mobilization strategies while establishing clear referral pathways between service providers across sectors. By creating these intentional linkages, the coordination platform maximizes public health impact while ensuring that vulnerable groups receive comprehensive support that addresses the multiple dimensions of their needs during emergencies.

Action: Implement strategies for effective cross-sectoral coordination

Lead: WASH and health sector leads with support from coordination specialists

Key integration areas:

- Coordinate hygiene promotion activities across sectors.
- Integrate with community mobilization strategies.
- Ensure representation of at-risk groups in coordination mechanisms.
- Establish clear referral mechanisms between:
  - WASH actors
  - healthcare facilities
  - other relevant sectors (nutrition, shelter, protection).

Technical coordination mechanisms:

- Joint technical working groups for specialized areas
- Shared technical standards and protocols
- Cross-training of staff across sectors
- Regular technical exchange forums
- Coordinated quality assurance processes

Implementation steps:

- Map technical overlap areas between WASH and health.
- Identify opportunities for integration and resource sharing.

- Develop integrated work plans with clear responsibilities.
- Establish joint monitoring mechanisms for cross-cutting activities.
- Document and share successes and challenges.

2.2.3.8 Community engagement and participation

Meaningful community engagement transforms affected populations from passive recipients to active participants in the emergency response. By establishing structured mechanisms for community input and leadership, the coordination platform ensures that interventions are culturally appropriate, address priority needs, and build upon existing capacities. This participatory approach not only improves the effectiveness and sustainability of WASH health interventions but also upholds the dignity and agency of affected communities, fostering ownership that extends beyond the emergency phase.

Action: Establish mechanisms for meaningful community engagement in coordination

Lead: WASH and health sector leads with community engagement specialists

Key engagement strategies:

- Actively engage local leaders and community-based organizations.
- Establish structured mechanisms for affected populations' participation.
- Reserve seats for community representatives in coordination bodies.
- Conduct regular consultations and dialogue sessions.
- Establish transparent feedback mechanisms.
- Build capacity of local organizations for effective advocacy.

Implementation steps:

- Map existing community structures and entry points.
- Develop a community engagement strategy with clear objectives.
- Create accessible communication channels for diverse groups.
- Schedule regular community feedback sessions.
- Document and share community perspectives in coordination forums.
- Track and report on response to community input.

2.3 Emergency WASH actions

The emergency WASH actions outlined in this section provide a framework for rapid response in the acute phase of a crisis, focusing on the first 90 days. The emergency actions (0–14 days) prioritize life-saving interventions, while the resilience actions (14–90 days) emphasize sustainability and resilience. Key actions include rapid assessments, ensuring access to safe water and sanitation, promoting hygiene, controlling disease vectors, and coordinating with the health sector. The section also guides the review and strengthening of public health policies and the transition to community-managed WASH services.

2.3.1 Emergency actions (0–14 days)

The emergency actions phase (0–14 days) is crucial for mitigating public health risks and preventing disease outbreaks during a humanitarian crisis. Rapid assessments are conducted to identify areas with the greatest health and sanitation strengths and needs, focusing on the status of healthcare facilities, water and sanitation infrastructure, and hygiene practices. Key activities include ensuring access to safe water and sanitation in healthcare settings, distributing essential hygiene and cleaning supplies, and promoting infection prevention and control measures. Coordination with health actors is prioritized to align WASH interventions with disease surveillance data, treatment protocols, and community health promotion efforts. The emergency actions set the stage for more comprehensive, health-focused WASH interventions in the subsequent phases of the emergency, aiming to protect and improve public health outcomes.

Key resources available in Annex 1:

- *Coordination timeline (first 45 days)* (Section 1.7): Step-by-step activation guide for national coordination.
- *Health system capacity mapping tool* (Section 3.5): Assessment framework for government health system integration.
- *Joint capacity building plan* (Section 3.6): Template for strengthening national and subnational capabilities.
- *WASH in healthcare facility improvement planning template* (Section 4.5): Systematic approach to facility-level improvements.
- *Performance review and learning tools* (Section 5.5): Framework for adaptive management and institutional learning.

2.3.1.1 Rapid WASH strengths and needs assessment

Purpose: Conducting a rapid WASH assessment targeting both strengths and needs is crucial for identifying areas and populations with the greatest health and sanitation risks. This assessment should be initiated within the first 72 hours of the emergency and completed within 14 days. The Practitioners' Toolkit (Annex 1) provides additional resources for this process, including the stakeholder identification checklist (Section 1.1), and various assessment tools can be found in Section 2 of the toolkit.

Timing: Begin assessment within the first 72 hours of the emergency and complete initial rapid assessment within 14 days.

Key steps:

1. Use existing standardized tools to identify areas and populations with the greatest health and sanitation needs and risks.
2. Conduct a multisectoral assessment, engaging experts from relevant fields and backgrounds, drawing on infection prevention and control (IPC) frameworks and best practices.
3. Gather qualitative data on cultural practices, social norms, and power dynamics influencing WASH access and outcomes by engaging community representatives and local organizations.
4. Rapidly analyse and disseminate assessment findings to inform community-level response planning and resource allocation.
5. Use harmonized questions and indicators from the WHO/UNICEF Joint Monitoring Programme to ensure comparability and alignment with global standards.

2.3.1.2 Access to safe and sufficient water

Purpose: Ensuring access to safe and sufficient water is critical to prevent waterborne diseases, maintain hydration, and support hygiene and healthcare functions during emergencies. The Practitioners' Toolkit (Annex 1) offers further guidance on water quality testing and treatment (Section 4.4) and community engagement in water supply management (Section 3.3).

Timing: Provide minimum safe water quantities within the first 72 hours and progressively increase access and quality throughout the first 14 days of the response.

Key steps:

1. Mobilize and deploy water trucking, treatment kits, storage receptacles, and purification supplies to affected areas, prioritizing the most vulnerable groups.
2. Set up and manage water trucking services in coordination with community members, ensuring equitable distribution and accessibility for all.
3. Test water quality at both source and point of use, and treat and protect water sources to maintain safety standards.
4. Ensure minimum water quantities are met, providing at least:
    a. 5 L per person per day for outpatients
    b. 40–60 L per person per day for inpatients in health facilities
    c. 15 L per person per day at the household level
5. Monitor and maintain water quality, with free residual chlorine levels of 0.2–0.5 mg/litre at the point of delivery.

In emergency contexts, it is possible to provide both immediate, life-saving water interventions, while prioritizing long-term resilience interventions. One such example is demonstrated in Case Study 2.1 (Afghanistan: Integrating

Case Study 2.1 Afghanistan: Integrating emergency response with groundwater sustainability

The 2018 drought in Afghanistan, the worst in over a decade, displaced an estimated 298,000 people, particularly from Badghis and Herat provinces. This emergency occurred against a backdrop of long-term water scarcity, climate change impacts, and four decades of conflict that damaged water infrastructure.

World Vision International implemented a dual-focus response that addressed both immediate water needs and long-term groundwater sustainability. They constructed drinking water networks for displaced populations while simultaneously building macro-catchment ponds in flood paths to capture runoff water. These large basins (approximately 60 metres in diameter with 5,600 cubic metre capacity) slowed water flow, increasing aquifer infiltration and creating positive environmental feedback loops that support long-term water security.

An assessment in Khwaja Charom village found that the macro-catchments not only reduced annual flooding but also raised the water table, reactivating previously dry *kariz* systems and wells. Concurrently, World Vision collaborated with government stakeholders to develop Afghanistan's national Operation and Maintenance of Rural Water Systems Strategy, establishing minimum standards for both humanitarian and development organizations. This policy framework incorporated provisions for climate change mitigation, environmental sustainability, and common benchmarks for all organizations working in WASH, helping to ensure that emergency water interventions prioritize water source conservation and groundwater recharge while meeting immediate needs.

Attribution: Adapted from Keam, 2021: 28–30 (see Annex 4).

emergency response with groundwater sustainability), in which World Vision International implemented a dual-focus response that addressed both immediate water needs and long-term groundwater sustainability. By constructing drinking water networks for displaced populations while simultaneously building macro-catchment ponds to capture runoff water, they created positive environmental feedback loops that support long-term water security. This case study highlights the importance of considering sustainability and resilience even in the initial emergency response phase.

2.3.1.3 Safe and acceptable sanitation facilities

Purpose: Providing safe and acceptable sanitation facilities is essential to prevent open defecation, reduce disease transmission, and ensure dignity and well-being in emergency-affected communities. The Practitioners' Toolkit (Annex 1) provides additional guidance on rapid sanitation assessments (Section 2.1) and community-led sanitation approaches (Section 4.4).

Timing: Provide basic, shared sanitation facilities within the first 72 hours and progressively increase access to safe, acceptable, and sustainable facilities throughout the first 14 days and beyond.

Key steps:

1. Coordinate with gender-based violence (GBV) counterparts to install gender-segregated emergency latrines in public places, such as camps,

schools, markets, and health facilities, aiming for a maximum of 50 people per latrine.

2. Construct temporary household latrines and support the rapid repair of existing toilets using locally available materials and designs.
3. Distribute culturally appropriate, gender-sensitive hygiene and menstrual health management kits to support the use and maintenance of sanitation facilities.
4. Promote community engagement in selecting sanitation technologies, siting facilities, and establishing operations and maintenance systems to ensure acceptability and sustainability.
5. Ensure the accessibility and safety of sanitation facilities for women, girls, people with disabilities, and other vulnerable groups through inclusive design and siting.

2.3.1.4 Promote key hygiene practices

Purpose: Promoting key hygiene practices, such as handwashing with soap and safe water storage and treatment, is critical to prevent the spread of waterborne and communicable diseases in emergency settings. The Practitioners' Toolkit (Annex 1) offers further guidance on hygiene promotion strategies (Section 4.4) and behaviour change communication (Section 4.4).

Timing: Begin hygiene promotion activities within the first 72 hours of the response and sustain them throughout the emergency and recovery phases.

Key steps:

1. Distribute context-appropriate and gender-sensitive hygiene kits, including soap, water containers, and menstrual hygiene and incontinence materials, to affected households.
2. Focus hygiene promotion on key behaviours that prevent disease transmission, such as handwashing at critical times, safe water handling, and food hygiene.
3. Launch community-level hygiene promotion campaigns using multiple channels, such as radio, posters, and interpersonal communication, to maximize reach and reinforce messages.
4. Target hygiene promotion to high-risk groups, such as caregivers of young children, the elderly, and people with disabilities, using tailored behaviour change approaches and communication methods.
5. Train community health workers, volunteers, and hygiene promoters on effective behaviour change techniques, including demonstrations, storytelling, and problem-solving.

2.3.1.5 Vector breeding and transmission control

Purpose: Controlling vector breeding sites and interrupting transmission pathways is essential to prevent the spread of vector-borne diseases such as malaria, dengue, and Zika in emergency settings. The Practitioners' Toolkit (Annex 1) provides further guidance on vector control strategies (Section 4.4) and community-based surveillance (Section 5.4).

Timing: Assess vector risks and implement control measures within the first 14 days of the response, and sustain efforts throughout the emergency and recovery phases.

Key steps:

1. Mobilize community members to identify and eliminate mosquito breeding sites by removing standing water and safely disposing of solid waste.
2. In coordination with health actors, distribute long-lasting insecticide-treated nets to affected households and promote their correct and consistent use.
3. Implement safe and effective chemical and biological vector control measures, such as indoor residual spraying and larviciding, in consultation with the community and relevant experts.
4. Establish community-based vector surveillance systems to monitor the presence and density of mosquitoes and other disease vectors, and to guide the targeting and adaptation of control interventions.
5. Promote the safe storage and handling of drinking water and food to prevent contamination by vectors and pests, using locally appropriate and affordable container covers and storage methods.

2.3.1.6 Health sector coordination

Purpose: Coordinating with the health sector is critical to ensure that WASH interventions are aligned with public health priorities, disease surveillance data, and healthcare delivery needs in emergency settings. The Practitioners' Toolkit (Annex 1) provides further guidance on WASH coordination mechanisms (Section 1.2) and WASH in healthcare facilities (Section 2.4).

Timing: Establish coordination mechanisms with health actors within the first 72 hours of the response and maintain regular communication and collaboration throughout the emergency and recovery phases.

Key steps:

1. Assess WASH-related disease risks and identify high-vulnerability groups, such as children under five, pregnant women, persons with disabilities, older persons, and people with compromised immune systems, in coordination with health experts.

2. Establish community-level joint surveillance and referral systems to enable the early detection, reporting, and control of WASH-related disease outbreaks, in collaboration with community health workers and volunteers.
3. Provide essential WASH facilities, supplies, and services at community health centres, oral rehydration points, and other frontline care delivery sites, in accordance with healthcare protocols and standards.
4. Map and strengthen the capacity of community-based health workforces to promote hygiene, deliver WASH-related health messages, and facilitate community engagement and participation in WASH interventions.
5. Establish and maintain clear referral pathways and communication channels between community health facilities and WASH service providers to ensure a timely and coordinated response to WASH-related health issues.

2.3.1.7 Review and strengthen public health sanitation policies

Purpose: Reviewing and strengthening public health sanitation policies is essential to ensure that emergency WASH interventions are aligned with national standards, regulations, and systems, and to promote the sustainability and resilience of sanitation services. The Practitioners' Toolkit (Annex 1) provides further guidance on policy review processes (Section 1.3) and sustainability planning (Section 3.4).

Timing: Conduct a rapid review of existing sanitation policies within the first 14 days of the response, and support policy strengthening efforts throughout the emergency and recovery phases.

Key steps:

1. Assess the comprehensiveness, clarity, and coherence of local sanitation legislation and standards along the entire sanitation service chain, from containment to treatment and safe disposal or reuse.
2. Identify policy gaps, inconsistencies, and implementation challenges that may hinder the effectiveness, equity, and sustainability of emergency sanitation interventions.
3. Ensure that sanitation policy frameworks are evidence-based, assign clear institutional roles and responsibilities, and include provisions for community participation and accountability.
4. Support the development or revision of emergency-specific sanitation policies and protocols to enable the rapid deployment of context-appropriate interventions in future crises.
5. Use policy review findings to inform the design and adaptation of emergency sanitation strategies, and to advocate for longer-term policy reforms and investments in resilient sanitation systems.

2.3.1.8 Realistic and incremental sanitation standards

Purpose: Setting realistic and incremental sanitation standards is critical to ensure that emergency interventions are context-appropriate, feasible, and sustainable, while progressively improving the quality and coverage of sanitation services. The Practitioners' Toolkit (Annex 1) provides further guidance on adaptive management (Section 1.3) and monitoring and evaluation (Section 5.2).

Timing: Establish initial minimum sanitation standards within the first 14 days of the response, and progressively raise standards throughout the emergency and recovery phases as conditions allow.

Key steps:

1. Base initial sanitation standards on a rapid assessment of public health risks, existing sanitation access and practices, and available resources and capacities on the ground.
2. Ensure that sanitation standards are aligned with global humanitarian guidelines, such as the Sphere standards, while being adapted to the local context and emergency phase.
3. Engage affected communities in setting and monitoring sanitation standards, ensuring that their needs, preferences, and constraints are reflected in the design and management of facilities and services.
4. Encourage the use of locally appropriate, affordable, and sustainable sanitation technologies and approaches that can be easily operated and maintained by communities.
5. Establish mechanisms for the regular review and adjustment of sanitation standards based on evolving needs, capacities, and lessons learned throughout the emergency and recovery phases.

2.3.2 Resilience actions (14–90 days)

The resilience actions phase (14–90 days) focuses on strengthening the resilience and sustainability of emergency WASH interventions by engaging and empowering local actors, systems, and resources. This phase prioritizes capacity building, community-led management, and alignment with long-term development goals. Case Study 2.2 (Yemen: Evidence-based water management in conflict zones) showcases how the International Organization for Migration (IOM) partnered with local authorities and technical experts to conduct groundwater assessments and develop sustainable water management strategies, demonstrating the importance of integrating local knowledge and capacity into emergency response efforts.

2.3.2.1 Strengthen local WASH capacity and resources

Purpose: Strengthening local WASH capacity and resources is essential to ensure the sustainability, resilience, and ownership of emergency health interventions, and to facilitate the transition to long-term development and service delivery. The Practitioners' Toolkit (Annex 1) provides further guidance on capacity mapping (Section 1.3) and community engagement (Section 3.3).

Timing: Begin capacity and resource assessments within the first 14 days of the response, and continue strengthening efforts throughout the emergency, recovery, and development phases.

Key steps:

1. Pre-position essential WASH and health supplies in strategic locations, in collaboration with local authorities and partners, to enable rapid deployment and distribution in case of an emergency.
2. Work with local partners to map, mobilize, and strengthen community-based WASH infrastructure, supply chains, and market systems, leveraging existing resources and capacities.
3. Engage community leaders and representatives in all aspects of the emergency WASH response, from planning and implementation to monitoring and evaluation, to ensure local ownership and sustainability.
4. Identify opportunities to support the development and expansion of local WASH market systems, including through capacity building, financial assistance, and public–private partnerships.

2.3.2.2 Community-based WASH training and capacity building

Purpose: Developing community-based WASH training and capacity building programmes is critical to empower local actors to lead and sustain emergency response and recovery efforts, and to promote long-term hygiene behaviour change and service management. The Practitioners' Toolkit (Annex 1) provides further guidance on training and staff development (Section 4.2).

Timing: Initiate community-based training and capacity building within the first 30 days of the response, and continue to provide ongoing learning and support throughout the emergency, recovery, and development phases.

Key steps:

1. Train local authorities, WASH service providers, and community-based health, education, and nutrition workers on key WASH topics, such as water safety, sanitation management, and hygiene promotion.
2. Strengthen the governance and coordination capacities of local WASH institutions and platforms, such as water user associations, sanitation committees, and multi-stakeholder forums.
3. Promote household water treatment and safe storage practices, using locally available materials and technologies, and building on existing community knowledge and preferences.
4. Shift from one-off, classroom-based training sessions to ongoing, on-the-job mentoring, peer learning, and experiential capacity building approaches that are tailored to local needs and contexts.

2.3.2.3 Transition to community-managed, climate-resilient WASH services

Purpose: Transitioning to community-managed, climate-resilient WASH and health services is essential to ensure the long-term sustainability, equity, and resilience of emergency interventions, and to promote local ownership and adaptation to changing climatic conditions. The Practitioners' Toolkit (Annex 1) provides further guidance on sustainability planning (Section 3.4) and community engagement (Section 3.3).

Timing: Initiate the transition to community-managed, climate-resilient WASH services within the first 90 days of the response, and continue to support and monitor the process throughout the recovery and development phases.

Key steps:

1. Support the participatory development and implementation of community-level water and sanitation safety plans that identify and mitigate key risks and vulnerabilities, including those related to climate change.
2. Facilitate inclusive, community-led planning processes for the design, construction, and management of sustainable, climate-resilient WASH infrastructure and services.
3. Establish community-based monitoring, feedback, and accountability mechanisms to ensure that WASH services are responsive to local needs, preferences, and grievances, and are adapted to evolving climatic conditions.
4. Provide ongoing technical, financial, and institutional support to community-based WASH service providers and management structures to ensure the long-term functionality, quality, and equity of services.

2.3.2.4 Align emergency WASH and long-term development

Purpose: Aligning emergency WASH interventions with long-term development priorities and plans is critical to ensure the sustainability, coherence, and impact of investments, and to promote a smooth transition from relief to recovery and resilience. The Practitioners' Toolkit (Annex 1) provides further guidance on strategic planning (Section 3.1).

Timing: Initiate the alignment of emergency WASH interventions with long-term development within the first 30 days of the response, and continue to update and adapt alignment strategies throughout the recovery and development phases.

Key steps:

1. Review existing local and national WASH policies, budgets, and strategies to identify opportunities for alignment with emergency WASH priorities, approaches, and standards.

2. Advocate for the integration of climate-resilient, risk-informed, and inclusive WASH approaches and technologies into long-term development plans and investments.
3. Promote participatory, accountable, and transparent WASH governance mechanisms that engage affected communities, particularly marginalized and vulnerable groups, in decision-making and oversight.
4. Establish and strengthen strategic partnerships between humanitarian and development actors, including government, civil society, and the private sector, to leverage comparative advantages and ensure a coordinated, sustainable WASH response.

2.3.2.5 Monitor and evaluate WASH outcomes

Purpose: Monitoring and evaluating WASH outcomes is essential to track progress, identify gaps and challenges, and inform evidence-based decision-making and adaptive management throughout the emergency response and recovery phases. The Practitioners' Toolkit (Annex 1) provides further guidance on monitoring and evaluation frameworks (Section 5.1).

Timing: Establish WASH monitoring and evaluation systems within the first 30 days of the response, and continue to collect, analyse, and use data throughout the emergency, recovery, and development phases.

Key steps:

1. Develop and implement a comprehensive monitoring and evaluation framework that tracks the coverage, quality, and use of WASH services, using both quantitative and qualitative indicators and methods.
2. Assess the short-term and long-term impacts of WASH interventions on key outcomes, such as hygiene behaviour change, disease reduction, and community resilience, using rigorous research and evaluation designs.
3. Strengthen the capacity of local WASH institutions and service providers to collect, analyse, and use monitoring and evaluation data for planning, management, and accountability purposes.
4. Use participatory monitoring and evaluation tools and approaches to gather real-time feedback from affected communities and ensure that WASH interventions are responsive to their needs, preferences, and concerns.
5. Establish clear benchmarks and targets for progressive improvements in WASH outcomes, and use monitoring and evaluation data to identify and prioritize corrective actions and adaptations.

2.3.2.6 Document and share lessons learned

Purpose: Documenting and sharing lessons learned from emergency WASH interventions is critical to build the evidence base, promote continuous learning and improvement, and inform future response strategies and best practices. The Practitioners' Toolkit (Annex 1) provides further guidance on knowledge management (Section 5.5).

Timing: Initiate the documentation and sharing of lessons learned within the first 90 days of the response, and continue to update and disseminate learning throughout the emergency, recovery, and development phases.

Key steps:

1. Capture and synthesize the perspectives and experiences of affected communities on the effectiveness, relevance, and sustainability of WASH interventions, using participatory assessment and feedback tools.
2. Facilitate cross-learning and knowledge exchange between communities, agencies, and sectors through peer-to-peer learning events, workshops, and online platforms.
3. Document and disseminate best practices, innovations, and lessons learned from emergency WASH interventions through case studies, guidance notes, and other knowledge products.
4. Advocate for the integration of community-based, locally led WASH approaches and learning into national and global policies, strategies, and programmes.
5. Establish and maintain repositories, networks, and communities of practice to enable the long-term access to and use and updating of WASH lessons learned and best practices.

2.4 Monitoring

2.4.1 Objectives

Monitoring integrated WASH and health interventions aims to track the implementation, quality, and effectiveness of coordinated efforts to prevent and control WASH-related diseases in emergencies. It provides essential data for decision-making, quality assurance, accountability, and learning at national and subnational levels.

2.4.2 Key monitoring activities

2.4.2.1 Engaging communities

Community participation is vital for relevant, context-specific monitoring of WASH health risks, needs, and outcomes. Affected people should be actively involved in designing indicators, collecting data, analysing results, and planning improvements.

- Consult diverse community members to identify locally appropriate indicators and monitoring approaches.
- Train and involve community actors in participatory data collection, analysis, and use.

- Establish community feedback and accountability mechanisms on WASH health services and facilities.
- Conduct inclusive community assessments to understand WASH-related health risks, behaviours, and barriers.
- Triangulate findings using household surveys, facility assessments, community scorecards, and focus group discussions for comprehensive understanding.
- Ensure data are disaggregated by sex, age, disability, and other vulnerability characteristics to inform equity-focused programming.
- Establish community dashboards and participatory review forums for visualizing data and supporting local decision-making and accountability.

2.4.2.2 Harmonizing indicators and systems

Standardized monitoring frameworks enable coherent data collection, analysis, and use across WASH and health actors. Indicators should align with national systems and global standards while being adapted to emergency contexts.

- Develop a core set of WASH health indicators for emergencies in line with national and global frameworks.
- Integrate key indicators into WASH and health information management systems at all levels.
- Harmonize monitoring tools, methods, and reporting timelines among WASH health stakeholders.
- Establish data sharing and protection protocols to enable joint analysis and use.
- Align selected indicators with Sustainable Development Goal (SDG) targets and WHO/UNICEF JMP standards to enable comparability and global benchmarking.

2.4.2.3 Strengthening community capacities

Building local monitoring skills and systems is key for ownership, sustainability, and resilience. Capacity development should target community members, health workers, and local authorities.

- Train community teams on WASH and health monitoring, using simple tools and practical methods.
- Mentor health facility staff to routinely monitor WASH services and practices.
- Establish community-managed monitoring systems for WASH facilities and behaviours.
- Strengthen local government capacities for WASH health data management and use.

- Build sustainable community capacity to collect, analyse, and use WASH monitoring data, providing training, mentoring, and support to community-based organizations, frontline workers, and local authorities.

2.4.2.4 Utilizing monitoring data

Regular review and use of monitoring data drives evidence-based action to improve the quality, coverage, and equity of WASH health interventions. This requires accessible information products, participatory forums, and feedback loops. Case Study 2.2 (Yemen: Evidence-based water management in conflict zones) highlights the critical importance of utilizing monitoring data to guide WASH interventions, even in highly challenging crisis contexts. In this example, IOM commissioned hydrogeological assessments and established groundwater monitoring to develop evidence-based water management strategies. By using this monitoring data, IOM was able to shift from short-term emergency water trucking to investing in more sustainable water infrastructure. This case demonstrates how monitoring evidence can drive strategic adaptations in WASH approaches to better address both immediate and longer-term needs. Key ways to utilize monitoring data include:

- Analyse monitoring data to assess WASH health service functionality, quality, and utilization.
- Produce user-friendly dashboards and reports to inform decision-making and advocacy.

Case Study 2.2 Yemen: Evidence-based water management in conflict zones

Yemen faces one of the world's worst water crises, exacerbated by conflict, with 15.3 million Yemenis lacking clean water and sanitation. As the lead WASH humanitarian agency in Marib, the International Organization for Migration (IOM) addressed the critical water situation where groundwater withdrawal is twice the recharge rate.

The conflict has driven Marib's population from 300,000 to over 1.1 million people, with 800,000 internally displaced persons seeking refuge in an area receiving just five days of rain annually. This influx severely strained already depleted aquifers, causing declining groundwater levels and increasing salinity.

To address this crisis sustainably, IOM partnered with the Deputy Governor of Marib and other water authorities to obtain approvals and ensure security for groundwater assessments despite ongoing conflict. IOM then commissioned Groundwater Relief to conduct hydrogeological assessments, establish baseline monitoring, and develop evidence-based water management strategies. This technical assessment analysed available information, conducted field studies on water infrastructure and quality, and established a pilot-scale groundwater monitoring programme, creating the first basis for estimating future water availability and identifying potential deficits. Using this evidence base, IOM shifted from emergency water trucking to developing durable infrastructure, including the Al Sowayda Water Supply Project with a 6-km transmission pipeline, 15-km distribution network serving four displacement sites, and a 300 cubic metre storage tank. This approach extended project lifecycle while creating a foundation for long-term water security.

Attribution: Adapted from Al-Basha, 2024: 119–21 (see Annex 4).

- Convene joint data review meetings with communities, health actors, and local authorities.
- Document and disseminate innovations and lessons learned to inform sector learning.
- Use community WASH monitoring data in local health and development planning and budgeting processes.

2.4.3 Key monitoring indicators

WASH and health monitoring indicators track the inputs, outputs, and outcomes of integrated programming. Key indicators include the following.

WASH in health facilities:

- Proportion of health facilities with functional WASH services meeting national standards
- Proportion of health facility staff trained on and applying WASH-IPC (infection prevention and control) protocols
- Percentage of WASH facilities in community healthcare settings meeting minimum standards

Outbreak detection and response:

- Number and timeliness of suspected outbreak alerts investigated and responded to
- Proportion of outbreak response plans with integrated WASH and health interventions

Hygiene and health behaviours:

- Proportion of households with knowledge of key hygiene practices for disease prevention
- Proportion of households with handwashing facilities with soap and water
- Proportion of people who report practising safe drinking water and food hygiene behaviours
- Percentage of people who have received critical hygiene messages and can demonstrate use of key hygiene items

WASH-related disease burden:

- Incidence and attack rates of priority WASH-related diseases (e.g. cholera, hepatitis E)
- Morbidity and mortality rates from WASH-related diseases, disaggregated by age and sex

Community access and functionality:

- Percentage of households with access to safely managed drinking water and sanitation services
- Maximum distance to water points and toilets
- Number of days that community water points and sanitation facilities are not functional

2.4.4 Monitoring methods and tools

- Health facility assessments (e.g. WASH FIT [Water and Sanitation for Health Facility Improvement Tool], IPC scorecards)
- Community-based disease surveillance and outbreak investigation reports
- Knowledge, attitude, and practice surveys on WASH and health behaviours
- Household surveys and interviews on WASH access, quality, and use
- HMIS data on WASH-related disease trends
- WASH facility functionality and service quality checklists and spot checks
- Standardized monitoring tools and templates for consistent data collection and reporting
- Locally tailored benchmarks and protocols adapted from global quality assurance frameworks

2.4.5 Monitoring roles and responsibilities

Community actors:

- Participate in defining local WASH health monitoring priorities and approaches.
- Collect and report monitoring data on community WASH health behaviours and outcomes.
- Analyse monitoring results and develop action plans to improve community WASH and health.
- Establish community-based working groups to co-lead monitoring efforts and tool refinement.

Implementing agencies:

- Establish and coordinate the implementation of harmonized WASH and health monitoring systems.
- Train and mentor staff and partners on data collection, quality assurance, and analysis.
- Compile, synthesize, and disseminate monitoring data for decision-making and advocacy.
- Facilitate monitoring, evaluation, and learning processes with stakeholders.
- Monitor WASH health financing and expenditures to assess resource gaps and advocate for support.

Government counterparts:

- Coordinate and oversee WASH and health monitoring processes at national and subnational levels.
- Integrate WASH health indicators into national epidemiological and early warning systems.
- Convene periodic WASH health data review and performance management meetings.

- Use monitoring data to inform emergency preparedness, response planning, and resourcing.

2.4.6 Monitoring timeline and deliverables

- Rapid WASH health assessments in the acute phase of emergencies and periodic updates.
- Monthly reporting of all WASH and health data collected during the emergency response, from health facilities and communities.
- Quarterly analysis and dissemination of WASH health monitoring trends and performance.
- Biannual joint review meetings to assess monitoring frameworks, methods, and use.
- Annual evaluation and learning workshops on WASH and health coordination in emergencies.

Key deliverables:

- WASH and health assessment and surveillance database, dashboards, and reports.
- WASH and health monitoring framework, methods, and tools for emergencies.
- Quarterly and annual WASH and health monitoring bulletins and info-graphics.
- WASH and health outbreak investigation and after action review reports.
- Operational research and learning products on WASH health monitoring and coordination.
- Community-specific bulletins and reporting products that distil key data and trends.
- Financial tracking tools integrated into monitoring deliverables.

CHAPTER 3

Integration in emergencies

Guideline for coordinating WASH with nutrition at the national level

3.1 Summary

This coordination guideline outlines seven critical actions that national decision-makers should take during the first 90 days of an emergency. Start with the Key actions table on next page to see what needs to happen and when. The table also directs you to detailed guidance in this chapter and the Practitioners' Toolkit (Annex 1).

This guideline provides essential guidance on coordination for national officials overseeing WASH and nutrition initiatives during emergencies. It supports rapid response while emphasizing long-term resilience, serving as one of four complementary guidelines designed as an integrated framework for WASH coordination with health and nutrition at both national and community levels. This guideline was developed by the WASH Road Map in consultation with numerous other professionals. A list of external sources consulted in the creation of these guidelines can be found in Annex 3.

3.1.1 Purpose

This guideline helps national-level officials and humanitarian coordinators integrate WASH and nutrition interventions during emergencies through structured, time-bound actions. It operationalizes a multisectoral approach to addressing the underlying causes of undernutrition, particularly during the critical first 1,000 days from conception to a child's second birthday. It upholds the rights outlined in the Humanitarian Charter and aligns with global commitments to advance universal health coverage and primary healthcare.

Who should use this: National-level policy makers, nutrition and WASH programme managers, cluster coordinators, UN agency technical leads, and senior representatives from international and national implementing organizations responsible for developing integrated strategies, strengthening cross-sectoral coordination mechanisms, and ensuring policy coherence between nutrition-specific and nutrition-sensitive interventions during humanitarian emergencies.

How to use these actions: Each action in the table is connected to specific sections in this guideline (see the 'Guideline sections' column) that provide detailed coordination frameworks, and to sections in the Practitioners' Toolkit

Key actions

Actions	*WASH*	*Nutrition*	*Timeframe*	*Guideline sections*	*Practitioners' Toolkit sections*
Establish community WASH and nutrition committee	Identify WASH representatives and define roles	Identify nutrition representatives and define roles	Within 48 hours	2.1, 2.2	1.1, 1.2
Conduct participatory community mapping and assessment	Assess WASH conditions, practices, and map community structures	Assess nutrition status, conduct rapid nutrition assessment practices, and map existing nutrition services	Days 1–5	2.2, 2.4, 3.1.1	1.3, 1.4, 2.1, 2.2, 2.3
Provide emergency WASH interventions integrated with nutrition	Ensure access to safe water, sanitation, hygiene; integrate WASH into nutrition service delivery points	Support nutrition-sensitive WASH interventions; integrate WASH messages into nutrition programming	Days 1–14	3.1.2, 3.1.3	2.1, 2.2, 2.3, 4.1, 4.4, 4.6, 4.10
Develop joint strategies and communication systems	Contribute to integrated strategy development; set up WASH feedback systems	Contribute to integrated strategy development; set up nutrition feedback systems	Days 5–14	2.5, 2.6, 3.1.4	3.1, 3.2, 5.3
Establish integrated monitoring and community coordination	Develop WASH indicators aligned with nutrition outcomes; support community coordination functions	Adapt nutrition indicators that capture WASH-sensitive measures; support community monitoring	Days 14–30	2.6, 3.1.4, 4	1.2, 3.3, 4.8, 4.9, 5.1, 5.3, 5.5
Mobilize community champions and expand to schools	Engage WASH champions and promote WASH in schools integrated with nutrition education	Engage nutrition champions and promote nutrition education in schools integrated with WASH	Days 14–60	2.6, 3.2.2	3.3, 4.2, 4.3, 4.4, 4.7
Strengthen local capacity and build sustainable partnerships	Build sustainable WASH capacity, forge partnerships, and plan transition strategies	Build sustainable nutrition capacity, develop partnerships, and plan for sustainability	Days 30–90	2.7, 3.2.1, 3.2.3	1.3, 1.4, 3.4, 3.6

in Annex 1 (see the 'Practitioners' Toolkit sections' column) that offer operational tools, templates, and checklists. Begin with the action most relevant to your current emergency phase, and then refer to the corresponding sections for guidance on implementation.

The guideline sections provide the strategic frameworks for establishing coordination platforms, conducting assessments, and building sustainable systems. The Practitioners' Toolkit (Annex 1) translates these frameworks into practical tools you can adapt and use immediately. Together, they support decision-makers in transitioning from urgent responses to resilient, locally led systems that create enabling environments for optimal nutrition outcomes.

3.1.2 Framework pillars

These five pillars structure the detailed guidance found throughout this guideline:

1. *National coordination*: Set up inclusive national mechanisms with diverse ministries, nutrition and WASH actors, and development partners.
2. *Strategic assessment*: Quickly identify critical WASH and nutrition links, vulnerability patterns, and existing national capacities.
3. *Integrated service delivery*: Provide services that address immediate WASH and nutrition needs while strengthening national food and water systems.
4. *National capacity building*: Develop sustainable government and partner capacity for nutrition-sensitive WASH programming.
5. *National monitoring*: Track integrated WASH and nutrition outcomes to ensure accountability, facilitate learning, and inform future strategies.

3.1.3 Adaptability

Adapt this guideline to align with existing national policies, strategies, and systems, rather than creating parallel structures. It works in both rural and urban settings and should be used in conjunction with district and community-level guidelines for a coherent, multi-level approach. The Practitioners' Toolkit (Annex 1) provides templates and tools that can be modified to suit your specific context.

3.1.4 Timeframe

This guideline focuses specifically on coordinated action during the first 90 days of an emergency at the national level:

- *Emergency actions (0–14 days)*: Urgent action to prevent disease outbreaks and malnutrition.
- *Resilience actions (14–90 days)*: Establishing mechanisms for transitioning to sustainable, locally led, nutrition-sensitive WASH systems.

These timeframes provide a coordination framework for establishing transition mechanisms rather than fixed deadlines for completing transitions, which remain context-dependent and may extend well beyond the initial emergency response period as emphasized in Sphere standards.

3.1.5 Cross-cutting issues

This guideline mainstreams climate resilience, protection, gender equity, and social inclusion, while clearly defining roles and responsibilities across government entities, humanitarian organizations, and community partners. It provides practical guidance to transform emergency response into sustainable progress, bridging the humanitarian–development divide at the national level.

3.2 Stakeholder coordination

Effective stakeholder coordination is essential for the successful integration of WASH and nutrition interventions at the national level. This guideline establishes a framework for engaging all relevant actors in planning, implementation, and monitoring activities across seven critical stakeholder categories: government authorities, humanitarian and development organizations, community and civil society representatives, private sector entities, academic and research institutions, UN agencies and donors, and inter-cluster coordination mechanisms. While numerous stakeholders contribute to this coordination platform, particular attention should be given to securing participation from both nutrition-focused and WASH-oriented entities to create an integrated approach addressing the complex relationship between water, sanitation, hygiene practices, and nutritional outcomes.

Quick reference: Key national-level templates available in Annex 1

Purpose	*Annex 1 Section*	*Use when …*
Multi-stakeholder coordination	1.1, 1.2, 1.5, 1.6	Setting up integrated WASH-nutrition platforms
Nutrition-sensitive assessments	2.1, 2.2, 2.3	Identifying WASH-nutrition linkages and risks
Integrated strategy development	3.1, 3.2, 3.6	Creating nutrition-sensitive WASH strategies
Joint implementation planning	4.1, 4.3, 4.4, 4.6	Coordinated campaign and outreach planning
Unified monitoring systems	5.1, 5.3, 5.5	Tracking integrated WASH-nutrition outcomes

NOTE: All templates in Annex 1 are designed for adaptation to different national contexts and government structures

Further practical guidance can be found in the Practitioners' Toolkit (Annex 1), including:

- Section 1.1: Stakeholder identification checklist
- Section 1.2: Coordination committee terms of reference (TOR) template
- Section 1.3: Stakeholder analysis and mapping tools
- Section 1.5: Stakeholder roles and responsibilities matrix
- Section 1.6: Coordination performance scorecard
- Section 1.7: Coordination timeline (first 45 days)

- Section 2.3: Nutrition-sensitive WASH risk assessment checklist
- Section 3.1: Integrated WASH-nutrition-health response planning template
- Section 3.2: Nutrition-sensitive WASH strategy development guide
- Section 3.3: Community engagement planning framework
- Section 3.4: Capacity assessment and building tools
- Section 3.6: Joint capacity building plan
- Section 4.1: Joint workplan and budget template
- Section 4.2: Training and staff development guides
- Section 4.3: Integrated outreach and campaign planning tools
- Section 4.4: WASH and nutrition behaviour change communication toolkit
- Section 4.6: Integrated outreach strategy template
- Section 5.1: Integrated monitoring framework
- Section 5.3: Community feedback mechanism checklist
- Section 5.5: Performance review and learning tools

The coordination mechanisms described in this guideline are implemented using these tools, which cover aspects such as stakeholder mapping, risk assessment, outreach planning, and performance tracking.

3.2.1 Stakeholder identification checklist

Figure 3.1 illustrates the key stakeholder groups that should be involved in the WASH and nutrition multi-stakeholder platform at the national level, including: government authorities, humanitarian and development organizations, community representatives, private sector, academic and research institutions, UN agencies and donors, and inter-cluster coordination. Each segment represents a distinct category of stakeholders essential for comprehensive emergency response. For a complete stakeholder identification checklist tailored to national WASH and nutrition coordination, please refer to Tool 1.1 in the Practitioners' Toolkit (Annex 1).

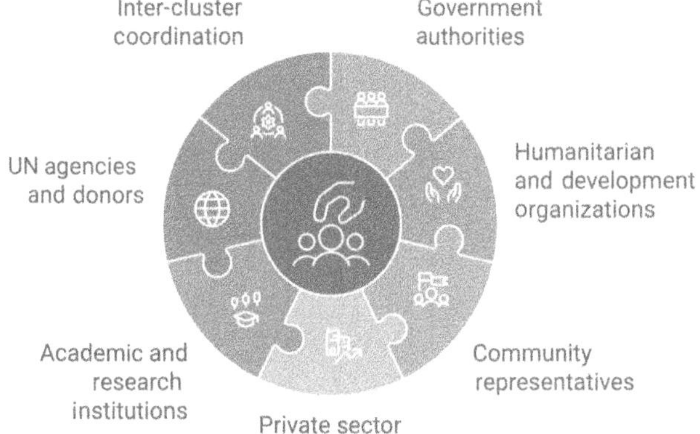

Figure 3.1 Multi-stakeholder coordination wheel with seven segments.

3.2.2 Strengthening meaningful participation

To enhance the effectiveness of the national WASH and nutrition coordination platform, priority should be given to allocating dedicated seats for community representatives, local civil society organizations, and local academic institutions in coordination groups and decision-making bodies. Formal partnership agreements or memoranda of understanding with research and training institutions are recommended to support capacity building, data analysis, and knowledge sharing activities. The coordination mechanism should implement participatory approaches that actively involve community members, including vulnerable and marginalized groups such as women's organizations and disability advocates, in needs assessments, solution development, and decision-making processes. Engaging this diverse range of stakeholders, especially those most affected by the crisis, is essential to ensuring an inclusive, effective, and locally relevant humanitarian response that addresses the complex interrelationship between WASH factors and nutritional outcomes at the national level. See Tool 3.3 in the Practitioners' Toolkit (Annex 1) for guidance on community engagement planning.

3.2.3 Coordination mechanisms

Critical action summary

Critical action	*Timeframe*	*Lead responsibility*
Activate national coordination platform	Within 48 hours	Government ministries with UNICEF/cluster support
Convene initial multi-stakeholder meeting	Within 48 hours	Platform co-chairs
Establish WASH-nutrition task force	By day 5	Platform co-chairs
Complete rapid stakeholder assessment	Days 1–3	Information management officer
Develop a comprehensive stakeholder matrix	By day 14	Information management team
Develop joint, multi-year response plan	By day 30	WASH-nutrition task force

3.2.3.1 Activate and structure the coordination platform

Establishing a robust coordination platform immediately after crisis onset creates the foundation for an effective integrated WASH and nutrition response. This initial structure must balance rapid deployment with thoughtful design, ensuring representation from government ministries, UN agencies, NGOs, and other stakeholders. Early activation of this platform within the first 48 hours provides the operational framework for all subsequent integrated actions and demonstrates organizational commitment to addressing nutritional vulnerabilities through coordinated WASH interventions.

Action: Establish national WASH and nutrition coordination platform within 48 hours

Key stakeholder roles summary

Stakeholder	*Coordination role*	*Implementation role*
Ministry of Health/ Nutrition	Co-lead national platform; chair nutrition sector meetings	Nutrition service standards; integration of WASH in nutrition protocols
WASH cluster/ Lead agency	Technical coordination; information management	Emergency WASH service delivery; water quality and hygiene promotion
UNICEF	Nutrition technical leadership; inter-agency coordination	Nutrition programming; WASH-nutrition integration support
World Food Programme	Food assistance coordination; supply chain management	Food distribution; nutrition programme implementation
Local government	Subnational coordination; resource mobilization	Service delivery oversight; community nutrition programmes
NGO partners	Field-level coordination; community liaison	Direct service implementation; community-based nutrition programmes
Community health workers	Local coordination; outreach coordination	Integrated nutrition and hygiene counselling; community screening

Note: For complete roles and responsibilities, see Annex 1, Section 1.5

Lead: Government ministries (WASH, Health, Nutrition) with WASH/ Nutrition cluster/sector support

Key steps:

- Determine appropriate coordination mechanism (stand-alone or integrated into existing structures).
- Establish co-leadership between government ministries and UNICEF/ Cluster or Sector lead agencies.
- Ensure reporting lines to WASH Cluster or Sector Coordinator and Office for the Coordination of Humanitarian Affairs (OCHA) inter-cluster coordinator, who relays information to the Humanitarian Coordinator/Humanitarian Country Team (HC/HCT).
- Formalize through inclusive Terms of Reference (ToRs) that align with IASC cluster coordination guidelines while adapting to the local context.

3.2.3.2 Manage stakeholder engagement and meetings

Effective emergency coordination depends on bringing diverse stakeholders together quickly to establish a common operating picture. The initial coordination meeting sets the tone for collaboration, helping to align priorities and define working methods among partners with different mandates and capacities.

By ensuring inclusive participation and efficient meeting management from the outset, the platform creates space for meaningful dialogue that balances urgent action with thoughtful planning, enabling stakeholders to contribute their expertise while maintaining focus on critical WASH and nutrition outcomes.

Action: Convene multi-stakeholder coordination meeting within 48 hours

Lead: Platform co-chairs

Key steps:

- Establish a shared understanding of the situation, WASH/nutrition linkages, needs, and capacities.
- Agree on joint priorities, objectives, and response strategies.
- Define inclusive decision-making processes and working methods.
- Ensure balanced representation across all stakeholder groups.

3.2.3.3 Technical coordination structures

Creating specialized coordination structures enhances the platform's ability to address both strategic and technical dimensions of WASH and nutrition integration. These complementary mechanisms – including the technical task force, strategic advisory group, and technical working groups – provide dedicated forums for expertise sharing, decision-making, and innovation. By establishing clear roles and reporting lines for each structure, the platform enables more efficient division of labour while maintaining coherence across the response, ensuring that specialized discussions translate into practical action at both national and subnational levels.

Action: Establish technical and operational coordination mechanisms

Lead: Platform co-chairs

Key components:

- WASH and nutrition task force with technical experts from government, UN, NGOs, and research institutions.
- Strategic advisory group (SAG) of key operational partners for strategic decision-making.
- Technical working groups for specific technical challenges (time-bound).
- Subnational coordination platforms with clear reporting lines.

Functions and responsibilities:

- *Task force*: Oversee joint assessments, develop integrated response plans, provide technical guidance.
- *SAG*: Guide strategic decision-making, oversee response planning, monitor implementation.
- *Technical working groups*: Address specific technical challenges and develop standards.

- *Subnational platforms*: Implement localized responses aligned with national strategy.
- *Information management team*: Support data collection, analysis, and visualization.

3.2.3.4 Stakeholder mapping and management

Comprehensive stakeholder mapping provides the intelligence foundation for strategic coordination and targeting of integrated WASH and nutrition interventions. This mapping process evolves from a rapid initial assessment to a detailed characterization of actors' capacities, coverage, and resources. By systematically tracking 'who is doing what, where, and when', the platform gains visibility into operational realities, enabling more effective gap analysis, partnership formation, and resource allocation. Regular updates to this stakeholder database support real-time decision-making while building institutional memory that strengthens both immediate response and longer-term sector development.

Action: Develop and maintain a comprehensive stakeholder mapping system

Lead: Information management officer

Implementation timeline:

- *Days 1–3*: Rapid stakeholder assessment (4W mapping)
- *By day 14*: Comprehensive stakeholder matrix
- *Ongoing*: Strategic application and regular updates

Key components:

- Government ministries and agencies (all levels)
- UN agencies, clusters, and coordination mechanisms
- NGOs, civil society networks, and community organizations
- Donors, private sector partners, and academic institutions

Responsibility assignment:

- *Information management officer*: Maintains database and visualizations.
- *Coordination team*: Lead joint discussions on the development and planning of crisis solutions.
- *Sector leads*: Analyse data to identify gaps and opportunities, and ensure accurate information from respective areas.
- *All partners*: Provide regular activity and capacity updates.

3.2.3.5 Policy alignment and joint planning

The emergency context presents both challenges and opportunities for aligning WASH and nutrition policy frameworks and operational plans. By conducting a systematic review of existing sectoral policies and strategies, the platform identifies integration gaps and opportunities that inform more coherent joint programming. This alignment process bridges immediate humanitarian action with longer-term development goals, ensuring that emergency response reinforces rather than undermines existing systems. The resulting joint response plan provides a roadmap for coordinated action that maximizes nutritional impact through strategic WASH interventions while building foundations for sustained integration beyond the crisis.

Action: Conduct policy review and develop joint response plan

Lead: WASH and nutrition task force

Key steps for policy review:

- Review existing sectoral policies, strategies, and plans.
- Identify gaps, challenges, and opportunities for integration.
- Ensure WASH is prioritized as a determinant of nutritional outcomes.
- Clarify institutional roles and mutual accountability mechanisms.

Joint response plan requirements:

- Time-bound, measurable objectives and targets for integrated outcomes
- Clear roles and responsibilities for implementation
- Sequenced interventions based on priorities, with flexibility to adapt
- Alignment with national policies, standards, and emergency response frameworks

Planning process:

- Base plan on policy review, stakeholder mapping, and needs assessment. See Tool 2.1 in the Practitioners' Toolkit (Annex 1) for joint assessment methodology.
- Ensure inclusive consultation process with affected communities.
- Develop a multi-year timeframe with short- and long-term objectives.
- Include resource mobilization strategy and sustainability considerations.

3.2.3.6 Monitoring, evaluation, and accountability

A unified monitoring system enables evidence-based coordination by tracking both sector-specific and integrated WASH and nutrition outcomes. This shared information architecture connects field-level implementation with strategic decision-making, providing timely data on coverage, quality, and impact to guide adaptive management. By embedding accountability mechanisms within the monitoring framework, the platform ensures that partners remain responsive to affected communities while maintaining standards. Regular joint analysis converts monitoring data into actionable insights that improve programme effectiveness and build the evidence base for integrated approaches to addressing malnutrition's underlying causes.

Action: Establish a unified information management and accountability system

Lead: Information management team with WASH and nutrition sector leads

Key components of the information management system:

- SMART indicators for tracking integrated WASH and nutrition outputs and outcomes. Refer to Tool 5.1 in the Practitioners' Toolkit (Annex 1) for monitoring framework guidance.
- Alignment with Ministry/UNICEF/OCHA reporting requirements and national health management information system (HMIS) and other relevant data systems.
- Collection of sex-, age-, and disability-disaggregated data.
- Regular joint analysis and information products. See Tool 1.6 in the Practitioners' Toolkit (Annex 1) for coordination performance scorecard.

National system integration requirements:

- Integrate WASH-nutrition monitoring with national nutrition surveillance systems.
- Align with existing HMIS nutrition indicators and reporting cycles.
- Connect to national nutrition cluster information management systems.
- Ensure compatibility with national early warning systems for nutrition.
- Link to national growth monitoring and promotion data systems.
- Coordinate with national nutrition information focal points.
- Use national nutrition survey protocols and anthropometric standards where available.

Accountability mechanisms:

- Monitoring of WASH and nutrition standards adherence through joint supervision.
- Transparent tracking and reporting of funding allocations, expenditures, and results.
- Accessible complaint and feedback mechanisms for affected populations. Refer to Tool 5.3 in the Practitioners' Toolkit (Annex 1) for feedback mechanism guidelines.
- Regular joint reviews to assess relevance, effectiveness, and sustainability.
- Quality assurance checks.

3.2.3.7 Transition and sustainability

Effective coordination platforms evolve throughout the emergency lifecycle, gradually reducing international assistance while maintaining national/local leadership from crisis onset. Planning for this transition from the outset helps ensure that emergency coordination mechanisms strengthen rather than replace national systems. By systematically building government capacity and empowering local organizations, the platform lays the foundations for sustainable coordination of integrated WASH and nutrition programming beyond the emergency phase. This deliberate transition approach maintains continuity of essential services while strengthening the institutional architecture needed for long-term improvements in nutritional outcomes through enhanced WASH services and practices.

Action: Plan for transition to sustainable coordination from the outset

Lead: Platform co-chairs with government counterparts

Key steps:

- Progressively transfer leadership to national and subnational authorities.
- Strengthen government capacity for multisectoral coordination.
- Empower local organizations for service delivery and monitoring.
- Provide sustainable institutional support for building local capacities.

3.3 Emergency WASH actions

The emergency WASH actions outlined in this section provide a roadmap for swift, coordinated, and context-specific interventions to address the critical water, sanitation, and hygiene needs of nutritionally vulnerable populations during humanitarian crises. The framework prioritizes life-saving measures in the emergency actions phase (0–14 days), followed by a concerted effort to integrate WASH interventions with local capacity, ensuring sustainable and resilient solutions in the 14–90 day timeframe. Key actions encompass rapid joint assessments, ensuring access to sufficient quantities of safe water, providing dignified sanitation facilities, promoting critical hygiene practices, and enhancing community-driven coordination. The section also emphasizes the importance of aligning WASH strategies with nutrition sector priorities and strengthening local systems for long-term impact.

3.3.1 Emergency actions (0–14 days)

The emergency actions phase (0–14 days) is critical for addressing the most pressing WASH needs of nutritionally vulnerable populations during a humanitarian crisis. Rapid joint assessments are conducted in collaboration with nutrition actors to identify areas and groups with the highest risk of malnutrition, focusing on the availability and accessibility of safe water, sanitation, and hygiene services. Key activities include ensuring access to sufficient quantities of safe water for drinking and cooking, providing gender-sensitive sanitation facilities, distributing hygiene kits tailored to the needs of families with young children, and promoting key hygiene practices that prevent the spread of diarrheal diseases. Coordination with nutrition actors is prioritized to align WASH interventions with programmes that manage acute malnutrition, support infant and young child feeding, and other nutrition-specific interventions. The emergency actions lay the foundation for more targeted, nutrition-sensitive WASH interventions in the subsequent phases of the emergency, aiming to protect and improve the nutritional status of vulnerable populations.

Key resources available in Annex 1:

- *Coordination timeline (first 45 days)* (Section 1.7): Rapid activation guide for integrated platforms.
- *Nutrition-sensitive WASH strategy development guide* (Section 3.2): Framework for developing evidence-based approaches.
- *Integrated outreach strategy template* (Section 4.6): Planning tool for coordinated nutrition messaging.
- *WASH and nutrition behaviour change communication toolkit* (Section 4.4): Comprehensive resource for unified messaging.
- *Integrated monitoring framework* (Section 5.1): System for tracking cross-sectoral outcomes.

3.3.1.1 Rapid joint WASH and nutrition assessment

Purpose: Conducting rapid joint WASH and nutrition assessments is crucial for identifying strengths, assets, and the most pressing needs and informing the design of effective, context-specific interventions. By engaging communities as active participants and using participatory tools alongside standard methodologies, responders can gain a holistic understanding of the local context, capacities, and priorities. This people-centred approach helps ensure that subsequent actions are relevant, acceptable, and sustainable.

Timing: Within the first 14 days of the emergency response.

Key steps:

1. Coordinate with the Nutrition Cluster, community representatives, and local sectors to identify high-risk populations and existing community structures and resources.
2. Review primary and secondary data to understand local capabilities, the impact of the crisis on local WASH, health, and nutrition outcomes, and cultural beliefs and practices that impact WASH services.
3. Conduct joint, multi-sector rapid assessments at the community level, ensuring the participation of diverse community members, to better understand local strengths and needs.
4. Engage the community as active participants throughout the assessment process.
5. Rapidly analyse and share assessment findings with community members and local partners to inform the design of locally acceptable, relevant, and sustainable interventions.

3.3.1.2 Life-saving, community-based WASH interventions

Purpose: Prioritizing life-saving, community-based WASH interventions in the acute phase of an emergency is critical for preventing disease outbreaks, mitigating malnutrition risks, and promoting dignity. By rapidly restoring access to safe water, providing appropriate sanitation and hygiene facilities, and promoting essential hygiene practices, responders can help protect the health and well-being of affected communities. Engaging local capacities and resources in the design and delivery of these interventions fosters ownership and lays the foundation for sustainable recovery.

Timing: Within the first 14 days of the emergency response.

Key steps:

1. Ensure equitable access to sufficient, safe water supply by supporting community-led rehabilitation of damaged water sources, providing appropriate household water treatment and storage options, promoting local water safety planning, and implementing temporary solutions such as kiosks or water trucking based on community preferences.
2. Rapidly provide safe, accessible, and appropriate sanitation facilities by constructing communal latrines with local designs and labour, installing gender-segregated and secure toilets, adapting facilities for vulnerable users, and establishing community-led systems for ongoing maintenance and cleaning.
3. Promote handwashing and safe hygiene practices by engaging community actors to lead behaviour change, co-designing and distributing appropriate handwashing stations and hygiene kits, conducting hygiene promotion at key community sites, and integrating hygiene messages into existing health and nutrition programming.
4. Enable safe food handling and storage at household and community levels by promoting hygienic preparation and storage methods, distributing essential cooking and storage supplies, and training food handlers while coordinating with community authorities for oversight.
5. Prioritize community support to the most nutritionally vulnerable groups, including pregnant and lactating women, children under five, malnourished families, marginalized households, and individuals with health conditions affecting their WASH and nutrition practices.
6. Jointly develop a community-level WASH and nutrition action plan that sets realistic community-defined targets, identifies and leverages local resources and structures, outlines roles for implementation and monitoring, and establishes shared indicators for measuring progress.

As demonstrated in Case Study 3.1 (Nigeria: Integrating WASH with maternal and child nutrition), integrating WASH and nutrition interventions through a targeted, community-based approach can lead to significant improvements in key practices and outcomes, even in complex crisis settings. The BabyWASH model provides a practical example of how to layer hygiene promotion,

Case Study 3.1 Nigeria: Integrating WASH with maternal and child nutrition

Nigeria has the world's second-highest prevalence of stunting (32% among children under 5), a situation exacerbated by conflict that has displaced over 136,600 persons in Yobe State alone. Global acute malnutrition rates exceeded emergency thresholds (10.9–14.1%), with inadequate WASH access identified as a major contributing factor.

Action Against Hunger implemented a BabyWASH approach in Nangere local government area, targeting 5,562 pregnant and lactating women with integrated interventions at cash distribution points. The programme provided handwashing materials (soap and tippy tap components), promoted child WASH and nutrition practices, and distributed complementary feeding items (child cups, bowls, utensils, and playmats). Additional WASH infrastructure was developed in communities with the highest numbers of vulnerable women.

After 18 months, external evaluation showed significant improvements in WASH knowledge, attitudes, and practices compared to non-intervention communities. Beneficiaries demonstrated better handwashing with soap (90.4% versus 74.9%), greater understanding of disease transmission, improved caretaker practices, and reduced diarrhea incidence in children (16.7% versus 23.0%). The prevalence of severe acute malnutrition, initially higher in the intervention area, declined significantly over the study period.

Attribution: Adapted from 'Case study: BabyWASH approach in Nigeria', in Dodos and Riems, 2023: 98 (see Annex 4).

provision of essential WASH supplies, and infant and young child feeding support to create an enabling environment for health and nutrition. Linking these activities to existing delivery platforms, such as cash distribution points, and prioritizing the most vulnerable households helps maximize coverage and impact.

3.3.1.3 Integrate WASH into community-based nutrition programmes

Purpose: Integrating WASH activities into ongoing community-based nutrition programmes is an effective way to reinforce key messages, improve service uptake, and optimize resource utilization. By leveraging existing delivery platforms, community structures, and trusted influencers, integrated programming can achieve greater coverage, continuity, and sustainability compared to siloed interventions. Joint, multi-purpose community engagements also minimize duplication and mitigate beneficiary fatigue in emergency contexts.

Timing: Start integrating WASH within the first 14 days of the emergency response and continue throughout the programme cycle.

Key steps:

1. Involve community health workers, volunteers, and peer educators in integrated WASH-nutrition activities by conducting joint household visits for counselling and support, organizing participatory cooking and hygiene sessions, facilitating community dialogues and support groups, and training volunteers to screen for acute malnutrition and refer families to nutrition and WASH services.

2. Support community-led construction and maintenance of WASH facilities at nutrition sites by engaging local labour to build culturally appropriate infrastructure, establishing WASH committees to oversee ongoing management, and encouraging cost-sharing through volunteer labour or in-kind contributions to promote local ownership.
3. Collaborate with community organizations, leaders, and influencers to develop culturally relevant WASH and nutrition behaviour change materials by adapting communication strategies to local beliefs, creating visual aids in local languages, identifying motivating factors for behaviour change, and selecting respected community figures to lead outreach efforts.

3.3.1.4 Strengthen community-driven coordination

Purpose: Strengthening community-driven coordination mechanisms is crucial for ensuring the relevance, effectiveness, and sustainability of emergency WASH and nutrition interventions. By actively engaging community representatives in multi-stakeholder platforms and empowering local structures to lead on planning, implementation, and monitoring, responders can promote a more localized, adaptive, and accountable response. Investing in community coordination capacities from the early stages of a crisis sets the stage for a smooth transition to longer-term, resilient WASH and nutrition systems.

Timing: Establish community coordination mechanisms within the first 14 days and strengthen them throughout the response and recovery phases.

Key steps:

1. Promote regular community-level coordination meetings that bring together WASH, nutrition, health, and community actors to jointly set goals, align household targeting with a focus on the most marginalized, identify emerging issues, and foster adaptive management through shared problem-solving.
2. Establish community feedback and accountability mechanisms – such as suggestion boxes, hotlines, scorecards, radio programmes, and participatory reviews – to ensure services remain accessible, responsive, and informed by community input.
3. Develop joint indicators and participatory monitoring tools that capture community perspectives through mapping, surveys, and storytelling, and use regular community meetings to review data, celebrate progress, and plan corrective actions collaboratively.

3.3.2 Resilience actions (14–90 days)

Integrating emergency WASH interventions with local capacity is crucial for building resilience and ensuring the sustainability of nutrition-sensitive WASH services beyond the acute crisis phase. This section focuses on the

14–90 day timeframe, wherein concerted efforts are made to engage, strengthen, and empower local actors, systems, and resources. Key strategies include assessing and building the capacity of local WASH and nutrition stakeholders, mobilizing community structures and champions, forging partnerships for resilience, and facilitating a smooth transition to community-managed, climate-resilient WASH services. Case studies, such as the one from Nigeria showcasing the BabyWASH approach, demonstrate the transformative potential of integrating WASH and nutrition interventions at the community level, leveraging local knowledge, preferences, and ownership for lasting impact.

3.3.2.1 Strengthen local government and community capacity

Purpose: Strengthening the capacity of local government institutions and community-based organizations to lead and sustain integrated WASH and nutrition interventions is critical for ensuring the continuity of services and progress towards long-term development goals. By providing targeted technical assistance, training, and mentoring to local actors, responders can catalyse sustainable improvements in WASH and nutrition governance, financing, service delivery, and community engagement. Supporting the development of local policies, plans, and budgets that prioritize integrated, nutrition-sensitive WASH programming helps institutionalize multisectoral approaches and ensures they remain a priority beyond the crisis period.

Timing: Begin capacity strengthening within the first 14 days of the response and continue throughout the recovery and development phases, with a focus on the 14–90 day period.

Key steps:

1. Work with local authorities to review and adapt policies, standards, and plans by conducting participatory policy analysis, providing technical support to embed community priorities into official guidance, and advocating for increased funding and decentralized support for community-led WASH and nutrition programming.
2. Strengthen the capacity of the local health, WASH, and nutrition workforce by training government staff as master trainers, creating peer learning and mentorship networks, and developing simple tools and job aids that frontline workers can use to promote integrated behaviours.
3. Support communities to develop costed, multi-year WASH and nutrition action plans by facilitating inclusive planning processes, conducting local capacity and resource mapping, and providing technical support in budgeting, resource mobilization, and implementation strategies.
4. Integrate community-defined indicators and participatory monitoring into local government systems by co-developing monitoring tools with communities, building local authority capacity to manage and use participatory data, and advocating for its inclusion in broader subnational and national information systems.

3.3.2.2 Mobilize community structures and champions

Purpose: Mobilizing trusted community structures and influential champions is a powerful way to accelerate uptake of improved WASH and nutrition behaviours and generate demand for quality services. By engaging local leaders, community-based organizations, and positive deviants as change agents, responders can tap into existing social capital, knowledge networks, and community-driven solutions. Investing in the capacity and motivation of these local actors to promote integrated WASH and nutrition practices helps create an enabling environment for sustainable behaviour change.

Timing: Begin identifying and engaging community structures and champions within the first 14 days of the response and continue to support and strengthen them throughout the 14–90 day period and beyond.

Key steps:

1. Engage traditional, religious, and civic leaders to promote improved WASH and nutrition practices by conducting stakeholder mapping, sensitizing leaders on key issues, and training them to serve as behaviour change champions and community mobilizers.
2. Form or strengthen inclusive community structures – such as WASH and nutrition committees, mother-to-mother support groups, including father support groups, and youth-led clubs – to lead local planning, peer education, and intergenerational behaviour change efforts.
3. Identify and support community role models and early adopters by using community feedback to select champions, providing training and incentives, and engaging them as peer educators and advocates for WASH and nutrition within their social networks.
4. Facilitate community-led design, construction, and management of WASH facilities by organizing participatory design sessions, training local artisans in construction and maintenance, and establishing systems like water user committees to sustain services.

As highlighted in Case Study 3.2 (Yemen: Solar-powered water infrastructure for nutrition security), investing in local capacity and fostering strategic partnerships with government authorities and community structures is critical for the long-term sustainability of WASH interventions in protracted crises. The solar-powered water system rehabilitation project demonstrates how appropriate technology choices, coupled with capacity building of local management committees and alignment with government institutions, can improve the resilience and cost-effectiveness of water supply in fragile contexts. By proactively engaging local authorities in joint planning, monitoring, and problem-solving, responders can build trust, ensure relevance to local priorities, and pave the way for government-led service delivery. While navigating complex stakeholder relationships in conflict settings can be challenging, transparent communication and a commitment to strengthening local systems can yield substantial results for sustainability.

Case Study 3.2 Yemen: Solar-powered water infrastructure for nutrition security

Yemen faces one of the world's largest humanitarian crises, with 20.7 million people requiring assistance and 15.3 million lacking clean water and sanitation. The ongoing conflict has severely damaged water infrastructure in a country already facing extreme water scarcity, with 70% of Yemenis lacking access to soap for handwashing and 11.2 million lacking basic water supplies.

Save the Children supported 26 healthcare facilities with WASH interventions, including rehabilitation of latrines and excreta disposal systems in 15 sites. The organization focused on replacing diesel-powered pumps with solar systems, converting 28 out of 39 rehabilitated water networks to solar power. While initially more expensive, these systems proved cheaper over time due to lower operating costs, addressing fuel availability challenges that previously drove families to seek unsafe water sources.

Save the Children also trained local water management committees in operation and maintenance, providing tools and spare parts for future repairs. They established connections between these committees and local water authorities to ensure institutional support for major breakdowns. Despite initial delays from local authority approval processes, Save the Children committed to building closer ties with local administrators through joint monitoring and transparency in budgeting. Over time, this deliberate relationship building significantly reduced waiting times for programme approval and enabled both sides to see shared success. It also allowed Save the Children to better align programme design with local needs and the longer-term planning goals of local authorities, essential for sustained nutrition impact.

Attribution: Adapted from Nyamoko, 2021: 32–33 (see Annex 4).

3.3.2.3 Forge community partnerships for resilience

Purpose: Forging diverse partnerships to support community-led initiatives is crucial for strengthening the shock-responsiveness and sustainability of local WASH and nutrition systems. By linking community structures with civil society organizations, research institutions, private sector actors, and development agencies, responders can mobilize a wider range of resources and capacities to scale up and sustain successful community-based models. Nurturing these multi-stakeholder coalitions also creates opportunities for mutual learning, innovation, and advocacy to influence broader policy and practice.

Timing: Identify and engage potential community partners within the first 30 days of the response and continue to strengthen partnerships throughout the 14–90 day period and beyond.

Key steps:

1. Support community-driven risk assessments, hazard mapping, and preparedness planning by training community members in participatory tools, facilitating analysis of WASH and nutrition vulnerabilities, and developing preparedness plans that assign clear roles and resources for mitigating WASH-related shocks.
2. Establish community-managed contingency funds and supply stockpiles by conducting feasibility and market assessments, training community

structures in transparent fund and supply management, and providing seed funding and linkages to financial institutions for sustainability.

3. Forge multi-stakeholder partnerships to support community-led WASH and nutrition initiatives by engaging local entrepreneurs, linking savings groups to credit and livelihoods, collaborating with schools and local media, and encouraging local organizations to scale successful models.
4. Strengthen coordination across community health, nutrition, and WASH systems by developing integrated referral protocols, promoting cross-training among community workers, establishing community-managed posts with basic WASH services, and creating local platforms for joint planning and accountability.

3.4 Monitoring

3.4.1 Objectives

Monitoring integrated WASH and nutrition interventions at the national level aims to track progress, identify gaps, inform decision-making, and strengthen accountability to affected populations. It focuses on assessing the relevance, coverage, quality, and effectiveness of integrated programming in emergency contexts.

3.4.2 Key monitoring activities

3.4.2.1 Engaging communities

Meaningful community participation throughout the monitoring process is critical for ensuring local relevance, ownership, and utilization of findings. Diverse community members, including women, children and marginalized groups, should be actively involved in designing assessments, collecting and analysing data, and using results to inform improvements.

- Train and engage community members, including women, children, and marginalized groups, in context-specific WASH and nutrition assessments.
- Collaborate with community representatives to select locally appropriate indicators, conduct joint analysis, and discuss findings through accessible feedback sessions.
- Implement community-level assessments using participatory data collection methods, such as household interviews, focus groups, and direct observation.
- Disaggregate data by sex, age, disability, and other relevant factors to identify and monitor disparities and inequities to capture specific vulnerabilities and track equitable access to services.
- Establish accessible feedback and complaint mechanisms (e.g. suggestion boxes, help desks, open community meetings) and ensure timely response to all complaints.

3.4.2.2 Harmonizing indicators and systems

Establishing a harmonized monitoring system enables comparable data, joint analysis, and evidence-based decision-making. Core indicators should be aligned with national and global monitoring frameworks while allowing flexibility to integrate context-specific indicators defined with communities.

- Develop a set of core WASH and nutrition indicators aligned with national systems and global frameworks like the Sustainable Development Goals (SDGs).
- Integrate key indicators into national and subnational WASH and nutrition information systems.
- Harmonize data collection tools, methodologies, and reporting timeframes across WASH and nutrition partners.
- Establish clear roles, accountability mechanisms, and data sharing protocols among monitoring stakeholders.
- Develop joint monitoring and evaluation plans with nutrition actors, defining shared roles, indicators, and follow-up mechanisms.

3.4.2.3 Strengthening community capacities

Building community capacities and systems for participatory monitoring empowers local actors to track progress, generate learning, and sustain outcomes in the long-term. This requires targeted skills training, ongoing mentoring, appropriate tools and technology, and effective feedback and accountability mechanisms.

- Train community monitoring teams on data collection, analysis and use, using simple, locally adapted tools and methods.
- Facilitate community-led monitoring of WASH and nutrition facilities, behaviours, and outcomes using participatory tools such as community scorecards, user satisfaction surveys, and community observation checklists through joint assessments, spot checks, and feedback mechanisms.
- Analyse monitoring data with communities using accessible formats to identify gaps, celebrate achievements, and agree on follow-up actions.
- Link community monitoring to subnational and national WASH and nutrition coordination and information management systems.
- Lead the development and implementation of community action plans based on monitoring findings.
- Support the transition of monitoring responsibilities to local committees (e.g. village WASH committees, mother care groups).
- Facilitate community-to-community learning exchanges and peer support networks to share promising practices and strengthen local ownership.

3.4.2.4 Utilizing monitoring data

Translating monitoring data into action is key to driving evidence-based decision-making, quality improvement, and accountability. This requires regular, participatory analysis of results, clear information products tailored to different audiences, and functioning knowledge management and learning systems.

- Analyse monitoring findings to assess the reach, quality, and equity of integrated interventions, identify barriers and enablers, and recommend improvements.
- Develop user-friendly dashboards, info-graphics, and reports to communicate results to diverse stakeholders.
- Convene periodic data review meetings with communities, government, and partners to jointly interpret findings and agree on course corrections.
- Document and disseminate promising practices, innovations, and lessons through knowledge products, learning events, and communities of practice.
- Monitor and report on the safety, privacy, cultural acceptability, and physical accessibility of facilities, particularly for women, children, and people with disabilities, using joint spot checks and interviews.
- Develop policy briefs and advocacy materials using monitoring data to influence WASH and nutrition policies, budgets, and national planning. Use monitoring findings to advocate for domestic resource allocation and long-term policy reforms that sustain integrated WASH and nutrition approaches.

3.4.3 Key monitoring indicators

Monitoring integrated WASH and nutrition programming requires a combination of output, outcome and process indicators. Key indicators are listed below.

WASH and nutrition outcomes:

- Prevalence of child stunting, wasting, and underweight
- Proportion of children 6–23 months receiving a minimum acceptable diet
- Prevalence of diarrhea and enteric infections in children under five
- Percentage of caregivers reporting sufficient time for child care

WASH access and practices:

- Proportion of households with access to a basic water supply, sanitation, and hygiene facilities
- Proportion of households practising safe drinking water storage and treatment
- Proportion of households with a handwashing facility with soap and water

- Proportion of households safely disposing of child feces
- Percentage of mother-child dyads practising key hygiene behaviours
- Functionality rate of water points and their distance to households (e.g. within 30-minute round trip)
- Percentage of open defecation-free-verified communities maintaining criteria
- Percentage of caregivers knowing how to prepare oral rehydration solution
- Proportion of caregivers practising safe food preparation and storage
- Functionality and user satisfaction of WASH services in integrated programmes

Service performance and capacity:

- Proportion of WASH facilities in health and nutrition centres meeting minimum standards
- Number of community health and nutrition workers trained on integrated WASH and nutrition
- Functionality of community-based WASH and nutrition management committees

3.4.4 Monitoring methods and tools

- Household surveys (e.g. standardized questionnaires on WASH and nutrition KAP, diarrhea prevalence)
- Health facility assessments (e.g. WASH FIT survey, health centre records review)
- Community assessments (e.g. participatory mapping, focus group discussions, interviews)
- Programme reports and coverage data (e.g. WASH beneficiaries, SAM/MAM admissions, IYCF counselling)
- Observation checklists (e.g. on handwashing, food hygiene, infant feeding demonstrations)

3.4.5 Monitoring roles and responsibilities

Community actors:

- Participate in designing and implementing community-level WASH and nutrition assessments.
- Collect, compile, and communicate monitoring data on agreed indicators.
- Analyse results and develop action plans to address identified gaps and priorities.
- Provide feedback on the quality, access, and use of WASH and nutrition services and facilities.
- Support the transition of monitoring responsibilities to local committees (e.g. village WASH committees, mother care groups).

Implementing agencies:

- Coordinate the implementation of harmonized monitoring systems and tools.
- Train staff and partners on data collection, quality assurance, analysis, and reporting.
- Compile data from different sources, conduct analysis, and develop information products.
- Facilitate data use for evidence-based planning, adaptive management, and learning.

Government counterparts:

- Coordinate and oversee monitoring processes at the national and subnational levels.
- Integrate WASH and nutrition indicators into sectoral monitoring frameworks and systems.
- Convene joint data analysis and performance review events with partners.
- Use monitoring evidence to inform policies, strategies, guidelines, and resource allocation.

3.4.6 Monitoring timeline and deliverables

- Community WASH and nutrition assessments conducted at least biannually
- Monthly monitoring visits and data collection at health facilities and communities
- Quarterly compilation of monitoring data and production of information products (e.g. dashboards)
- Biannual data review and action planning workshops at subnational and national levels
- Annual WASH and nutrition sector performance review and planning meeting
- WASH and nutrition knowledge products developed and disseminated semi-annually (e.g. bulletins, reports)

Key deliverables:

- Integrated WASH and nutrition monitoring and evaluation framework and indicators
- WASH and nutrition assessment and survey reports (baseline, midline, endline)
- Monthly/quarterly WASH and nutrition sector monitoring dashboards and info-graphics
- Minutes of data review meetings with performance improvement action points
- Community WASH and nutrition scorecards and monitoring reports
- Case studies, learning briefs, and other knowledge products documenting practices and innovations
- Policy briefs and advocacy materials using monitoring data to influence WASH and nutrition policies, budgets, and national planning

CHAPTER 4

Integration in emergencies

Guideline for coordinating WASH with health at the community level

4.1 Summary

This coordination guideline outlines eight critical actions that community-level implementers should take during the first 90 days of an emergency. Start with the Key actions table on next page to see what needs to happen and when. The table also directs you to detailed guidance in this chapter and the Practitioners' Toolkit (Annex 1).

This guideline provides essential guidance on coordination for community-level implementers overseeing WASH and health initiatives during emergencies. It supports rapid response while emphasizing long-term resilience, serving as one of four complementary guidelines designed as an integrated framework for WASH coordination with health and nutrition at both national and community levels. This guideline was developed by the WASH Road Map in consultation with numerous other professionals. A list of external sources consulted in the creation of these guidelines can be found in Annex 3.

4.1.1 Purpose

This guideline helps frontline workers, community leaders, and local organizations integrate WASH and health interventions during emergencies through structured, time-bound actions. It provides a people-centred approach for rapidly improving WASH services in health facilities and communities, while strengthening local stakeholder capacity to sustain these services in the long term. It upholds the rights outlined in the Humanitarian Charter and aligns with global commitments to advance universal health coverage and primary healthcare.

Who should use this: Frontline workers, community leaders, facility managers, local NGO staff, and field-based technical advisers implementing WASH and health interventions at the community level. This benefits explicitly health facility administrators, community health workers, WASH committee members, and field officers from implementing agencies who are directly responsible for coordinating and delivering integrated services within affected communities.

How to use these actions: Each action in the table is connected to specific sections in this guideline (see the 'Guideline sections' column) that provide

Key actions

Actions	*WASH*	*Health*	*Timeframe*	*Guideline sections*	*Practitioners' Toolkit sections*
Activate health facility-led coordination platform	Identify WASH representatives and align with health facility priorities	Lead coordination platform with senior facility management and support from local government	Within 48 hours	2.1	1.1, 1.2, 1.5
Conduct rapid community and facility assessments	Assess WASH conditions in communities and health facilities; map stakeholders and capacities	Provide input on health risks and priorities; assess health facility WASH conditions	Days 1–10	2.2, 2.3, 3.1.1	1.3, 2.1, 2.2, 2.4, 2.6, 3.4, 3.5
Implement priority WASH interventions and behaviour change	Provide water, sanitation, hygiene interventions; promote critical hygiene behaviours	Provide guidance on health-related WASH priorities; support hygiene promotion in health settings	Days 1–14	3.1.2, 3.1.3	4.4, 4.5, 2.4
Develop localized action plans and establish partnerships	Align WASH activities with health programme objectives; engage community leaders in WASH planning	Incorporate WASH messages into health programmes; establish strategic partnerships with development actors	Days 5–21	2.4, 2.3, 3.1.6	3.1, 3.2, 3.3, 3.7, 4.1
Strengthen local governance and establish monitoring systems	Build capacity of local WASH committees; set up referral pathways between WASH and health services	Build capacity of community health workers; establish accountability and information sharing systems	Days 10–30	2.5, 2.8, 3.1.4, 3.1.5	3.4, 3.6, 4.2, 5.1, 5.2, 5.3, 5.4
Establish facility-based WASH improvement teams and secure high-level support	Support WASH assessments and improvements in health facilities; align with national standards	Oversee facility WASH improvements; engage senior ministry leadership for resource commitments	Days 7–30	2.6, 2.7	2.4, 2.5, 2.6, 4.5
Develop sustainable systems and market solutions	Build local WASH market systems; support community-managed WASH services transition	Integrate WASH into health system strengthening; support health facility sustainability planning	Days 30–90	2.9, 3.2.1, 3.2.2, 3.2.4	3.3, 3.4, 4.8, 4.9
Facilitate learning and establish resilience measures	Capture community perspectives on WASH improvements; document innovations and adaptations	Document health facility WASH improvements; establish emergency preparedness systems	Days 45–90	3.2.3, 2.9	5.5, 5.6, 4.7, 4.9

detailed coordination frameworks, and to Annex 1, the Practitioners' Toolkit (see the 'Practitioners' Toolkit sections' column), that offers operational tools, templates, and checklists. Begin with the action most relevant to your current emergency phase, and then refer to the corresponding sections for guidance on implementation.

The guideline sections provide the strategic frameworks for establishing coordination platforms, conducting assessments, and building sustainable systems. The Practitioners' Toolkit (Annex 1) translates these frameworks into practical tools you can adapt and use immediately. Together, they support implementers in transitioning from urgent responses to resilient, community-managed systems that leverage local resources while meeting immediate health protection needs.

4.1.2 Framework pillars

These five pillars structure the detailed guidance found throughout this guideline:

1. *Community engagement*: Engaging health facility staff, community representatives, and local partners as active participants in all stages of WASH improvement.
2. *Local assessment*: Assessing WASH infrastructure, practices, and skills at the facility and community level to identify critical gaps.
3. *Coordinated implementation*: Implementing priority actions to upgrade WASH services, change behaviours, and establish a culture of hygiene and safety.
4. *Local capacity building*: Building the capacity of health workers and community partners to operate and maintain WASH infrastructure.
5. *Community monitoring*: Supporting health facilities and communities in establishing systems for ongoing data collection, review, and quality improvement.

4.1.3 Adaptability

Adapt this guideline to align with local healthcare practices, social norms, and existing community structures, rather than creating parallel systems. It works effectively in both rural and urban settings across diverse cultural contexts and should be used in conjunction with national-level guidelines for a coherent, multi-level approach. The Practitioners' Toolkit (Annex 1) provides templates and tools that can be modified to suit your specific context.

4.1.4 Timeframe

This guideline focuses specifically on coordinated action during the first 90 days of an emergency at the community level:

- *Emergency actions (0–14 days)*: Urgent action to prevent disease outbreaks and reduce mortality.

- *Resilience actions (14–90 days)*: Establishing mechanisms for transitioning to sustainable, community-managed WASH and health systems.

These timeframes provide a coordination framework for establishing transition mechanisms rather than fixed deadlines for completing transitions, which remain context-dependent and may extend well beyond the initial emergency response period as emphasized in Sphere standards. By engaging local stakeholders from the outset and integrating with local health and development systems, communities emerge from crises stronger and better equipped.

4.1.5 Cross-cutting issues

This guideline mainstreams climate resilience, protection, gender equity, and social inclusion, while clearly defining roles and responsibilities across government entities, humanitarian organizations, and community partners. It provides practical guidance to transform emergency response into sustainable progress, bridging the humanitarian–development divide at the national level.

4.2 Stakeholder coordination

Effective coordination of WASH and health interventions at the community level requires engagement of a diverse range of local stakeholders who directly interface with families and individuals. This guideline section outlines the approach to stakeholder coordination with special emphasis on health facilities as focal points for integrated WASH and health interventions and community outreach. This approach recognizes that sustainable improvements in health outcomes require collaborative efforts between clinical care providers and environmental health practitioners.

Quick reference: Key community-level templates available in Annex 1

Purpose	*Annex 1 section*	*Use when …*
Community coordination setup	1.2, 2.5, 4.9	Establishing local coordination structures
Participatory assessments	2.1, 2.4, 2.6	Mapping and evaluating community and facilities
Local action planning	3.7, 4.1, 4.5	Developing community-owned implementation plans
Health facility improvements	4.5, 4.7, 5.2	Enhancing WASH in healthcare settings
Community monitoring	5.1, 5.3, 5.4, 5.6	Developing participatory tracking and feedback systems

Note: All templates in Annex 1 are designed for adaptation to different community contexts and government structures.

Further practical guidance can be found in the Practitioners' Toolkit (Annex 1), including:

- Section 1.1: Stakeholder identification checklist
- Section 1.2: Coordination committee terms of reference (TOR) template
- Section 1.3: Stakeholder analysis and mapping tools
- Section 1.4: Social network analysis guide
- Section 1.5: Stakeholder roles and responsibilities matrix
- Section 2.1: Participatory community mapping guide
- Section 2.4: Health facility WASH assessment checklist
- Section 2.5: Committee setup checklist
- Section 2.6: WASH-IPC monitoring checklist
- Section 3.3: Community engagement planning framework
- Section 3.4: Capacity assessment and building tools
- Section 3.6: Joint capacity building plan
- Section 3.7: Community-level joint action plan template
- Section 4.1: Joint workplan and budget template
- Section 4.2: Training and staff development guides
- Section 4.3: Integrated outreach and campaign planning tools
- Section 4.5: WASH in healthcare facility improvement planning template
- Section 4.7: Integrated risk communication and community engagement plan
- Section 4.9: Community coordination timeline and task checklist
- Section 5.1: Integrated monitoring framework
- Section 5.2: Outbreak investigation and response checklist
- Section 5.3: Community feedback mechanism checklist
- Section 5.4: Supportive supervision checklist
- Section 5.5: Performance review and learning tools
- Section 5.6: Monthly reporting format for community committees

These tools support community-level coordination, covering aspects such as participatory mapping, committee setup, joint action planning, risk communication, and feedback mechanisms.

4.2.1 Stakeholder identification checklist

Figure 4.1 illustrates seven key stakeholder groups essential for effective community WASH and health coordination: government authorities, humanitarian and development organizations, community representatives, private sector, academic and research institutions, UN agencies and donors, and inter-cluster coordination. A detailed stakeholder identification checklist is provided in Tool 1.1 of the Practitioners' Toolkit (Annex 1).

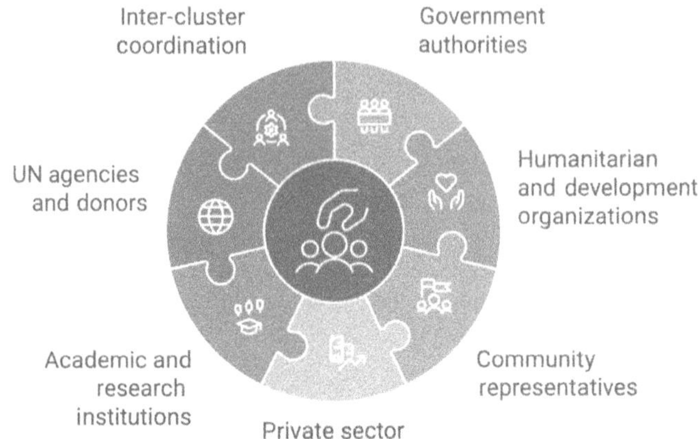

Figure 4.1 Multi-stakeholder coordination wheel with seven segments.

4.2.2 Strengthening meaningful participation

For effective community WASH and health coordination, leadership roles and decision-making authority should be allocated to health facility staff, community representatives, and local officials to prevent external agency domination. The coordination platform should actively reduce participation barriers for marginalized populations through inclusive meeting practices, accessible information formats, and leadership opportunities, with dedicated seats for representatives of vulnerable groups. As demonstrated in the Syria case study (Case Study 4.1), engaging children as active participants rather than passive recipients can lead to more effective and sustainable WASH interventions.

Case Study 4.1 Syria: Child-centred hygiene promotion during COVID-19

Save the Children implemented the COVID-19 Hygiene Promotion Initiative in north-west Syria, planning interventions before the pandemic's arrival in this remote region. This proactive approach allowed community members and children to operationalize activities within 10 days of the first detected case.

COVID-19 prevention information was contextualized into five key messages: hand-washing, drinking safe water, using and maintaining latrines, social distancing, and using masks or avoiding face touching. When face-to-face activities became impossible due to pandemic restrictions, the programme rapidly adapted to remote modalities, including radio sessions and information leaflets on bread bundles.

Children played a crucial role in programme design and implementation, contributing ideas for radio sessions and even selecting the programme name. Their input made hygiene messages more accessible and engaging for peers while increasing their self-confidence and self-expression. After the programme concluded, both children and adults continued sharing hygiene information with their communities, demonstrating sustained behaviour change.

Attribution: Adapted from 'Case study: COVID-19 response in Syria', in Jeffery, 2023: 166–68 (see Annex 4).

The Syria example shows how children's direct involvement in programme design and implementation made hygiene messages more accessible and engaging for their peers while building their own confidence and self-expression. Developing sustained partnerships with local academic and training institutes helps produce evidence, build capacity, and expand effective practices at the community level. Collaboration with trusted male and female community leaders, including informal leaders such as elders, is crucial for facilitating programme entry, building trust, and shifting WASH and health behaviour norms. The coordination mechanism should focus on building the capacity of local teams to effectively engage stakeholders, lead multisectoral initiatives, and make evidence-based decisions. Social accountability mechanisms, such as community scorecards and participatory monitoring (see Tool 5.3), empower communities to hold health facilities accountable for service quality and sustainability. Community dialogues and self-help initiatives foster local ownership. At the same time, the joint engagement of medical and administrative staff in planning activities creates a shared sense of ownership over WASH health improvements in facilities and surrounding communities.

4.2.3 Coordination mechanisms

Critical action summary

Critical action	*Timeframe*	*Lead responsibility*
Activate health facility-led coordination platform	Within 48 hours	Senior facility management
Map and engage local stakeholder structures	By day 5	Platform leadership team
Establish strategic partnerships with development actors	By day 7	Platform coordination team
Develop localized multisectoral action plans	By day 14	Platform with community input
Establish accountability and information sharing systems	By day 10	Platform monitoring team
Form facility-based WASH improvement teams	By day 7	Facility management

4.2.3.1 Activate the coordination platform

The activation of an inclusive, health facility-led WASH coordination platform within the first 48 hours of an emergency is crucial for ensuring a rapid and well-coordinated response. Led by senior facility management with support from local government and partners, this platform should include representatives from key departments, civil society, and the community. Developing clear terms of reference and convening regular meetings to assess needs, set priorities, and track progress will help establish effective coordination from the outset.

Action: Establish inclusive health facility-led WASH coordination platform within 48 hours

Lead: Senior facility management with support from local government and partners

Key steps:

- Activate the coordination platform led by senior facility management.
- Include representatives from key departments, local government, civil society, and community.
- Ensure diverse stakeholder engagement with clear roles and responsibilities.
- Develop clear terms of reference outlining purpose and accountability mechanisms (see Annex 1 Section 2.5).
- Convene regular meetings to assess needs, set priorities, and track progress.
- Share meeting minutes with all stakeholders for transparency.

Representation requirements:

- Allocate leadership roles for women, youth, and marginalized groups.
- Dedicate specific seats for representatives of vulnerable populations.
- Strive for gender balance in leadership positions.
- Include technical experts in WASH and health.

Adaptations for low-resource and fragile settings

When community capacity is limited:

- Start with simplified coordination structures (3–5 key representatives vs. full committees).
- Use visual communication tools and verbal agreements rather than written documents.
- Leverage existing informal networks (religious groups, market associations, extended families).
- Focus on one or two essential actions rather than comprehensive programming.

In fragile contexts:

- Prioritize flexible, mobile service delivery over fixed infrastructure.
- Establish rapid communication systems using local radio, mobile networks, or traditional signalling.
- Work through respected neutral actors (religious leaders, elders, traditional healers).
- Plan for service continuity during disruptions with pre-positioned supplies and alternative delivery methods.

Adapting to resource constraints:

- Use low-cost, locally available materials for WASH infrastructure.

- Train community volunteers using peer-to-peer learning models.
- Implement graduated cost-sharing based on household economic capacity.
- Focus on behaviour change interventions with minimal material requirements.

4.2.3.2 Local stakeholder engagement

Mapping and engaging existing local structures and stakeholder groups is essential for building on community capacities and ensuring locally relevant interventions. The platform leadership team, supported by community mobilization specialists, should identify and involve key structures such as development committees, health management teams, WASH committees, women's groups, and community health worker networks. Establishing WASH subcommittees, assigning leadership roles to community representatives, and providing orientation on roles and responsibilities will help decentralize coordination and decision-making.

Action: Map and engage existing local structures and stakeholder groups

Lead: Platform leadership team with community mobilization specialists

Key structures to engage:

- Development committees and local governance bodies
- Health management teams and health committees
- WASH committees and water user associations
- Women's groups and youth organizations
- Religious and traditional leadership structures
- School committees and parent associations
- Community health worker networks

Decentralization strategies:

- Establish WASH subcommittees at village or catchment level.
- Provide clear mandates and support to local committees.
- Link local committees to facility platform and national mechanisms.
- Assign leadership roles to community representatives.
- Build capacity for effective engagement in decision-making.

Implementation steps:

- Conduct mapping of existing structures (see Annex 1 Section 1.3).
- Assess capacity and representation of local structures.
- Develop an engagement strategy for each key stakeholder group.
- Establish two-way information flow mechanisms.
- Provide orientation on roles and responsibilities.
- Schedule regular coordination between levels.

4.2.3.3 Strategic partnerships

Establishing strategic partnerships with development actors can bring valuable technical expertise, resources, and sustainability perspectives to the emergency response. The platform coordination team, with support from facility management, should identify key partners such as NGOs, UN agencies, private sector entities, and academic institutions. The Syria case study (Case Study 4.1) highlights how strategic partnerships between Save the Children and local communities enabled rapid adaptation of hygiene promotion activities when face-to-face interactions became impossible due to COVID-19 restrictions, demonstrating the importance of flexible, collaborative approaches during emergencies. Defining clear roles, formalizing partnerships through memoranda of understanding (MOUs), and developing transition plans will help ensure effective collaboration and sustainable outcomes.

Action: Establish strategic partnerships with development actors

Lead: Platform coordination team with support from facility management

Key partners to engage:

- NGOs and civil society organizations
- UN agencies with relevant mandates
- Private sector entities and businesses
- Academic and research institutions
- Technical resource partners

Partnership development steps:

- Identify partners with technical expertise and resources.
- Define the supporting role of external actors.
- Avoid creating parallel structures that undermine local leadership.
- Formalize partnerships through memoranda of understanding.
- Develop clear transition plans for external support.

MOU components:

- Roles and responsibilities of each partner
- Resource commitments and limitations
- Information sharing protocols
- Decision-making processes
- Sustainability and transition considerations
- Monitoring and accountability mechanisms

4.2.3.4 Localized action planning

Developing localized, multisectoral WASH and health action plans is critical for ensuring a targeted and context-specific response. The platform coordination team, with community input and technical guidance, should base plans on facility assessments and community priorities. Key components include situation analysis, measurable targets, specific activities with timelines and responsibilities, resource requirements, and monitoring frameworks. Emphasizing local ownership, mobilizing partners to address gaps, and using plans for advocacy will help drive implementation.

Action: Develop localized, multisectoral WASH and health action plans

Lead: Platform coordination team with community input and technical guidance

Planning process:

- Base plans on facility assessments and community input.
- Develop time-bound, locally resourced action plans (see Annex 1 Section 3.7).
- Integrate WASH activities into broader health and development plans.
- Leverage multisectoral collaboration opportunities.
- Pool resources across sectors when appropriate.

Plan components:

- Situation analysis and priority issues
- Clear objectives and measurable targets
- Specific activities with timeline and responsible parties
- Resource requirements and funding sources
- Capacity building needs and approaches
- Monitoring and evaluation framework
- Risk management strategies

Implementation requirements:

- Clear definition of roles for each activity
- Emphasis on local ownership and capacity development
- Mobilization of partners to address capacity gaps
- Wide dissemination in accessible formats and languages
- Use as advocacy tool for political and financial support

4.2.3.5 Accountability and information sharing

Strengthening accountability, transparency, and information sharing systems is essential for ensuring effective coordination and continuous improvement. The platform monitoring team, supported by information management specialists, should establish clear targets and indicators, integrate them into existing systems, and create data sharing protocols. Setting up safe and responsive feedback mechanisms, regularly reviewing progress, and transparently reporting on resources will help promote accountability to affected communities.

Action: Strengthen accountability, transparency, and information sharing systems

Lead: Platform monitoring team with support from information management specialists

Accountability mechanisms:

- Establish clear targets and indicators for WASH health action plan.
- Integrate indicators into existing monitoring systems (see Annex 1 Section 2.6).
- Agree on common data definitions and collection methodologies.
- Create protocols for data sharing across stakeholders.
- Schedule periodic coordination meetings to review progress.
- Establish transparent reporting on financial resources.

Feedback system requirements:

- Safe, accessible, and responsive grievance mechanisms
- Multiple channels appropriate to context and literacy levels
- Clear processes for investigation and resolution
- Regular communication about how feedback is being addressed
- Protection of confidentiality and privacy
- Documentation and analysis of feedback trends

Information management steps:

- Designate information focal points at all levels.
- Establish regular reporting timelines and formats.
- Create simple, standardized data collection tools.
- Develop visualization tools for data presentation.
- Build capacity for data collection and analysis.
- Use information products to influence decision-making.
- Clarify that committees are responsible for supervising activities, mobilizing resources, and informing partners at their respective levels.

4.2.3.6 Facility-based WASH improvement

Establishing dedicated WASH improvement teams within health facilities can drive rapid enhancements in infrastructure and practices. Facility management, supported by WASH technical specialists, should form teams with staff from various departments, community representatives, and technical advisers. Key responsibilities include leading assessments, developing improvement plans, monitoring progress, training staff, and engaging communities. Providing clear terms of reference, conducting baseline assessments, and regularly reporting will help institutionalize WASH improvements.

Action: Establish facility-based WASH improvement teams

Lead: Facility management with support from WASH technical specialists

Team composition:

- Dedicated clean clinic teams at each health facility
- Staff from various clinical and support departments
- Representation from both medical and administrative staff
- Community liaisons and patient representatives
- Technical advisers as needed

Team responsibilities:

- Lead WASH assessments at facility level.
- Develop and implement action plans for improvement.
- Monitor and maintain WASH infrastructure and practices.
- Train staff on WASH protocols and standards.
- Engage patients and communities in WASH improvements.
- Document and share learning and best practices.

Implementation steps:

- Identify and appoint team members with clear terms of reference.
- Provide orientation and training on roles and responsibilities.
- Conduct baseline assessment of facility WASH conditions.
- Develop prioritized improvement plan with clear targets.
- Implement regular monitoring and maintenance systems (see Annex 1 Section 2.6).
- Schedule regular team meetings and reporting.

4.2.3.7 High-level support and buy-in

Securing high-level institutional support is crucial for mobilizing resources and ensuring the sustainability of WASH and health coordination efforts. Platform leadership, with support from senior health officials, should engage senior ministry leadership, facility directors, and district authorities to build ownership and commitment. Presenting evidence on the health impact and cost-effectiveness of WASH interventions, aligning with national priorities, and celebrating leadership commitment will help garner high-level buy-in.

Action: Secure high-level institutional support for WASH and health coordination

Lead: Platform leadership with support from senior health officials

Key steps:

- Conduct initial evaluation of WASH conditions in health facilities.
- Present results to senior Ministry of Health leadership.
- Secure endorsement and resource commitments from authorities.

- Engage facility directors and district health authorities.
- Build understanding and ownership of WASH improvements.
- Host stakeholder workshops to familiarize them with assessment tools.

Advocacy strategies:

- Link WASH improvements to health outcome priorities.
- Present evidence on cost-effectiveness of integrated approaches.
- Highlight disease reduction potential of WASH interventions.
- Demonstrate alignment with national health priorities.
- Use visual documentation of current conditions.
- Share success stories from other locations.

4.2.3.8 Monitoring systems and learning

Establishing robust monitoring systems and feedback loops is essential for tracking progress, identifying gaps, and continuously improving the response. The platform monitoring team, supported by district health officers, should monitor key elements such as adherence to standards, infrastructure functionality, staff practices, disease surveillance, community satisfaction, and sustainability. Implementing supportive supervision, facilitating peer learning, and regularly reviewing data will help promote adaptive management and accountability.

Action: Establish robust monitoring systems and feedback loops

Lead: Platform monitoring team with support from district health officers

Key monitoring elements:

- Adherence to standard operating procedures for WASH and infection prevention and control (IPC) (see Annex 1 Section 2.6)
- Infrastructure functionality and maintenance
- Staff knowledge and practice of WASH standards
- Disease surveillance and outbreak detection
- Community engagement and satisfaction
- Sustainability of improvements

Supportive supervision approach:

- Regular supportive supervision by trained district officers
- Joint monitoring visits with multiple stakeholders
- Peer-to-peer learning and exchange
- Emphasis on improvement rather than inspection
- Documentation and sharing of good practices
- Capacity building through on-the-job coaching

Learning and adaptation mechanisms:

- Regular review and reflection meetings
- Documenting lessons learned and challenges

- Adaptation of approaches based on monitoring data
- Experience sharing across facilities and communities
- Continuous staff development and skill building

4.2.3.9 Sustainability and resilience

Promoting sustainability, learning, and resilience is crucial for ensuring the long-term impact of WASH and health interventions beyond the emergency phase. Platform leadership, together with facility management and local authorities, should develop strategies for resource mobilization, capacity building, and emergency preparedness. Identifying sustainable funding sources, strengthening local maintenance systems, documenting best practices, and integrating resilience measures will help build long-term WASH and health system strengthening.

Action: Promote sustainability, learning, and resilience

Lead: Platform leadership with facility management and local authorities

Resource sustainability strategies:

- Determine long-term resource needs for WASH infrastructure.
- Identify sustainable funding sources with facility and local officials.
- Advocate for integration in facility and district budgets.
- Explore pooled resource options across facilities and sectors.
- Develop innovative financing mechanisms.

Capacity building for sustainability:

- Continuously build staff and community capacity for operations.
- Promote local innovation to reduce external dependence.
- Identify and mentor WASH champions in various sectors.
- Create peer support networks for knowledge sharing.
- Develop locally appropriate maintenance systems and supply chains.

Resilience building approaches:

- Document and share lessons learned and best practices.
- Participate in learning exchanges at various levels.
- Integrate emergency preparedness in WASH planning.
- Build local capacity for rapid response to disruptions.
- Consider climate change and environmental sustainability.
- Ensure that national committees conduct regular reviews of strategy implementation to identify areas for improvement.

4.3 Emergency WASH actions

This section outlines the critical WASH interventions needed in the acute phase of an emergency to rapidly address public health risks and prevent the spread of diseases. It covers key aspects of emergency WASH response, including rapid assessments, prioritized interventions, hygiene promotion, local governance capacity strengthening, disease risk mitigation, and community-driven planning. The section emphasizes the importance of community engagement, participatory methods, and multisectoral coordination to ensure that WASH actions are relevant, acceptable, and effective in meeting the immediate needs of affected populations.

4.3.1 Emergency actions (0–14 days)

The emergency actions phase focuses on quickly identifying and addressing the most pressing WASH needs in collaboration with affected communities. It involves rapid assessments to understand the local context, capacities, and priorities, followed by the implementation of priority interventions to reduce public health risks. Key activities include ensuring access to safe water, providing appropriate sanitation facilities, distributing essential hygiene items, and promoting critical hygiene behaviours.

Key resources available in Annex 1:

- *Community coordination timeline and task checklist* (Section 4.9): Step-by-step implementation guide for first 90 days.
- *Participatory community mapping guide* (Section 2.1): Visual assessment tool requiring minimal literacy.
- *Community feedback mechanism checklist* (Section 5.3): Setting up accessible complaint and suggestion systems.
- *Supportive supervision checklist* (Section 5.4): Quality assurance framework for community-level interventions.
- *Monthly reporting format for community committees* (Section 5.6): Simple template for progress tracking.

4.3.1.1 Rapid WASH assessments with communities

Purpose: Conducting rapid WASH assessments in partnership with affected communities is essential for gaining a comprehensive understanding of the local situation and informing the design of context-specific interventions. These assessments involve the active participation of community members, leaders, and representatives from diverse groups to ensure that all voices are heard and that the most vulnerable are not left behind. Rapid assessments also provide an opportunity to build trust and rapport with the community, laying the foundation for more collaborative and sustainable WASH and health interventions.

Timing: Initiate rapid assessments within the first 72 hours of the emergency and complete the process within 14 days, with regular updates as the situation evolves.

Key steps:

1. Mobilize community leaders, health workers, and volunteers to jointly assess WASH conditions, practices, and locally available resources using participatory methods such as transect walks, focus group discussions, and community mapping.
2. Prioritize the assessment of high-risk households and vulnerable groups, such as those with undernourished children or limited WASH access, to identify critical gaps and inform response targeting based on both needs and vulnerabilities.
3. Engage diverse community members, particularly women, youth, and marginalized groups, to understand their specific WASH needs, challenges, and priorities.
4. Analyse assessment findings with community representatives to co-develop local WASH improvement plans that are inclusive and responsive to the needs of women, children, the elderly, and persons with disabilities.
5. Identify and engage local influencers to champion behaviour change and promote community ownership of WASH improvements.
6. Conduct comprehensive assessments of WASH status in health facilities across multiple dimensions, including infrastructure, supplies, practices, and protocols, to identify priority areas for improvement.

4.3.1.2 Implement prioritized WASH interventions

Purpose: Based on the findings of the rapid assessments, the next step is to work with the community to prioritize and implement the most critical WASH and health interventions. Prioritized activities may include ensuring access to safe water through emergency repairs or temporary solutions, providing appropriate sanitation facilities, and promoting critical hygiene behaviours such as handwashing with soap. Importantly, the implementation of these interventions should actively involve the community, building on their existing knowledge, skills, and resources.

Timing: Begin implementing priority interventions within 72 hours of initial assessments, progressively expanding coverage and quality based on evolving needs and capacities.

Key steps:

1. Based on assessment results, work with community leaders and existing WASH committees to select and implement quick impact interventions that address the most pressing risks, such as distributing household water treatment products, constructing emergency latrines, or establishing handwashing stations in public spaces.
2. Identify and rapidly mobilize local resources, skills, and capacities for WASH improvements. Engage community members to contribute

labour, materials, and ideas, providing tools, technical guidance, and skill building to enable locally driven action.

3. Distribute essential WASH supplies, such as soap, water containers, and menstrual hygiene products, to the most vulnerable households. Pair distributions with culturally appropriate demonstrations and information on proper use, maintenance, and critical hygiene behaviours.
4. Continuously monitor WASH interventions through community feedback mechanisms, regular spot checks, and simple indicators (e.g. latrine usage rates and handwashing station functionality). Adapt approaches based on monitoring data and community input.
5. Prioritize the implementation of critical WASH actions at the health facility level, such as ensuring functional hand hygiene stations at points of care, proper decontamination of medical devices, safe management of healthcare waste, and adequate environmental cleaning.
6. Rapidly repair existing water and sanitation systems if possible or set up temporary solutions such as water trucking, treatment kits, and storage receptacles to ensure access to sufficient safe water and sanitation. Transition to more durable, locally manageable options as soon as feasible.

4.3.1.3 Promote participatory hygiene behaviour change

Purpose: Promoting sustainable hygiene behaviour change is a critical component of any emergency WASH response, as it helps prevent the spread of waterborne and communicable diseases. To be effective, hygiene promotion activities must be designed and implemented in a participatory manner, actively engaging the community in the process. Participatory methods such as community dialogues, peer education, and social marketing campaigns can be used to raise awareness, build skills, and create a supportive environment for the adoption of positive hygiene practices.

Timing: Launch hygiene promotion activities within the first 14 days of the response, using assessment data to prioritize target behaviours and audiences. Intensify and adapt promotion efforts based on community feedback and disease surveillance data.

Key steps:

1. Engage community members to design and launch context-specific hygiene promotion campaigns. Identify and train trusted local influencers – community health workers, teachers, and religious leaders – to model and promote key behaviours.
2. Develop and disseminate targeted hygiene messages and materials tailored for pregnant women, young children, the elderly, persons with disabilities, and individuals with chronic illness. Focus on WASH practices that prevent common childhood illnesses such as diarrhea and respiratory infections.

3. Support community volunteers to establish community-led monitoring systems using simple, observable indicators (e.g. household soap availability and observed handwashing at critical times). Provide regular feedback to communities to inform and adapt promotion strategies.
4. Integrate hygiene promotion into existing community-based platforms, such as care groups, savings associations, and schools, to maximize reach and reinforce key messages across multiple touchpoints.
5. Engage health facility staff and community health workers in participatory sessions to identify key hygiene behaviours and practices to target for improvement. Co-design facility-based behaviour change strategies that leverage existing IPC protocols and community health promotion activities.

4.3.1.4 Strengthen the capacities of local WASH governance

Purpose: Strengthening local WASH and health governance capacities is crucial for ensuring that WASH interventions are sustainable, accountable, and responsive to community needs. This involves working with existing community structures, such as WASH committees and leaders, to build their skills and knowledge in areas such as participatory planning, resource mobilization, monitoring, and maintenance of WASH facilities. By investing in local governance capacities from the outset of an emergency, responders can help build the foundation for a more resilient and locally led WASH sector in the long term.

Timing: Within the first 30 days, work with local leaders to establish or reactivate representative WASH committees. Provide ongoing capacity building and support to committees throughout the emergency, recovery, and development phases.

Key steps:

1. Work with local leaders to establish or reactivate community WASH committees, ensuring diverse representation from women, youth, and marginalized groups. Develop clear roles, responsibilities, and action plans.
2. Provide hands-on training and mentoring to committee members in participatory planning, problem-solving, resource mobilization, and monitoring. Use adult learning techniques such as demonstrations, role plays, and peer exchange to build skills.
3. Connect WASH committees with local government authorities and nutrition partners to advocate for WASH prioritization in emergency response plans and funding allocations. Facilitate joint planning and coordination meetings.
4. Facilitate community-led asset mapping to identify existing WASH resources, key service providers, and local influencers. Encourage committees to document and share lessons learned using storytelling, photos, and videos to support peer learning and motivation.

Case Study 4.2 Nigeria: Community-led WASH management in nutrition centres

In conflict-affected Borno state, Nigeria, Save the Children operates the Molai health stabilization centre, which treats approximately 60 children under five monthly for acute malnutrition with medical complications. The centre exemplifies effective WASH and health integration in a humanitarian setting.

Save the Children provided comprehensive WASH infrastructure, including a solar-powered twin water tank system (5,000 litres each), an underground reservoir (1,600 litre capacity), gender-segregated latrines for staff, and five semi-flush latrines for patients. Water user committees were established with gender-balanced membership (five women, five men) and trained on operations and maintenance of water points. These committees took ownership of maintaining WASH infrastructure, contributing to the sustainability of services beyond the emergency phase.

The integration of WASH with nutrition services included hygiene promotion sessions for mothers of admitted children and the distribution of hygiene kits. Water quality was ensured through rigorous monitoring, with online chlorine dosing pumps at the centre maintaining appropriate disinfection levels. For communities affected by cholera outbreaks that lacked online chlorination systems, Save the Children implemented bucket chlorination and the distribution of water purification tablets as an immediate solution while developing longer-term systems. This tiered approach to water quality monitoring and treatment demonstrates adaptive strategies that protect the most vulnerable populations while building sustainable systems.

Attribution: Adapted from 'Case study: Molai health stabilization centre in Borno, Nigeria', in Sorensen and Snel, 2023: 73–75 (see Annex 4).

5. Strengthen the capacity of health facility management teams to lead and sustain WASH improvements. Provide training and ongoing support in WASH assessment, action planning, resource mobilization, and monitoring. Encourage peer learning and experience sharing among facilities.

Case Study 4.2 (Nigeria: Community-led WASH management in nutrition centres) highlights the importance of establishing inclusive and sustainable local governance structures for WASH service delivery. By setting up gender-balanced water user committees and providing them with training and resources to manage WASH facilities, the intervention fostered community ownership and responsibility. This participatory approach ensured that WASH services were tailored to the community's needs and increased the likelihood of their continued operation and maintenance beyond the emergency phase.

4.3.1.5 Assess and mitigate WASH-related disease risks

Purpose: Assessing and mitigating WASH-related disease risks involves conducting a comprehensive analysis of potential disease transmission pathways and identifying the most at-risk groups. Based on this assessment, responders can develop targeted interventions to break the chain of disease transmission, such as improving water quality, promoting safe hygiene practices, and ensuring proper waste disposal. These interventions should be designed and implemented in collaboration with affected communities, building on their existing knowledge, practices, and resources.

Timing: Conduct initial risk assessments within the first 14 days of the response, updating regularly based on disease surveillance data and community feedback. Implement priority risk mitigation measures within 30 days.

Key steps:

1. Collaborate with community health workers and local health facilities to identify and track households at high risk of WASH-related diseases, particularly children with severe acute malnutrition.
2. Coordinate with nutrition actors to ensure high-risk households receive targeted WASH interventions, including hygiene promotion, water treatment, and improved sanitation access. Jointly develop criteria and referral protocols for integrated WASH and nutrition support.
3. Establish community-based referral systems between WASH, health, and nutrition services, ensuring that caregivers of undernourished children receive hygiene kits and WASH information during treatment. Train community health workers and volunteers on referral processes and counter-referral tracking.
4. Support oral rehydration therapy points, handwashing stations, and safe play spaces at nutrition treatment sites, ensuring a clean environment for vulnerable children and caregivers. Provide WASH training and supplies to nutrition staff and community volunteers.
5. Strengthen health facility disease surveillance systems to rapidly detect and respond to potential WASH-related disease outbreaks. Establish clear reporting and response protocols and provide training to health facility staff on early warning signs and outbreak control measures.

4.3.1.6 Plan the improvement of community-driven WASH

Purpose: Engaging communities as active partners in planning and prioritizing WASH improvements is key to effective emergency response. This involves creating spaces and processes for community members to assess their WASH needs and priorities and develop locally appropriate solutions. The resulting community-driven WASH improvement plans should be based on a realistic assessment of available resources and capacities and aligned with the broader emergency response strategy. By fostering community ownership and leadership in planning and implementing WASH improvements, responders can help ensure that interventions are sustainable, acceptable, and responsive to evolving needs.

Timing: Initiate participatory planning sessions within the first 30 days of the response, updating and adapting plans regularly based on monitoring data and community feedback.

Key steps:

1. Based on assessment findings, facilitate participatory planning sessions where community members jointly analyse WASH challenges, identify solutions, and develop context-specific improvement plans.

2. Prioritize low-cost, feasible interventions that leverage local knowledge, skills, and resources. Encourage communities to take incremental, achievable actions rather than waiting for external assistance.
3. Identify capacity gaps and training needs, delivering tailored, hands-on capacity development through local trainers and peer-to-peer learning approaches. Establish partnerships with local vocational institutes and universities to support capacity building efforts.
4. Ensure that emergency WASH plans contribute to long-term resilience by aligning with broader community development goals and integrating sustainability considerations. Work with health, education, and nutrition partners to embed WASH across sectors.
5. Advocate for the inclusion of community WASH priorities in local government recovery and development plans. Support health facilities to develop facility-based WASH improvement plans that progressively meet national standards.

4.3.2 Resilience Actions (14–90 days)

As the emergency response progresses, it is critical to focus on integrating WASH and health interventions with local capacities and systems to ensure their sustainability and long-term impact. Key aspects of this integration process include strengthening local WASH governance structures, building the capacity of local actors to manage and maintain WASH services, promoting sustainable behaviour change, and developing market-based solutions for WASH products and services. By investing in local capacities and systems, responders can help build the foundation for a more resilient and locally led WASH sector.

4.3.2.1 Develop sustainable community WASH governance

Purpose: Developing sustainable community WASH governance structures involves working with communities to establish or strengthen inclusive and accountable mechanisms for managing and overseeing WASH services. These structures should be representative of the diverse groups within the community, with clear roles and responsibilities for planning, implementing, and monitoring WASH interventions. Community WASH governance structures should also be linked to and recognized by formal institutions and systems to ensure their sustainability and scalability.

Timing: Provide ongoing support to community WASH committees throughout the emergency, recovery, and development phases, with a focus on progressively building their autonomy and sustainability.

Key steps:

1. Provide ongoing coaching and organizational development support to community WASH committees. Facilitate visioning and strategic planning exercises to define long-term goals and sustainability strategies.

2. Establish clear by-laws, leadership transition processes, and financial transparency mechanisms to enhance committee accountability. Ensure committees track and document infrastructure functionality, service access, and equity of use.
3. Develop community-led monitoring systems that use participatory tools to inform decision-making and ensure continuous service improvements. Establish feedback loops where monitoring data is reviewed in regular action planning meetings.
4. Strengthen peer-to-peer learning networks, facilitating cross-community exchanges, competitions, and storytelling events to spread promising practices and foster collective action.
5. Establish knowledge management systems to enable community leaders and WASH committees to document, share, and scale up best practices and innovations.
6. Engage municipal authorities and advocate for their ongoing support and investment in sustaining health facility WASH infrastructure and services. Establish clear roles, responsibilities, and coordination mechanisms between health facilities and local government WASH departments.

4.3.2.2 Strengthen local WASH market systems

Purpose: Strengthening local WASH market systems involves working with local entrepreneurs, businesses, and service providers to develop and deliver affordable, quality, and sustainable WASH products and services that meet the community's needs. Market-based approaches should be designed and implemented in a way that is inclusive, equitable, and responsive to the needs of the most vulnerable and marginalized groups. By strengthening local WASH market systems, responders can help create a more resilient and self-sustaining WASH sector.

Timing: Conduct initial market assessments within the first 30 days of the response, and continuously work to strengthen local WASH markets throughout the emergency, recovery, and development phases.

Key steps:

1. Conduct market assessments to identify constraints and opportunities in local WASH supply chains. Assess the availability, quality, and affordability of essential WASH products and services.
2. Provide business coaching, training, and facilitated market linkages to existing and aspiring WASH enterprises. Prioritize women and youth-led businesses and offer targeted support to overcome entry barriers. Facilitate access to financing through savings groups, microfinance institutions, and small business grants.
3. Partner with community WASH committees to design and pilot market-based models for sustainable WASH services (e.g. sanitation enterprises and water kiosks). Use community feedback and monitoring to refine these models.

4. Work with local authorities and community leaders to strengthen the policy and regulatory environment for WASH enterprises, advocating for measures that support service expansion and consumer protection.
5. Identify and address health facility WASH supply chain bottlenecks, working with local suppliers and service providers to improve the availability, quality, and affordability of essential WASH commodities and services. Establish facility-level procurement and inventory management systems for WASH supplies.
6. Provide hands-on training and support to local personnel responsible for sustaining WASH interventions, such as water quality monitoring, operation and maintenance of water systems, and supply chain management. Progressively transfer skills and responsibilities to local actors.

Case Study 4.3 (West Bank: Portable wastewater treatment for healthcare settings) showcases an innovative approach to strengthening local WASH market systems in fragile and resource-constrained environments. By leveraging public–private partnerships and locally appropriate technologies, the project developed a decentralized, low-cost, and sustainable solution for managing wastewater in small communities, schools or healthcare facilities. Priced comparably to a small family car, BluElephants offer exceptional value given their long-term impact. While recent international humanitarian funding cuts may limit their deployment in all humanitarian responses, their cost-effectiveness and sustained benefits make them valuable tools for bridging the gap between crisis response and development resilience. The case study highlights the importance of engaging local actors in designing and delivering WASH interventions to ensure their relevance, acceptability, and sustainability.

Case Study 4.3 West Bank: Portable wastewater treatment for healthcare settings

The BluElephant wastewater treatment system was developed through public–private partnerships led by Jotem Water Solutions to address water scarcity in resource-constrained areas. Using membrane bioreactor technology with anaerobic, aerobic, and anoxic zones, the system treats wastewater to European standards suitable for irrigation and sanitary use.

Designed for portability, there are two units within a standard shipping container and key features include low power consumption (500 W nominal, 2 kW peak), easy maintenance (requiring only a one-day training), and efficient self-cleaning using common cleaning products. The system can process 5–6 m^3 of wastewater per day, supporting the daily needs of 80–160 people with over 97% purification efficiency.

As of early 2023, two units were under testing in the Netherlands and three more in the West Bank, located near healthcare facilities. Commercial release is anticipated in 2025 or 2026. With its decentralized, low-maintenance model and minimal infrastructure requirements, BluElephant offers a practical and scalable solution for healthcare and community settings in areas lacking reliable wastewater treatment systems.

This innovation represents a significant advancement in integrated WASH and health programming at the community level. By enabling local ownership and operation, BluElephant supports improved health, sanitation, and environmental outcomes in both development and humanitarian contexts.

Attribution: Adapted from Jansen, 2024: 124–25 (see Annex 4).

4.3.2.3 Facilitate participatory learning and adaptation

Purpose: Facilitating participatory learning and adaptation involves creating spaces and processes for communities, responders, and other stakeholders to reflect on their experiences, share knowledge, and make informed decisions about how to adjust and improve WASH interventions over time. Participatory learning and adaptation approaches should capture diverse perspectives and be linked to decision-making processes and feedback loops. This requires building the capacity of communities and responders to engage in ongoing reflection, experimentation, and adjustment.

Timing: Establish participatory learning and adaptation mechanisms within the first 90 days of the response, and maintain and strengthen these processes throughout the emergency, recovery, and development phases.

Key steps:

1. Establish community-led learning and reflection platforms, using participatory tools and methods to jointly analyse monitoring data, document lessons learned, and adjust strategies accordingly.
2. Support community members in capturing and sharing knowledge through diverse media and channels, such as storytelling, videos, radio programmes, and community theatre, ensuring broad dissemination of good practices and innovations.
3. Synthesize key learnings into simple, action-oriented materials and guidance, and distribute them widely through community meetings, local media, and stakeholder forums.
4. Organize periodic multi-stakeholder review and planning meetings with community representatives, local authorities, and partners to track progress, identify challenges and opportunities, and jointly develop solutions. Use community-generated evidence to inform sector-level planning, policymaking, and advocacy.
5. Facilitate participatory action research and learning exchanges within and among health facilities to identify, test, and scale up effective WASH improvement practices. Support health facility staff to document and share their experiences through case studies, learning briefs, and conference presentations.

4.3.2.4 Transition to local systems for sustainable services

Purpose: Transitioning to local systems for sustainable WASH and health service delivery is a gradual process that requires careful planning, capacity building, and partnership development. It involves progressively shifting roles and responsibilities for WASH and health service delivery from external actors to local institutions, service providers, and communities while strengthening the enabling environment for sustainable and equitable WASH access. The transition process should be informed by a thorough assessment of existing capacities, resources, and incentives of local actors and guided by a clear vision developed in consultation with all relevant stakeholders.

Timing: Develop and implement transition plans with local stakeholders within the first year of the response, with a phased approach that gradually transfers roles, responsibilities, and resources to local actors over a multi-year period.

Key steps:

1. Assess the capacity of local governments, utilities, and other service providers to assume long-term management of WASH services. Identify institutional gaps and training needs, and develop joint capacity building plans to address critical weaknesses.
2. Facilitate dialogue and negotiation between community WASH committees, local authorities, and service providers to develop and formalize transition plans through memoranda of understanding or partnership agreements. Clarify roles, responsibilities, and resource commitments, and agree on a timeline and process for phased handover.
3. Provide technical assistance and capacity building to local authorities and service providers in key areas such as planning, budgeting, performance monitoring, and customer engagement. Prioritize skills transfer to local counterparts to enable sustained service management.
4. Ensure emergency WASH infrastructure and services are properly integrated into local systems, with adequate provisions for sustainable operation and maintenance. Align infrastructure designs, technologies, and management arrangements with national policies, standards, and processes. Avoid abrupt handovers that could lead to service disruptions or failures.
5. Establish dedicated WASH focal points within local government and service provider institutions, with clear job descriptions, performance targets, and reporting lines. Provide ongoing mentoring, training, and peer support to enable them to effectively carry out their roles and responsibilities.
6. Monitor and support the transition process, using agreed-upon performance metrics and milestones to track progress and identify areas for improvement. Provide backstopping and technical assistance as needed to ensure continuity and quality of services.

Case Study 4.4 (Iraq: Solar-powered WASH solutions in critical public facilities) illustrates the importance of investing in sustainable and climate-resilient WASH infrastructure in critical public institutions. It demonstrates the potential of renewable energy solutions, such as solar-powered water pumps and lighting systems, to improve the reliability, affordability, and environmental sustainability of WASH services in resource-constrained and conflict-affected contexts. The case study emphasizes the importance of taking a holistic and multisectoral approach to WASH interventions in public facilities, addressing technical, behavioural, institutional, and financial dimensions of sustainability.

Case Study 4.4 Iraq: Solar-powered WASH solutions in critical public facilities

Iraq faces significant water scarcity and climate change impacts, affecting WASH services in schools and healthcare facilities. A comprehensive survey by WHO and UNICEF found 48% of schools and 31% of healthcare facilities lacked basic water services, while approximately half lacked adequate sanitation and hygiene facilities.

To address these challenges, UNICEF implemented a programme to increase climate-resilient WASH services through solar power systems. The initiative equipped 199 schools and four healthcare facilities with solar panels (twelve 450 W panels per site) to power water pumps and lighting in latrines, significantly reducing reliance on unstable electricity supplies.

The programme incorporated smart water meters alongside solar systems to measure consumption and detect leakages, creating an evidence base for water conservation while ensuring reliable supply. Enterprise performance management software was developed to increase system efficiency, create reports on performance and budgets, and track project portfolios. Additionally, 50 youth (nine female) received training in solar system installation, supporting green job creation while providing sustainable water access in critical facilities. This skills development approach not only supported immediate implementation but also created pathways to employment in the private sector, building local technical capacity for maintaining green WASH infrastructure beyond the project period.

Attribution: Adapted from Al-Khateeb, 2024: 122–123 (see Annex 4).

4.4 Monitoring

4.4.1 Objectives

By monitoring integrated community WASH and health interventions it is possible to track progress, identify gaps, and promote accountability to affected populations. Community-led monitoring empowers local actors to assess and improve the coverage, quality, and outcomes of WASH and health services.

4.4.2 Key monitoring activities

4.4.2.1 Engaging communities

Participatory monitoring by community members is critical for local ownership, relevance, and use of data. Affected people should be at the centre of deciding what to measure, how to measure it, and how to act on the findings.

- Consult diverse community groups to define context-specific WASH and health monitoring priorities, indicators, and methods.
- Establish inclusive community monitoring teams with women, youth, and marginalized groups in lead roles.
- Train and mentor community monitors to collect, analyse, and communicate WASH and health data using participatory tools.
- Use participatory methods such as community mapping, focus groups, and ranking exercises to identify key indicators.

- Facilitate community validation and interpretation of monitoring results to inform local action and advocacy.
- Conduct quarterly community meetings to review findings, celebrate progress, identify bottlenecks, and co-develop action plans using visual tools like colour-coded scorecards or maps.

4.4.2.2 Harmonizing indicators and systems

Aligned monitoring frameworks enable coherent tracking of WASH and health progress and gaps. Community-level indicators should be harmonized with national systems while reflecting local realities and information needs.

- Develop a core set of community WASH and health indicators that integrate with national frameworks like the Sustainable Development Goals (SDGs).
- Ensure indicators align with WHO/UNICEF Joint Monitoring Programme definitions and capture household, institutional, and service-level WASH data.
- Disaggregate all data by gender, age, disability, and vulnerability to inform targeted interventions.
- Standardize and streamline data collection tools, methods, and reporting formats across community to national levels.
- Integrate community monitoring data into subnational and national WASH and health information management systems.
- Establish data sharing and coordination protocols between community, health facility, and government monitoring systems.
- Use digital platforms for real-time data collection, visualization, and action planning where feasible.

4.4.2.3 Strengthening community capacities

Building local capacities for participatory monitoring is key for quality, sustainability, and resilience. Skills and systems should be strengthened through learning-by-doing, peer exchange, and integration with wider processes.

- Assess and build on existing community structures and processes for participatory planning, monitoring, and action.
- Develop simple, visual monitoring tools and guidance adapted to local needs, languages, and literacies.
- Provide hands-on training and coaching for community monitors, with emphasis on data collection, management, analysis, and use.
- Train local leaders, WASH committees, and volunteers to independently use mobile apps and other tools for data management.
- Facilitate community-to-community learning and scale up of good monitoring practices through exchange visits, joint events, and media.
- Establish peer mentoring, refresher sessions, and joint analysis workshops to support continuous learning.

4.4.2.4 Utilizing monitoring data

Monitoring data should inform real-time decision-making and quality improvements at all levels. This requires user-friendly formats, inclusive spaces for data analysis and use, and effective feedback loops.

- Analyse monitoring data to assess progress, equity, and effectiveness of community WASH and health interventions.
- Produce accessible monitoring reports, dashboards, and scorecards for community, facility, and government stakeholders.
- Convene participatory forums for community representatives, health workers, and authorities to review results and agree on actions.
- Use monitoring data to inform social accountability efforts such as participatory budgeting, community scorecards, and citizen report cards.
- Display findings publicly through community meetings, local media, and bulletin boards.
- Advocate for community monitoring evidence to inform higher-level WASH and health policies, plans, budgets, and adaptations.
- Establish safe, accessible grievance redress and complaint response mechanisms with transparent follow-up procedures.

4.4.3 Key monitoring indicators

Community WASH and health monitoring tracks inputs, outputs, and outcomes of integrated services.

Access and use of WASH and health services:

- Proportion of households with access to and use of basic drinking water and sanitation services
- Proportion of households with basic handwashing facilities with soap and water available
- Proportion of people who know and practise key hygiene behaviours for disease prevention
- Percentage of households safely handling/storing drinking water
- Percentage of fecal waste safely managed from containment to disposal
- Percentage of households living within 500 metres of an improved water source

Functionality and quality:

- Proportion of community water points functional at time of visit
- Proportion of community sanitation facilities clean, private, and well-maintained
- Proportion of community health facilities with functional WASH services and supplies

- Percentage of water samples with turbidity <5 NTU and residual chlorine in the range 0.5–1.0 mg/L
- Average daily water availability per person (minimum 20 L)
- People per communal latrine (≤20); people per public latrine (≤50)

Governance and sustainability:

- Existence and regular meeting of community WASH and health committees with inclusive membership
- Proportion of WASH and health facilities with up-to-date management/maintenance plans and records
- Proportion of WASH and health services with user fee collection and transparent financial management
- Percentage of WASH facilities meeting national design, construction, and performance standards

Health and disease outcomes:

- Prevalence of diarrhea and other WASH-related diseases in the community, especially among children under five
- Proportion of children under five who are stunted or wasted
- WASH-related disease outbreaks detected and responded to within 48 hours
- Trends in under-five diarrhea rates as a proxy for WASH impact on child health

4.4.4 Monitoring methods and tools

- Community WASH and health mapping, transect walks, and observation checklists
- Participatory community scorecards and social audits for WASH and health services
- Household surveys and interviews on WASH and health knowledge, attitudes, and practices
- Structured observations of handwashing, latrine use, and waste disposal practices
- Self-reports and demonstrations for hygiene practices
- Community health worker and facility records on WASH-related disease cases and trends
- WASH management committee records, minutes, and financial reports
- Sanitary inspections, water quality testing, and IPC audits at health facilities
- Facility-based assessments of:
  - PPE availability and use
  - cleaning/disinfection protocols for surfaces and equipment
  - presence of waste segregation systems and sharps containers
  - availability of adequate cleaning supplies and laundry systems

4.4.5 Monitoring roles and responsibilities

Community actors:

- Identify WASH and health priorities and indicators to monitor based on local context and needs.
- Collect, compile, and report monitoring data through community volunteers and structures.
- Analyse monitoring results and develop action plans to address gaps and sustain achievements.
- Provide feedback to service providers and authorities on WASH and health service quality and responsiveness.
- Participate in multi-stakeholder review forums and learning exchanges to share monitoring outcomes and advocate for change.

Implementing agencies:

- Co-design and support setup of participatory community monitoring systems for WASH and health.
- Train and mentor community monitors on data collection, management, analysis, and reporting.
- Conduct regular supervision visits to ensure data quality and provide technical backup.
- Facilitate community–facility dialogue and planning based on monitoring results.
- Aggregate and report community monitoring data for higher-level sectoral processes.

Government counterparts:

- Coordinate and oversee community-based WASH and health monitoring as part of national systems.
- Integrate community monitoring indicators and data into subnational and national databases.
- Convene joint review and performance management meetings with community representation.
- Allocate resources to sustain and scale community monitoring within government programmes.
- Utilize community monitoring evidence to inform WASH and health policies, strategies, and guidelines.

4.4.6 Monitoring timeline and deliverables

- Rapid community WASH and health assessments in acute emergency phase, updated quarterly
- Monthly monitoring visits and data collection by community monitoring teams

- Bi-monthly community review meetings to analyse monitoring data and plan actions
- Quarterly community monitoring reports submitted to subnational coordination mechanisms
- Annual participatory evaluations of community WASH and health monitoring systems and outcomes

Key deliverables:

- Community WASH and health monitoring framework, manual, tools, and training pack
- Database and dashboard for community WASH and health monitoring data across all sites
- Quarterly community WASH and health monitoring bulletins and scorecards for stakeholder review
- Biannual reports on community monitoring system functionality, data quality, and use
- Learning briefs and multimedia products documenting community monitoring outcomes and innovations
- Policy recommendations and inputs for institutionalizing community-led monitoring in national WASH and health strategies

CHAPTER 5

Integration in emergencies

Guideline for coordinating WASH with nutrition at the community level

5.1 Summary

This coordination guideline outlines eight critical actions that community-level implementers should take during the first 90 days of an emergency. Start with the Key actions table on next page to see what needs to happen and when. The table also directs you to detailed guidance in this chapter and the Practitioners' Toolkit (Annex 1).

This guideline provides essential guidance on coordination for community-level implementers overseeing WASH and nutrition initiatives during emergencies. It supports rapid response while emphasizing long-term resilience, serving as one of four complementary guidelines designed as an integrated framework for WASH coordination with health and nutrition at both national and community levels. This guideline was developed by the WASH Road Map in consultation with numerous other professionals. A list of external sources consulted in the creation of these guidelines can be found in Annex 3.

5.1.1 Purpose

This guideline helps frontline workers, community leaders, and local organizations integrate WASH and nutrition interventions during emergencies through structured, time-bound actions. It operationalizes a multisectoral approach to address the underlying causes of undernutrition at the household and individual level, particularly during the critical first 1,000 days from conception to a child's second birthday. It upholds the rights outlined in the Humanitarian Charter and aligns with global commitments to advance universal health coverage and primary healthcare.

Who should use this: Community-level implementers, including local health and nutrition workers, WASH promoters, community mobilizers, field supervisors, and representatives from community-based organizations. This serves as a practical resource for those directly engaged in household-level interventions, outreach activities, and community-based management of integrated WASH and nutrition programmes.

How to use these actions: Each action in the table is connected to specific sections in this guideline (see the 'Guideline sections' column) that provide

Key actions

Actions	*WASH*	*Nutrition*	*Timeframe*	*Guideline sections*	*Practitioners' Toolkit sections*
Establish community WASH and nutrition committee	Identify WASH representatives and engage community leaders	Identify nutrition representatives and engage community health workers	Within 1 week	2.1	1.1, 1.2, 4.8
Conduct participatory community assessment and map existing structures	Assess WASH conditions, practices, and capacities; map WASH-related community structures	Assess nutrition status, practices, and capacities; map nutrition-related community networks	Days 3–10	2.2, 2.3, 3.1.1	1.3, 1.4, 2.1, 2.2, 2.3, 3.4
Implement minimum WASH package and integrate with nutrition programmes	Provide water, sanitation, hygiene interventions tailored to nutrition needs; align with nutrition programme objectives	Incorporate WASH messages and activities into nutrition programmes; provide guidance on nutrition-sensitive WASH priorities	Days 1–14	3.1.2, 3.1.3	2.1, 2.2, 2.3, 4.4, 4.6, 4.10
Develop joint strategies and engage community actors	Contribute WASH expertise to integrated strategy development; involve community members in WASH intervention design	Contribute nutrition expertise to integrated strategy development; involve community members in promoting nutrition-sensitive WASH practices	Days 7–21	2.4, 3.1.4	3.1, 3.2, 3.3, 4.1, 4.7
Establish communication mechanisms and school-based integration	Set up communication and referral pathways between WASH and nutrition services; promote WASH in schools integrated with nutrition education	Set up communication pathways between nutrition and WASH services; promote nutrition education in schools integrated with WASH	Days 10–30	2.5, 2.6, 3.2.3	4.3, 4.7, 5.2, 5.3
Strengthen local capacity and align with national systems	Build capacity of local WASH committees; ensure community-level WASH interventions adhere to national standards	Build capacity of community nutrition volunteers; ensure community nutrition interventions align with national strategies	Days 30–90	3.2.1, 3.2.2	3.4, 3.6, 4.2, 4.8, 4.9
Support innovations and promote nutrition-sensitive programming	Document local WASH innovations; promote nutrition-sensitive WASH programming approaches	Document local nutrition innovations; integrate nutrition considerations into WASH strategies throughout response	Days 30–90	3.2.4, 3.2.6	3.2, 4.4, 5.5
Establish monitoring systems and plan transition	Collect and respond to community feedback on WASH interventions; transition ownership to community structures	Collect and respond to community feedback on nutrition interventions; transition ownership to local structures	Days 14–90	2.7, 2.8, 3.2.5, 5	5.1, 5.3, 5.5, 5.6, 3.4

detailed coordination frameworks, and to Annex 1 the Practitioners' Toolkit (see the 'Practitioners' Toolkit sections' column) that offers operational tools, templates, and checklists. Begin with the action most relevant to your current emergency phase, and then refer to the corresponding sections for guidance on implementation.

The guideline sections provide the strategic frameworks for establishing coordination platforms, conducting assessments, and building sustainable systems. The Practitioners' Toolkit (Annex 1) translates these frameworks into practical tools you can adapt and use immediately. Together, they support implementers in transitioning from urgent responses to resilient, community-managed systems that create enabling environments for good nutrition through improved WASH.

5.1.2 Framework pillars

These five pillars structure the detailed guidance found throughout this guideline:

1. *Community engagement*: Engaging communities as active partners in assessing, designing, implementing, and monitoring WASH and nutrition interventions.
2. *Local assessment*: Identifying WASH-related nutritional risks and the most vulnerable groups at the household level.
3. *Coordinated implementation*: Implementing priority actions that create an enabling environment for good nutrition through improved WASH.
4. *Local capacity building*: Building the capacity of community health workers, caregivers, and local structures to sustain integrated interventions.
5. *Community monitoring*: Supporting communities in establishing systems to track WASH and nutrition outcomes and facilitate continuous improvement.

5.1.3 Adaptability

Adapt this guideline to align with local feeding practices, hygiene norms, and existing community structures, rather than creating parallel systems. It is effective in both rural and urban settings across diverse cultural contexts and should be used in conjunction with national-level guidelines for a coherent, multi-level approach. The Practitioners' Toolkit (Annex 1) provides templates and tools that can be modified to suit your specific context.

5.1.4 Timeframe

This guideline focuses specifically on coordinated action during the first 90 days of an emergency at the community level:

- *Emergency actions (0–14 days)*: Urgent action to prevent WASH-related nutritional deterioration.

- *Resilience actions (14–90 days)*: Establishing mechanisms for transitioning to sustainable, community-managed WASH and nutrition systems.

These timeframes provide a coordination framework for establishing transition mechanisms rather than fixed deadlines for completing transitions, which remain context-dependent and may extend well beyond the initial emergency response period, as emphasized in Sphere standards. Investing in local capacity and participatory planning from the outset enables communities to emerge from crises with strengthened capabilities to deliver lasting WASH and nutrition services.

5.1.5 Cross-cutting issues

This guideline mainstreams climate resilience, protection, gender equity, and social inclusion, while clearly defining roles and responsibilities across government entities, humanitarian organizations, and community partners. It provides practical guidance to transform emergency response into sustainable progress, bridging the humanitarian–development divide at the national level.

5.2 Stakeholder coordination

Community-level coordination of WASH and nutrition interventions depends on the active engagement of local stakeholders and institutions. This guideline section emphasizes the importance of local ownership and contextual understanding in stakeholder coordination. Effective community-level coordination bridges the gap between national policies and household practices, ensuring that interventions are culturally appropriate, accessible, and sustainable within local contexts.

Quick reference: Key community-level templates available in Annex 1

Purpose	*Annex 1 section*	*Use when ...*
Community committee establishment	1.2, 2.5, 4.8	Setting up integrated WASH-nutrition coordination
Household and community assessments	2.1, 2.2, 2.3	Understanding local WASH-nutrition challenges
Integrated planning and strategy	3.2, 3.7, 4.1	Creating community-driven action plans
Behaviour change implementation	4.3, 4.4, 4.6, 4.10	Delivering integrated messaging and training
Community-led monitoring	5.1, 5.3, 5.6	Tracking progress and community satisfaction

Note: All templates in Annex 1 are designed for adaptation to different community contexts and government structures

Further practical guidance can be found in the Practitioners' Toolkit (Annex 1), including:

- Section 1.1: Stakeholder identification checklist
- Section 1.2: Coordination committee terms of reference (TOR) template
- Section 1.3: Stakeholder analysis and mapping tools
- Section 1.4: Social network analysis guide
- Section 1.5: Stakeholder roles and responsibilities matrix
- Section 2.1: Participatory community mapping guide
- Section 2.2: Household WASH and health survey
- Section 2.3: Nutrition-sensitive WASH risk assessment checklist
- Section 2.5: Committee setup checklist
- Section 3.2: Nutrition-sensitive WASH strategy development guide
- Section 3.3: Community engagement planning framework
- Section 3.4: Capacity assessment and building tools
- Section 3.6: Joint capacity building plan
- Section 3.7: Community-level joint action plan template
- Section 4.1: Joint workplan and budget template
- Section 4.2: Training and staff development guides
- Section 4.3: Integrated outreach and campaign planning tools
- Section 4.4: WASH and nutrition behaviour change communication toolkit
- Section 4.6: Integrated outreach strategy template
- Section 4.8: Community WASH and Nutrition committee TOR template
- Section 4.9: Community coordination timeline and task checklist
- Section 4.10: Outreach worker training package on WASH and nutrition
- Section 5.1: Integrated monitoring framework
- Section 5.3: Community feedback mechanism checklist
- Section 5.4: Supportive supervision checklist
- Section 5.5: Performance review and learning tools
- Section 5.6: Monthly reporting format for community committees

These tools support community-level assessment, planning, implementation, and monitoring of integrated WASH and nutrition interventions, ensuring local ownership and sustainability.

5.2.1 Stakeholder identification checklist

Figure 5.1 illustrates seven vital stakeholder groups that should be involved in the community-level WASH and nutrition multi-stakeholder platform: government authorities, humanitarian and development organizations, community representatives, private sector, academic and research institutions, UN agencies and donors, and inter-cluster coordination. A detailed stakeholder identification checklist is provided in Tool 1.1 of the Practitioners' Toolkit (Annex 1).

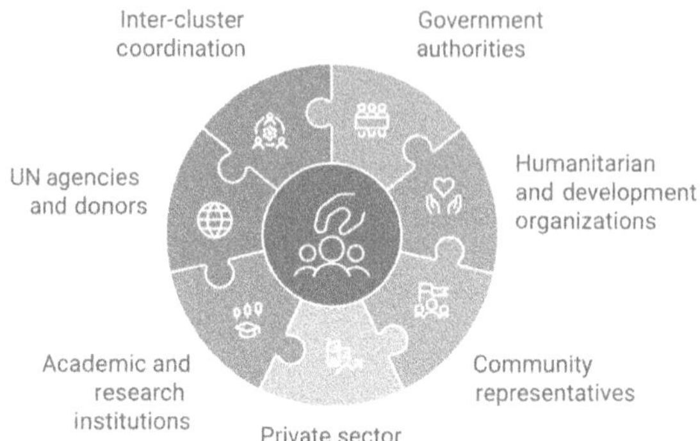

Figure 5.1 Multi-stakeholder coordination wheel with seven segments.

5.2.2 Strengthening meaningful participation

At the community level, strengthening WASH and nutrition coordination requires allocating leadership roles and decision-making authority to community representatives and local officials while preventing external agency domination. Coordination teams should actively reduce participation barriers for marginalized populations through inclusive meetings, accessible information formats, and dedicated leadership opportunities. Sustained partnerships with local academic and training institutes are valuable for producing contextually relevant evidence, building local capacity, and expanding effective practices. Collaboration with trusted male and female community leaders and influencers, including informal leaders such as elders, is essential to facilitate programme entry, build community trust, and shift WASH and nutrition behaviour norms. The coordination platform should invest in building the capacity of local teams to effectively engage stakeholders, lead multisectoral initiatives, and make evidence-based decisions. Employing social accountability mechanisms, such as community scorecards and participatory monitoring (see Annex 1 Section 5), empowers communities to monitor WASH and nutrition service quality, while community dialogues and self-help initiatives foster local ownership and the sustainability of integrated interventions.

5.2.3 Coordination mechanisms

Critical action summary

Critical action	*Timeframe*	*Lead responsibility*
Establish community WASH and nutrition committee	Within first week	Community leader with WASH/ nutrition sector support
Conduct participatory community mapping	By day 10	Committee with technical support
Map existing community platforms and networks	By day 14	Committee with community leaders

(*Continues*)

(Continued)

Critical action	*Timeframe*	*Lead responsibility*
Develop joint WASH-nutrition strategies	By day 21	Committee with technical advisers
Establish two-way communication mechanisms	By day 14	Committee with communication specialists
Engage schools as integration entry points	By week 3	Committee with education partners

5.2.3.1 Establish a community coordination committee

Establishing an inclusive community WASH and nutrition committee within the first week lays the foundation for effective coordination at the local level. Co-led by community leaders and sector representatives, this committee ensures balanced representation from all key stakeholder groups. With clear terms of reference outlining roles and decision-making processes, the committee fosters a shared understanding of the situation and priorities, setting the stage for joint action.

Action: Establish an inclusive community WASH and nutrition committee within the first week

Lead: Community leader with WASH and nutrition sector representatives

Key steps:

- Set up a committee to coordinate integrated response efforts at the local level.
- Ensure co-leadership between community leaders and sector representatives.
- Include representatives from all key stakeholder groups (see Annex 1 Section 4.8).
- Develop terms of reference with clear roles and decision-making processes.
- Foster shared understanding of situation and priorities.
- Establish a regular meeting schedule appropriate to the emergency phase.

Adaptations for low-resource and fragile settings

When community capacity is limited:

- Start with simplified coordination structures (3–5 key representatives vs. full committees).
- Use visual communication tools and verbal agreements rather than written documents.
- Leverage existing informal networks (religious groups, market associations, extended families).
- Focus on one or two essential actions rather than comprehensive programming.

In fragile contexts:

- Prioritize flexible, mobile service delivery over fixed infrastructure.
- Establish rapid communication systems using local radio, mobile networks, or traditional signalling.
- Work through respected neutral actors (religious leaders, elders, traditional healers).
- Plan for service continuity during disruptions with pre-positioned supplies and alternative delivery methods.

Adapting to resource constraints:

- Use low-cost, locally available materials for WASH infrastructure.
- Train community volunteers using peer-to-peer learning models.
- Implement graduated cost-sharing based on household economic capacity.
- Focus on behaviour change interventions with minimal material requirements.

5.2.3.2 Participatory community assessment

Conducting participatory community mapping and assessment provides a solid evidence base for designing locally relevant interventions. Led by the WASH and nutrition committee with technical support from specialists, this process engages diverse community members in identifying risks, capacities, and priorities. A mix of qualitative and quantitative methods, such as focus groups, transect walks, and household surveys, ensures a comprehensive understanding of the local context that informs joint analysis and action planning.

Action: Conduct participatory community mapping and assessment

Lead: Committee with technical support from WASH and nutrition specialists

Key assessment methods:

- Participatory mapping to identify WASH and nutrition vulnerabilities
- Focus group discussions with diverse community segments
- Key informant interviews with community leaders and service providers
- Household surveys for quantitative data collection
- Observation of practices and infrastructure

Priority assessment areas:

- Water sources, access, quality, and management
- Sanitation facilities, practices, and barriers
- Hygiene knowledge, practices, and enabling factors
- Nutritional status of vulnerable groups
- Feeding practices and food security conditions

- Care practices and gender dynamics
- Barriers to optimal WASH and nutrition behaviours

For guidance on assessment methodologies, refer to Annex 1 Section 2.1 (Participatory community mapping) and Annex 1 Section 2.2 (Household WASH and nutrition survey).

Implementation steps:

- Train community members as assessment facilitators.
- Develop locally appropriate assessment tools (see templates in Annex 1 Section 2).
- Ensure inclusive participation across age, gender, and diversity.
- Analyse findings jointly with community representatives.
- Validate results through community feedback sessions.
- Use findings to inform integrated response planning.

5.2.3.3 Leveraging existing community structures

Mapping and engaging existing community platforms and networks capitalizes on local resources and relationships to amplify WASH and nutrition messages and mobilize collective action. Led by the community WASH and nutrition committee, this process identifies trusted structures, such as care groups, youth clubs, and faith-based organizations, that can serve as strategic entry points for integrated programming. By building the capacity of local leaders and influencers, the coordination platform can catalyse sustainable social and behaviour change.

Action: Map and engage existing community platforms and networks

Lead: Committee with support from community leaders and social mobilizers

Key platforms to identify:

- Care groups and mother support networks
- Savings associations and economic cooperatives
- Faith-based groups and religious institutions
- Traditional leadership structures
- Youth groups and school committees
- Water management committees
- Community health volunteer networks

Engagement strategies:

- Map existing structures, their reach, and influence.
- Engage community leaders and influencers for message dissemination.
- Utilize community events and gatherings for integrated messaging.
- Build on existing trust relationships and local knowledge.
- Strengthen capacity of local networks for sustained engagement.

Implementation steps:

- Conduct stakeholder and social network analysis (see Annex 1 Sections 1.3 and 1.4).
- Identify strategic entry points for integration.
- Develop an engagement plan with each key platform.
- Train platform leaders on integrated WASH and nutrition approaches.
- Establish regular information exchange mechanisms.
- Monitor effectiveness of engagement strategies.

5.2.3.4 Integrated strategy development

Developing joint, multisectoral WASH and nutrition strategies and plans ensures that interventions are coordinated, complementary, and responsive to community needs and priorities. Led by the community WASH and nutrition committee with technical support from WASH and nutrition advisers, this participatory process translates assessment findings into practical action plans with clear targets, responsibilities, and timelines. The resulting strategy document serves as a roadmap for integrated programming, linking short-term emergency response to longer-term resilience and development goals.

Action: Develop joint, multisectoral WASH and nutrition strategies and plans

Lead: Committee with technical advisers from WASH and nutrition sectors

Strategy components:

- Shared objectives and primary outcomes based on assessment findings
- Integrated interventions addressing underlying causes of malnutrition
- Context-specific behaviour change approaches leveraging community assets
- Harmonized communication messages and delivery channels
- Costed, multisectoral workplans with clear responsibilities
- Links to long-term resilience and development goals

For guidance on developing integrated WASH and nutrition action plans, refer to Annex 1 Section 3.1 (Response planning template) and Annex 1 Section 3.2 (Nutrition-sensitive WASH strategy development guide).

Planning process:

- Analyse assessment findings to identify priority needs and opportunities.
- Facilitate community-led prioritization of interventions.
- Design integrated activities addressing multiple objectives.
- Identify resources, capacities, and gaps.
- Develop detailed implementation plans with timelines.
- Establish a monitoring framework with community-validated indicators.

5.2.3.5 Communication and feedback mechanisms

Establishing two-way communication, referral, and feedback systems is essential for fostering dialogue, trust, and accountability between communities and WASH and nutrition actors. Led by the community WASH and nutrition committee with support from communication specialists, this process identifies accessible and appropriate channels for information sharing, community input, and complaint resolution. By actively soliciting and responding to community feedback, coordination mechanisms can adapt interventions to local needs and concerns, strengthening the relevance, quality, and acceptability of integrated programming.

Action: Establish two-way communication, referral, and feedback systems

Lead: Committee with support from communication specialists

Key communication channels:

- Focus groups and community dialogues
- Call-in radio shows and community radio
- Community meetings and information boards
- Mobile messaging and phone trees
- Community volunteers and outreach workers

Referral pathway development:

- Map all WASH, nutrition, and health services in the area.
- Develop clear protocols for identification and referral of cases.
- Train community volunteers on identification of WASH and nutrition issues.
- Create simple referral forms and tracking systems.
- Establish follow-up mechanisms for referred cases.

Feedback mechanism requirements:

- Multiple accessible channels (verbal, written, technological)
- Options for anonymous feedback
- Clear procedures for handling different types of feedback
- Designate focal points for receiving and responding to feedback
- Regular analysis of feedback trends to inform programming
- Transparency about actions taken in response to feedback

For guidance on designing feedback and accountability systems, refer to Annex 1 Section 5.3 (Community feedback mechanism checklist).

Implementation steps:

- Design contextually appropriate feedback tools (see Annex 1 Section 5.3).
- Train committee members and service providers on feedback handling.
- Raise community awareness about feedback channels.

- Establish a documentation and analysis system.
- Schedule regular reviews of feedback data.
- Report back to the community on actions taken.

5.2.3.6 School-based integration

Engaging schools and educational institutions as integration entry points allows for the promotion of lifelong WASH and nutrition habits among children and adolescents, who are key agents of change within their households and communities. Led by the community WASH and nutrition committee in collaboration with education partners, this process leverages school-based platforms, such as health clubs, parent-teacher associations, and school feeding programmes, to deliver integrated messaging, services, and capacity building. By creating links between school and community initiatives, coordination mechanisms can amplify the reach and impact of WASH and nutrition interventions.

Action: Engage schools and educational institutions as integration entry points

Lead: Committee with education partners, school administration, and parent-teacher associations

Key integration opportunities:

- WASH in schools infrastructure and maintenance
- School feeding and nutrition programmes
- Student hygiene clubs and peer education
- Teacher training on integrated WASH and nutrition
- Parent education through school platforms
- School gardens and nutrition demonstration sites

Implementation steps:

- Assess existing school WASH and nutrition conditions.
- Develop comprehensive school improvement plans.
- Train teachers and school administrators as change agents.
- Establish student clubs and peer education programmes.
- Engage parent-teacher associations in programme design.
- Create links between school and community programmes.

Community outreach strategies:

- Use schools as platforms for community education sessions.
- Organize joint demonstrations and campaigns.
- Train students as household change agents.
- Host community events at school facilities.
- Involve community members in school programme implementation.

5.2.3.7 Review and adapt coordination mechanisms

Establishing processes for regular review and adaptation of coordination mechanisms is critical for ensuring the ongoing relevance, effectiveness, and accountability of integrated WASH and nutrition efforts. Led by the community WASH and nutrition committee with support from WASH and nutrition specialists, this reflective process assesses the performance of coordination structures and identifies opportunities for improvement and course correction. By institutionalizing a culture of continuous learning and adaptation, community-level coordination can remain agile and responsive to evolving needs and challenges.

Action: Establish processes for regular review and adaptation of coordination mechanisms

Lead: Committee with support from WASH and nutrition sector coordination specialists

Review areas:

- Progress against shared objectives and targets
- Effectiveness of coordination structures and processes
- Quality of information sharing and joint planning
- Inclusivity and community representation
- Adaptability to changing context and needs

Review process:

- Schedule periodic coordination reviews (frequency based on emergency phase).
- Collect feedback from diverse stakeholders.
- Analyse strengths, weaknesses, and gaps in coordination.
- Document lessons learned and good practices.
- Identify improvement opportunities and adjustments needed.

Adaptation mechanisms:

- Regular review of committee composition and representation
- Adjustment of meeting frequency and formats as needed
- Refinement of communication and information sharing processes
- Streamlining of coordination structures as emergency stabilizes
- Documentation and institutionalization of effective practices

5.2.3.8 Transition and sustainability

Developing transition and exit strategies from the outset of the emergency response is essential for building the foundation for locally led, resilient WASH and nutrition outcomes beyond the crisis phase. Led by the community WASH and nutrition committee with support from development partners and local authorities, this process focuses on strengthening the capacities of community-based institutions, systems, and actors to assume increasing responsibility for integrated programming. By investing in local leadership, resource mobilization, and knowledge management, coordination mechanisms can facilitate a smooth and sustainable handover of WASH and nutrition efforts to permanent community structures.

Action: Develop transition and exit strategies from the outset of emergency response

Lead: Committee with support from development partners and local authorities

Key transition elements:

- Identification and capacity building of local actors for leadership
- Progressive shift of decision-making to community structures
- Transfer of resource management responsibilities to local entities
- Integration of emergency response into long-term development plans
- Sustainable financing mechanisms for continued activities

Capacity building approaches:

- Skill transfer through mentorship and shadowing
- Formal training and learning opportunities
- Learning exchanges between communities
- Documentation of processes and approaches
- On-the-job coaching and supportive supervision

For guidance on capacity assessment and building, refer to Annex 1 Section 3.4 (Capacity assessment and building tools).

Implementation steps:

- Include transition planning in emergency actions strategy.
- Identify capacity needs and develop capacity building plan.
- Establish milestones and benchmarks for progressive transition.
- Monitor readiness for increasing local responsibility.
- Document and celebrate transition achievements.
- Maintain light support structures after formal exit.

5.3 Emergency WASH actions

The emergency WASH actions outlined in this section provide a roadmap for swift, coordinated, and context-specific interventions to address the critical water, sanitation, and hygiene needs of nutritionally vulnerable populations during humanitarian crises. The framework prioritizes life-saving measures in the emergency actions phase (0–14 days), followed by a concerted effort to integrate WASH interventions with local capacity, ensuring sustainable and resilient solutions in the 14–90 day timeframe.

5.3.1 Emergency actions (0–14 days)

The emergency actions phase (0–14 days) is critical for swiftly addressing the most pressing WASH needs and risks faced by nutritionally vulnerable populations in emergencies. Key actions include conducting rapid joint assessments, implementing a minimum WASH package, integrating WASH into community-based nutrition programmes, and collaborating with local actors for harmonized, localized interventions. These foundational steps aim to protect the nutritional status and well-being of affected communities while fostering community engagement and ownership from the outset.

Key resources available in Annex 1:

- *Community WASH and nutrition committee TOR template* (Section 4.8): Framework for establishing integrated coordination.
- *Outreach worker training package on WASH and nutrition* (Section 4.10): Comprehensive capacity building curriculum.
- *Integrated outreach and campaign planning tools* (Section 4.3): Coordinated implementation framework.
- *Community feedback mechanism checklist* (Section 5.3): Accountability systems for integrated programming.
- *Monthly reporting format for community committees* (Section 5.6): Simple tracking system for community committees.

5.3.1.1 Rapid WASH and nutrition assessments at the community level

Purpose: Conducting rapid WASH and nutrition assessments at the community level is essential for identifying priority risks, needs, and capacities to inform the design of context-specific, nutrition-sensitive WASH interventions. By engaging community members as active participants and combining qualitative and quantitative methods, these assessments provide a holistic understanding of the local WASH and nutrition situation to guide immediate response actions.

Timing: Initiate rapid assessments within the first 72 hours of the emergency, and complete data collection, analysis, and dissemination within the first 10 days.

Key steps:

1. Engage community leaders, health workers, caregivers, and representatives of at-risk groups in planning and implementing assessments by leveraging their local knowledge to map water points, sanitation practices, and existing WASH infrastructure, and community-based nutrition programmes.

2. Use participatory tools such as focus groups and community mapping alongside standardized methodologies like Standardized Monitoring and Assessment of Relief and Transitions (SMART), WASH KAP (Knowledge, Attitude and Practice), MUAC (mid-upper arm circumference), and IYCF (infant and young child feeding) assessment, surveys to capture community needs, priorities, perceptions, and capacities for integrated WASH and nutrition programming.
3. Assess key household and community-level WASH and nutrition risk factors and assets, including disease prevalence, access to safe water and sanitation, hygiene and food handling practices, environmental cleanliness, and infant and young child feeding behaviours.
4. Analyse findings collaboratively with nutrition, health, and food security actors to identify priority risks, target groups, and opportunities for integrated interventions, and build a shared understanding of how WASH conditions influence nutritional outcomes.
5. Establish assessment coordination structures and identify available local data collection capacity within the first 72 hours, followed by a secondary data review and selection of appropriate, locally adapted assessment tools and methods by day 3.
6. Mobilize and train gender-balanced and inclusive community assessment teams by day 5, and conduct primary data collection between days 3 and 10 using mixed methods and, where needed, remote approaches to ensure timely, safe, and comprehensive data gathering.

5.3.1.2 Minimum implementation of WASH package in collaboration with the community

Purpose: Implementing a locally adapted, nutrition-sensitive minimum WASH package in collaboration with affected communities is a priority intervention to prevent disease outbreaks and create an enabling environment for good nutrition in the initial emergency phase. This multi-pronged package combines the provision of critical WASH infrastructure and supplies with the promotion of key hygiene practices and community mobilization strategies.

Timing: Roll out the minimum WASH package within the first 14 days of the emergency, prioritizing the most at-risk communities and groups.

Key steps:

1. Rapidly restore access to safe drinking water by rehabilitating damaged water points with community input, distributing treatment kits and storage containers to vulnerable households, and promoting locally appropriate household water treatment and storage practices.

2. Support the construction and use of hygienic, accessible, and culturally acceptable sanitation facilities by facilitating community-led approaches like CLTS (community-led total sanitation), installing gender-segregated emergency latrines with handwashing and menstrual hygiene management (MHM) facilities, distributing latrine construction materials to vulnerable households, and ensuring all facilities are inclusive and safe for all users.
3. Promote critical hygiene behaviours through community-driven efforts by engaging local leaders and institutions in behaviour change campaigns, conducting hygiene demonstrations at schools and public spaces, co-designing inclusive hygiene kits and handwashing stations, and using local media and influencers to reinforce messages.
4. Ensure a clean and safe household environment for young children by encouraging safe child feces disposal, supporting access to BabyWASH facilities, promoting clean play and feeding areas, and distributing cleaning kits with caregiver training.
5. Build caregiver capacity for safe food preparation and feeding through participatory cooking demonstrations, breastfeeding and complementary feeding promotion, and the distribution of food hygiene kits with hands-on support for households with young children.
6. By day 14, collaborate with the community WASH and nutrition coordination committee to launch a locally tailored minimum service package based on rapid assessment findings, ensuring that interventions reflect community priorities and foster active participation and ownership.
7. Promote active participation and ownership through interventions that build on the findings of rapid assessments and community priorities.

Case Study 5.1 (Syria: Integrating WASH with shelter for nutritional well-being) illustrates how comprehensive shelter solutions with integrated WASH facilities can address multiple dimensions of well-being in displacement settings. By rehabilitating existing structures with water tanks, latrines connected to cesspits, and kitchen workspaces for hygienic food preparation, CARE International created dignified living environments for families previously living in inadequate conditions. The profound impact on beneficiaries, as demonstrated by 'Mohamed's' family transitioning from a livestock stall to a proper home with toilet facilities, highlights how integrated WASH-shelter interventions contribute significantly to psychological well-being and dignity. This holistic approach recognizes that nutritional security requires not just food accessibility, but also safe water, proper sanitation, and appropriate spaces for hygienic food preparation and consumption.

Case Study 5.1 Syria: Integrating WASH with shelter for nutritional well-being

In north-west Syria, approximately 1.7 million internally displaced persons live in 1,400 unplanned sites, with 900,000 in tents or makeshift shelters years after the initial displacement. Living in inadequate, non-durable shelters without proper WASH facilities increases protection risks, particularly gender-based violence, and creates health hazards that impact nutrition.

CARE International implemented 'dignified shelter solutions' incorporating private latrines and showers with necessary WASH infrastructure. Working within political and logistical constraints that limited construction materials, CARE rehabilitated existing structures and upgraded basic units with water tanks, latrines connected to cesspits, and kitchen workspaces for hygienic food preparation.

The impact on beneficiaries was profound, as illustrated by 'Mohamed' who was initially forced to house his family in a livestock stall. After CARE's intervention, which included a toilet connected to a cesspit, he reported his son's excitement: 'My son, when he saw the toilet, he could not believe his eyes ... The place turned from a livestock stall into a house, our house.' This transformation demonstrates how integrated WASH facilities contribute significantly to dignity and psychological well-being.

Attribution: Adapted from Keyyali, 'Case study: Dignified shelter solutions in northwest Syria', in Webb, 2023: 122–23 (see Annex 4).

5.3.1.3 WASH integration into community-based nutrition programmes and platforms

Purpose: Integrating WASH activities into ongoing community-based nutrition programmes and platforms is a key strategy for amplifying the reach, effectiveness, and sustainability of behaviour change interventions. By leveraging trusted delivery channels, capitalizing on existing community mobilization efforts, and harmonizing key messages, integrated programming can achieve greater impact while minimizing duplication and beneficiary fatigue.

Timing: Initiate WASH integration within nutrition programmes in the first 14 days of the response, and continue to strengthen integration approaches throughout the emergency and recovery phases.

Key steps:

1. Train and equip community health workers, nutrition volunteers, and growth monitoring promoters to deliver integrated WASH and nutrition messages during household and community visits, refer children with WASH-related illnesses to appropriate WASH, health or nutrition services, and conduct joint home visits with WASH promoters to reinforce behavioural links.
2. Incorporate WASH content into existing care groups and nutrition platforms by embedding hygiene messages into curricula, training model mothers and champions to promote improved behaviours, and establishing referral systems between nutrition groups and WASH committees. Ensure that programmes provide support for artificial feeding and

that admitted households are provided with sufficient safe water for preparing formula and for hygiene.

3. Provide a comprehensive WASH package in health and nutrition facilities by installing and maintaining handwashing stations and drinking water points, ensuring safe hygiene and food handling conditions, and distributing WASH kits with caregiver education for children with acute malnutrition.
4. Engage schools and educational platforms to promote lasting WASH and nutrition habits by integrating context-specific content into school activities, training teachers as role models, and upgrading school WASH facilities to be child-friendly and gender-sensitive.

5.3.1.4 Collaboration with community actors and authorities for harmonized, localized interventions

Purpose: Collaborating with community actors and authorities from the earliest stages of the emergency WASH response is critical for fostering local ownership, capacity, and resilience. By engaging community leaders, organizations, and influencers as active partners in assessment, planning, and implementation, responders can ensure that interventions build upon indigenous knowledge, priorities, and resources. This localized approach lays the foundation for a more sustainable, adaptive, and accountable response.

Timing: Within the first seven days, map key community stakeholders and convene initial coordination meetings. Continue to regularly engage community actors in programme design, implementation, and monitoring throughout the response.

Key steps:

1. Establish inclusive, multi-stakeholder WASH and nutrition coordination mechanisms at subnational and local levels by engaging community leaders, government, civil society, and private sector actors in joint planning, implementation, and regular progress reviews.
2. Develop localized tools, targeting criteria, communication materials, and monitoring systems that reflect community needs and beliefs, and harmonize messages, behaviour change approaches, and service delivery models to ensure consistency and cultural relevance.
3. Mobilize and strengthen existing community structures – such as health committees, women's groups, youth clubs, and faith-based networks – by providing training, resources, and mentoring to lead outreach, monitoring, and referral activities.
4. Support the establishment or revitalization of community-based management systems for WASH infrastructure by building the technical, financial, and organizational capacity of water committees, sanitation groups, and school clubs to ensure sustainable service delivery.

Case Study 5.2 Iraq: Community-driven WASH in conflict-affected schools

The 2014–17 conflict in Iraq continues to affect millions, with Zakho District in Dohuk Governorate hosting over 100,000 internally displaced persons (IDPs), straining school infrastructure. Schools average 300–400 students with 40–50 per class, often in multiple shifts, with inadequate WASH facilities impacting education quality, particularly for girls.

Save the Children improved WASH facilities in schools, focusing on gender-segregated bathrooms to address safety concerns. The organization recognized that historically, Iraqi parents rarely engaged with schools, while facility maintenance decisions were centralized at regional levels, creating delays in service provision.

Save the Children supported community mobilization for school improvements, helping communities recognize the need for new school buildings and WASH facilities. They mobilized both funds and labour for construction and maintenance, addressing the challenge of transitioning from historically centralized education systems (where schools were provided free by the government using oil revenues) to locally supported ones necessary in resource-constrained, conflict-affected contexts. Student input revealed that bathrooms often became gathering places where bullying occurred, particularly affecting children from different backgrounds (IDPs versus host community). These insights guided designs prioritizing safety, accessibility, and dignity, essential for educational continuity and student well-being.

Attribution: Adapted from Enwiya, 2021: 42–43 (see Annex 4).

5. Within the first seven days, map key community actors and assets, hold initial coordination meetings to align approaches and prioritize actions, and regularly update localization strategies to remain responsive to evolving needs and community feedback.

Case Study 5.2 (Iraq: Community-driven WASH in conflict-affected schools) underscores the significance of mobilizing community support and resources for school WASH improvements in conflict-affected settings. By actively involving students in the design process, the intervention ensured that the facilities met their specific needs, addressed safety and dignity concerns, and promoted a more inclusive learning environment. This community-driven approach not only fosters local ownership and sustainability but also contributes to improved educational outcomes and student well-being.

5.3.2 Resilience actions (14–90 days)

Building on the emergency actions efforts, the 14–90 day period focuses on strengthening the integration of emergency WASH interventions with local capacities for long-term resilience and sustainability. Key strategies include assessing and building the technical, organizational, and financial capacities of local WASH and nutrition actors, mobilizing community assets and champions, forging multi-stakeholder partnerships, and planning for a smooth transition to community-managed, risk-informed services.

5.3.2.1 Transition to local leadership and ownership

Purpose: Progressively transitioning leadership and ownership to local actors promotes the sustainability, scalability, and resilience of WASH and nutrition interventions by empowering communities to drive their own development agenda. This process involves working closely with community representatives to develop phased transition plans, providing regular training and mentoring to local structures, advocating for meaningful community participation in coordination platforms, and facilitating the development of sustainable management and financing models. Conducting participatory capacity self-assessments with key community structures helps tailor capacity building plans and transition strategies to enable local actors to take on increasing levels of responsibility for WASH and nutrition interventions.

Timing: Initiate the transition planning process within the first 30 days of the response, and gradually transfer responsibilities to local actors throughout the recovery and development phases, as conditions allow.

Key steps:

1. Work with community representatives to develop a phased transition plan that outlines a clear timeline and process for gradually handing over responsibility for managing and maintaining WASH infrastructure, promoting healthy practices, and monitoring progress to local actors.
2. Provide regular, on-the-job training, mentoring, and accompaniment to community health workers, WASH committees, school health clubs, and other local structures involved in WASH and nutrition service delivery and promotion. Use adult learning methods that build skills and confidence through hands-on practice, problem-solving, and peer support.
3. Advocate for meaningful community participation and leadership in subnational WASH and nutrition coordination platforms, ensuring that local priorities, perspectives, and innovations inform wider planning, resource allocation, and policy decisions.
4. Facilitate community-driven processes to develop sustainable management and financing models for WASH and nutrition services, such as tariff systems, cross-subsidies, or collective savings schemes. Link community initiatives with government programmes, market-based solutions, and long-term funding streams where possible.
5. Conduct participatory capacity self-assessments with key community structures to identify strengths, gaps, and support needs. Use the findings to tailor capacity building plans and transition strategies that enable local actors to take on increasing levels of responsibility for WASH and nutrition interventions.

5.3.2.2 Align community-level interventions with national systems

Purpose: Aligning community-level WASH and nutrition interventions with national standards, policies, and systems ensures coherence, consistency, and sustainability of local efforts, while leveraging external resources and expertise to support community-driven initiatives. This involves reviewing and adapting policies, standards, and plans to support community-based programming, strengthening the capacity of the local WASH and nutrition workforce, engaging community representatives in multi-stakeholder review and planning processes, and establishing clear roles and coordination mechanisms for local government actors. Integrating community-defined indicators and participatory monitoring approaches into local government WASH and nutrition information systems is also crucial for ensuring that community priorities and perspectives inform decision-making at all levels.

Timing: Review relevant national frameworks and engage key stakeholders in alignment dialogues within the first 30 days of the response. Continue to harmonize community-level interventions with evolving national systems throughout the recovery and development phases.

Key steps:

1. Review national WASH and nutrition policies, strategies, guidelines, and protocols to identify opportunities for aligning community-level interventions. Work with relevant government stakeholders to adapt national frameworks to the local context while maintaining core standards and principles.
2. Support subnational authorities to contextualize national WASH and nutrition training curricula, job aids, and behaviour change materials for frontline workers and community volunteers. Ensure that capacity building resources reflect local languages, customs, and learning needs.
3. Engage community representatives and local government counterparts in multi-stakeholder review and planning processes to feed local priorities, lessons learned, and solutions into subnational and national WASH and nutrition policies and programmes.
4. Establish clear roles, responsibilities, and coordination mechanisms for local government actors involved in managing and regulating community WASH-nutrition services. Strengthen institutional capacities and accountability systems to ensure sustained support for community-led initiatives.
5. Orient community leaders, WASH committees, and nutrition volunteers on relevant national standards and guidelines. Collaboratively identify areas where local practices and preferences may diverge and develop appropriate strategies to harmonize approaches while respecting community norms and promoting positive behaviours.

5.3.2.3 Coordination and referral mechanisms between community and facility WASH and nutrition services

Purpose: Strengthening coordination and referral mechanisms between community-based and facility-based WASH and nutrition services improves the continuum of care, optimizes resource utilization, and supports harmonized planning, implementation, and monitoring of interventions. This involves establishing clear protocols for identifying, referring, and following up on WASH-related illnesses and malnutrition cases, integrating key WASH and nutrition indicators into community-based surveillance and health information systems, setting up accessible community feedback mechanisms, conducting periodic joint assessments and reviews, and mapping available services to develop practical solutions that leverage existing resources and capacities.

Timing: Establish initial coordination and referral protocols within the first 30 days of the response, and continuously strengthen linkages and collaborative processes throughout the emergency, recovery, and development phases.

Key steps:

1. Establish clear, context-specific protocols for identifying, referring, and following up on WASH-related illnesses. Ensure WASH promoters are informed about available nutrition services and eligibility criteria, and, where feasible, provide training to WASH promoters on identifying and referring cases of acute malnutrition in coordination with community-based health workers and local health facilities.
2. Integrate key WASH and nutrition indicators into community-based surveillance, growth monitoring, and health information systems. Build the capacity of frontline workers to collect, analyse, and use integrated data to inform decision-making and response actions.
3. Set up and promote hotlines, SMS reporting, or other accessible community feedback mechanisms to enable timely identification and resolution of WASH and nutrition issues and gaps. Regularly review and act upon community input in coordination with relevant local authorities and service providers.
4. Conduct periodic joint assessments and reviews of community and facility-based WASH and nutrition services to identify bottlenecks, document good practices, and develop collaborative improvement plans. Use quality improvement methods to test, scale up, and institutionalize effective coordination and referral approaches.
5. Map available WASH and nutrition services at community and facility levels. Analyse barriers and enablers to effective coordination and work with community and government stakeholders to develop practical solutions that leverage existing resources, capacities, and systems.

5.3.2.4 Identify and support community-led innovations and adaptations

Purpose: Identifying and supporting community-led innovations and adaptations in WASH and nutrition programming fosters local ownership, relevance, and scalability of interventions, while leveraging community creativity and resourcefulness to address context-specific challenges and opportunities. This process involves engaging community members in participatory research and human-centred design processes, documenting and building upon indigenous knowledge and practices, mobilizing community champions to promote key messages and model positive practices, facilitating peer-to-peer learning and exchange, and establishing participatory learning and action cycles to iteratively identify, prioritize, and find solutions to local WASH and nutrition challenges.

Timing: Establish participatory innovation and learning processes within the first 45 days of the response, and continue to identify, test, and scale up promising community-led solutions throughout the emergency, recovery, and development phases.

Key steps:

1. Engage community members, particularly women, youth, and marginalized groups, in participatory research and human-centred design processes to co-create WASH technologies, products, and behaviour change approaches that address local needs, preferences, and challenges.
2. Document, validate, and build upon indigenous knowledge, beliefs, and practices related to WASH and nutrition. Identify positive norms and innovations that can be leveraged to promote optimal behaviours and address harmful misconceptions or taboos.
3. Mobilize community champions, such as respected elders, religious leaders, or traditional healers, to promote key WASH and nutrition messages and role model positive practices. Equip them with culturally relevant and technically accurate communication tools, talking points, and pedagogical skills.
4. Facilitate peer-to-peer learning, exchange visits, and healthy competition between communities to cross-fertilize ideas, spread successful innovations, and stimulate collective action. Use community-driven metrics, rewards, and recognition systems to validate and incentivize local achievements.
5. Establish participatory learning and action cycles within community structures to iteratively identify, prioritize, and find solutions to local WASH and nutrition challenges. Provide flexible seed funding, technical support, and partnership brokering to enable communities to test, refine, and scale up promising approaches.

Case Study 5.3 (Jordan: Refugee-led environmental health for nutrition security) presents a compelling example of a community-led innovation

Case Study 5.3 Jordan: Refugee-led environmental health for nutrition security

The Azraq refugee camp in Jordan, established in 2014 for Syrian refugees, covers approximately 15 square km and houses around 36,500 people. In a country where only 7% of municipal waste is recycled, the influx of 650,000 registered Syrian refugees further strained solid waste management systems.

World Vision has provided solid waste management services in Azraq since 2017, implementing a comprehensive approach that addresses environmental hygiene, an often overlooked dimension of nutrition-sensitive WASH programming. The programme provides a two-bin system for recyclable and non-recyclable waste for every eight households, conducts behaviour change campaigns for proper sorting, manages daily waste collection, and operates a solar-powered 'green centre' for processing collected materials.

The initiative employs 40 incentive-based volunteers for daily collection and sorting, with an additional 150 volunteers rotating monthly for behaviour change activities, creating valuable livelihood opportunities that strengthen community resilience. Approximately 17 tonnes of waste are generated daily, with over 15% being recyclable. These materials are sold to local vendors, with proceeds reinvested to cover about 20% of programme costs, creating a partial cost-recovery model that enhances financial sustainability while improving environmental health conditions essential for good nutrition outcomes.

Attribution: Adapted from Kocharyan, 2021: 30–31 (see Annex 4).

that addresses the critical, yet often neglected, issue of environmental hygiene in nutrition-sensitive WASH programming. By empowering refugees to design and manage a comprehensive solid waste management system, the intervention not only improves environmental health conditions but also creates valuable livelihood opportunities and establishes a partial cost-recovery model. This innovative approach demonstrates how identifying and supporting community-led adaptations can foster local ownership, enhance resilience, and contribute to the long-term sustainability of WASH and nutrition interventions in humanitarian settings.

5.3.2.5 Community-driven WASH and nutrition assessments and planning

Purpose: Transitioning to community-driven, comprehensive WASH and nutrition assessments and planning enhances the relevance, effectiveness, and sustainability of interventions by building local capacity to identify and address evolving needs and priorities. This involves working with community WASH-nutrition committees and local authorities to identify information needs and planning priorities, building the capacity of community members to design and lead assessments, facilitating inclusive processes to analyse findings and develop multi-year action plans, supporting communities to mobilize resources, and promoting a culture of continuous learning and adaptation within community structures.

Timing: As the situation stabilizes and local capacities grow, work with communities to plan and conduct in-depth WASH and nutrition assessments and develop long-term, costed action plans.

Key steps:

1. Work with community WASH-nutrition committees and local authorities to identify evolving information needs, knowledge gaps, and strategic planning priorities. Jointly define the scope and objectives of in-depth sectoral or multisectoral assessments.
2. Build the capacity of community members to design, lead, and participate in comprehensive WASH and/or nutrition assessments, with an emphasis on developing data collection skills, ethical research practices, and participatory analysis techniques.
3. Facilitate inclusive, community-driven processes to analyse assessment findings, identify root causes of WASH and nutrition vulnerabilities, and develop multi-year, costed action plans. Ensure the active participation of women, youth, people living with disabilities, and other marginalized groups in priority-setting and decision-making. Refer to Annex 1 Section 3.1 (Response planning template) and Section 3.2 (Nutrition-sensitive WASH strategy development guide) for guidance on participatory planning processes and tools.
4. Support communities to mobilize internal and external resources to implement their WASH and nutrition action plans. Broker strategic partnerships with government agencies, development donors, private sector actors, and civil society organizations to address funding, policy, and technical support gaps.
5. Promote a culture of continuous learning, experimentation, and adaptation within community structures. Embed participatory monitoring, evaluation, and knowledge management systems within local planning and implementation processes to enable real-time feedback, joint reflection, and evidence-based adjustments to WASH and nutrition interventions.

5.3.2.6 Promote nutrition-sensitive WASH programming

Purpose: Promoting nutrition-sensitive WASH programming is critical for addressing the underlying determinants of malnutrition, such as inadequate access to safe water, sanitation, and hygiene. This requires a multisectoral and integrated approach that brings together WASH, health, nutrition, and other relevant sectors to design and implement mutually reinforcing interventions. Nutrition-sensitive WASH interventions should be designed and implemented in a participatory and context-specific manner, taking into account the cultural beliefs, practices, and preferences of the communities they serve.

Timing: Integrate nutrition considerations into WASH strategies, plans, and interventions from the early stages of the emergency response, and continue to strengthen the nutrition sensitivity of WASH programming throughout the transition and development phases.

Key steps:

1. Integrate context-specific nutrition objectives and indicators into community WASH strategies and plans, prioritizing actions that improve food hygiene, environmental sanitation, and infant and young child feeding practices. Engage communities in identifying and addressing critical nutrition–WASH linkages through participatory assessment, planning, and monitoring processes.
2. Collaborate with food security, agriculture, and health actors to jointly design and implement multisectoral nutrition-sensitive WASH interventions, such as the promotion of safe food handling practices, the improvement of WASH conditions in markets and food processing areas, and the integration of WASH into care group and Positive Deviance/Hearth programmes.
3. Strengthen multisectoral coordination platforms and advocate for the inclusion of nutrition-sensitive WASH objectives, activities, and indicators in local government plans, budgets, and monitoring systems. Work with nutrition and health stakeholders to establish joint targeting criteria, delivery mechanisms, and referral protocols for households at high risk of malnutrition.
4. Integrate nutrition-sensitive WASH messaging and practices into routine health and nutrition services, particularly those targeting pregnant and lactating women, caregivers of children under two, and other nutritionally vulnerable groups. Train and equip frontline health workers to deliver practical, contextually relevant WASH and nutrition counselling and support as part of primary healthcare and nutrition programmes.
5. Monitor and evaluate the implementation and effectiveness of nutrition-sensitive WASH interventions, using a combination of output, outcome, and impact indicators. Conduct joint reviews and evaluations with nutrition and health stakeholders to assess the contribution of WASH to nutrition outcomes, identify lessons learned, and inform evidence-based policy and programming decisions.

5.4 Monitoring

5.4.1 Objectives

Monitoring community-level WASH and nutrition interventions aims to assess progress, quality, and equity of integrated services, promote accountability to affected people, and inform decision-making and adaptations. Participatory, locally led monitoring is critical for fostering ownership and sustainability.

5.4.2 Key monitoring activities

5.4.2.1 Engaging communities

Meaningful community involvement throughout the monitoring cycle is essential for relevant, actionable insights. Diverse community members should take the lead in prioritizing indicators, collecting data, analysing results, and planning improvements.

- Engage community leaders, volunteers, and representatives in designing WASH and nutrition assessments that reflect local priorities and capacities.
- Train and support community monitoring teams to collect and interpret WASH and nutrition data using participatory methods.
- Facilitate community-led analysis and validation of monitoring findings through accessible formats and inclusive dialogues.
- Establish feedback and accountability systems using:
  - community meetings and participatory review spaces
  - suggestion boxes, hotlines, or local helpdesks
  - tools like social audits, scorecards, or citizen report cards.
- Ensure findings are shared and interpreted jointly by communities and duty-bearers.
- Identify and strengthen existing community capacities, positive practices, and indigenous knowledge to reinforce locally led WASH and nutrition solutions.

5.4.2.2 Harmonizing indicators and systems

Standardized monitoring frameworks and tools enable coherent measurement and comparison of WASH and nutrition progress. Indicators should be locally relevant while aligning with national and global reporting systems.

- Develop a contextualized WASH and nutrition monitoring framework with a core set of indicators harmonized with national systems.
- Integrate community-level indicators into subnational and national WASH and nutrition information management systems.
- Harmonize data collection tools, quality controls, and reporting formats across community, district, and national levels.
- Establish data sharing and coordination mechanisms to promote joint analysis and use of monitoring information.

5.4.2.3 Strengthening community capacities

Investing in community-based monitoring systems and skills is vital for local ownership, quality, and sustainability. Capacity strengthening should emphasize practical application, learning-by-doing, and participatory approaches.

- Train community monitors on data collection, management, analysis, and use, using adult learning methods and on-the-job mentoring.
- Develop simple, visual monitoring tools and guides adapted to local contexts, languages, and literacies.
- Facilitate community-to-community learning exchanges and peer mentoring to spread effective monitoring practices.
- Advocate for policies and resources to sustain and scale up community-led WASH and nutrition monitoring systems.

5.4.2.4 Utilizing monitoring data

Translating monitoring data into action is key to achieving results and accountability. This requires user-friendly information, participatory interpretation, and functioning feedback loops to decision-makers at all levels.

- Analyse monitoring data to assess the coverage, quality, and equity of community WASH and nutrition interventions and identify bottlenecks.
- Monitor for unintended consequences, such as:
  - disruption to local markets or services
  - environmental sustainability issues (e.g. waste management, water use)
  - protection risks or power imbalances affecting women and marginalized groups.
- Triangulate WASH and nutrition monitoring data with information from relevant sectors, including:
  - health and disease surveillance from local health authorities
  - food security and livelihoods assessments
  - school health and education records
  - protection monitoring and community feedback mechanisms.
- Produce accessible, visual monitoring reports, dashboards, and scorecards tailored to different local stakeholders and decision-makers.
- Convene participatory spaces for communities, authorities, and partners to review monitoring results and jointly plan improvements.
- Strengthen linkages between community monitoring systems and higher-level decision-making, planning, and resource allocation.
- Use community evidence to advocate for improved WASH and nutrition policies and programming at national levels. Collaborate with research institutions and coordination platforms to scale successful community-led models.

5.4.3 Key monitoring indicators

Community WASH and nutrition indicators track the status, progress, and outcomes of integrated interventions:

Nutrition and health status:

- Prevalence of stunting, wasting, and underweight among children under five years
- Proportion of infants 0–5 months exclusively breastfed
- Proportion of children 6–23 months receiving a minimum acceptable diet
- Prevalence of anaemia among pregnant and lactating women and young children
- Incidence and prevalence of diarrhea and other WASH-related diseases in children under five

WASH practices and services:

- Proportion of households practising safe water handling and storage
- Proportion of households safely storing drinking water
- Proportion of households with access to basic sanitation facilities and using them
- Proportion of households practising safe disposal of child feces
- Proportion of households with handwashing facilities with soap and water
- Percentage of households with clean and safe play spaces for children under two
- Proportion of caregivers practising proper food hygiene behaviours
- Proportion of schools and health centres with functional WASH facilities meeting standards

Community mobilization and governance:

- Existence and functionality of community WASH and nutrition committees and plans
- Number of community members trained on integrated WASH and nutrition promotion
- Community satisfaction with WASH and nutrition services and participation in decision-making

5.4.4 Monitoring methods and tools

- Community WASH and nutrition mapping, transect walks, and participatory observations
- Household surveys and interviews on WASH and nutrition practices and coverage
- Focus group discussions to assess community perceptions, barriers, and priorities
- Community scorecards and social audits of WASH and nutrition services and duty-bearers
- Review of local health facility and school records on WASH and nutrition indicators
- WASH and Nutrition Committee meeting minutes and activity tracking forms

5.4.5 Monitoring roles and responsibilities

Community actors:

- Identify and prioritize key WASH and nutrition issues, indicators, and monitoring questions.
- Collect and compile monitoring data through community structures and processes.
- Analyse and validate monitoring results and develop action plans to address gaps.
- Share monitoring findings with subnational and national coordination platforms.

Implementing agencies:

- Co-design and set up participatory, community-based WASH and nutrition monitoring systems.
- Train and coach community monitors on data collection, analysis, and use.
- Provide supportive supervision and quality assurance for community monitoring activities.
- Facilitate community-led learning, reflection, and adaptation processes.
- Synthesize monitoring data for higher-level sectoral reporting and knowledge management.

Government counterparts:

- Coordinate and oversee community-based WASH and nutrition monitoring in line with national policies.
- Integrate community monitoring indicators into subnational and national information systems.
- Convene joint monitoring and performance review events with community participation.
- Allocate resources to sustain and scale up community-led WASH and nutrition monitoring.
- Use community monitoring evidence for policy, strategy, and programme improvements.

5.4.6 Monitoring timeline and deliverables

- Quarterly community WASH and nutrition assessments in the initial emergency phase
- Monthly monitoring visits and data collection by community monitoring teams
- Bi-monthly community review and action planning meetings based on monitoring results
- Quarterly consolidation of community monitoring data and submission to subnational coordination platforms
- Annual participatory evaluations and learning events for community WASH and nutrition monitoring

Key deliverables:

- Community WASH and nutrition monitoring framework, tools, and training materials
- Quarterly community WASH and nutrition monitoring reports and scorecards
- Case studies and learning briefs on community WASH and nutrition monitoring approaches and results
- Annual reports on the functionality and performance of community WASH and nutrition monitoring systems
- Policy briefs and advocacy materials on institutionalizing and scaling up community-led monitoring
- Advocacy briefs and learning products based on community-generated evidence
- Documentation of innovations and good practices from community WASH and nutrition integration

CHAPTER 6

Transforming WASH response

Toward integration, localization, and sustainability

This compendium, designed as a practitioner-oriented guide, addresses a critical gap in the current humanitarian coordination framework by providing specific protocols and tools to integrate WASH, health, and nutrition interventions. The framework's foundation rests on three core principles that transform traditional emergency response: integration that breaks down sectoral silos to address interconnected challenges holistically; strengths-based approaches that recognize and build upon existing local capabilities rather than focusing solely on deficits; and integrated coordination that creates synergies between sectors while empowering local leadership. By operationalizing these principles, practitioners can shift from fragmented, externally driven responses to cohesive, locally owned solutions that meet both immediate needs and long-term resilience. It empowers a diverse array of stakeholders, from implementers to decision-makers, to carefully consider the essential steps required at both the community and national levels to achieve sustainable development. These approaches are particularly effective in resource-constrained environments, enabling practitioners to maximize impact and sustainability even when international funding is limited.

Integration by design: Coordination guidelines for resilient WASH programming in humanitarian contexts (Chapter 1) establishes the conceptual foundation through the climate, conflict, and pandemics (CCP) framework, which examines how these three pressures interact to create complex humanitarian challenges. This chapter provides analytical tools for understanding crisis dynamics while emphasizing community assets and capacities as starting points for intervention design. The value of this integrated approach lies in its ability to address root causes rather than symptoms, creating pathways that connect emergency response to sustainable development outcomes.

Integration in emergencies: Guideline for coordinating WASH with health at the national level (Chapter 2) guides national officials through seven critical actions during the first 90 days: activating coordination platforms, conducting integrated assessments, providing emergency services, establishing monitoring systems, implementing cross-sectoral coordination, addressing specialized needs, and strengthening local capacity. The value of integrated coordination emerges through unified decision-making structures that align WASH interventions with health priorities, fostering policy coherence and resource optimization while enhancing government capacity for future crisis response.

Integration in emergencies: Guideline for coordinating WASH with nutrition at the national level (Chapter 3) operationalizes multisectoral approaches to address the underlying causes of undernutrition through seven coordinated actions: establishing coordination committees, conducting participatory assessments, providing integrated emergency interventions, developing joint strategies, establishing monitoring systems, mobilizing community champions, and building sustainable partnerships. Integrated coordination at this level creates nutrition-sensitive WASH programming that addresses the critical first 1,000 days while simultaneously strengthening national food and water systems.

Integration in emergencies: Guideline for coordinating WASH with health at the community level (Chapter 4) focuses on eight frontline actions: activating health facility-led coordination, conducting rapid assessments, implementing priority interventions, developing localized action plans, strengthening local governance, establishing facility-based improvement teams, developing sustainable systems, and facilitating learning. The value of community-level coordination lies in creating direct linkages between clinical care and environmental health while fostering local ownership and technical capacity for sustained service delivery.

Integration in emergencies: Guideline for coordinating WASH with nutrition at the community level (Chapter 5) outlines eight essential actions for household-level impact: establishing community committees, conducting participatory assessments, implementing minimum WASH packages, developing joint strategies, creating communication mechanisms, enhancing local capacity, supporting innovations, and establishing monitoring systems. Integrated coordination fosters enabling environments for good nutrition through improved WASH while promoting community leadership and sustainable behaviour change.

The Practitioners' Toolkit for Integrated WASH in Emergencies (Annex 1) is a unique resource that translates strategic guidance into immediately usable tools and resources. It is divided into five sections: coordination tools, assessment tools, planning and strategy tools, implementation tools, and monitoring and feedback tools. With over 30 practical templates and checklists, the toolkit ensures that integrated approaches can be operationalized effectively, regardless of context, providing the concrete mechanisms necessary to move from concept to implementation.

Current WASH trends and future directions

The humanitarian WASH landscape is undergoing a fundamental transformation driven by declining international funding, evolving coordination mechanisms, and technological advancements. The significant drop in development assistance necessitates a strategic shift toward government-led response mechanisms and domestic resource mobilization. This change requires humanitarian actors to transition from primary implementers to catalysts for strengthening government capacity, while emergency interventions must build upon, rather than bypass, existing systems.

Moving forward, success demands reduced dependence on traditional funding sources and improved self-sufficiency at all levels. This transition requires intentional private sector partnerships that view market-based solutions as essential components of sustainable WASH service delivery. Furthermore, leveraging artificial intelligence and digital technologies creates opportunities to enhance efficiency, reduce costs, and expand professional capabilities while decreasing reliance on external technical assistance.

These coordination guidelines represent more than emergency response protocols; instead, they provide a roadmap for transforming how the global WASH sector approaches crisis response, local ownership, and sustainable development. By emphasizing integration, community leadership, and systems strengthening from the outset of emergencies, these guidelines chart a course toward a more resilient, locally driven, and technologically enhanced future for WASH programming worldwide. The framework's ultimate value lies not in its individual components but in its integrated approach, which fosters lasting change through coordinated action across all levels of intervention.

The WASH sector is increasingly acknowledging the limitations of relying solely on donor funding. New analysis examining recently announced decreases in humanitarian funding suggests that overall reductions in humanitarian assistance could result in an annual decrease of US$41–60 bn (15–22 per cent relative to 2023 levels), with health programmes experiencing a particularly severe 44 per cent reduction in budget allocation (Sabow et al., 2025). These stark reductions underscore the need to develop alternative financing mechanisms. Achieving Sustainable Development Goal 6 by 2030 ('Ensure availability and sustainable management of water and sanitation for all') is becoming increasingly challenging due to anticipated cuts in global funding. In this context, new financing strategies, like blended finance that combines public and private capital to support water, sanitation, and hygiene projects, are crucial (Dietvorst, 2018). Organizations such as Aqua for All and IRC WASH are substantially investing in blended finance operations with the objective of mobilizing private finance and increasing the sustainability of WASH services. The operations aim to establish a more diversified and resilient funding base for the sector (Aqua for All, 2024).

Building local resilience and ownership

Encouraging local financial and institutional independence is key to guaranteeing the sustainability of WASH services. In Nigeria, low-income households have been enabled to construct toilets with the support of community savings and credit groups, through soft loans and exchange systems. This allows communities to take charge of their sanitation needs and become less reliant on external support (Jurji and Ogunjobi, 2023). This grassroots approach aligns with emerging best practices in efficient resource utilization. Recent analysis highlights the importance of zero-based budgeting and system optimization in maximizing impact with limited resources (Sabow et al., 2025). Furthermore, innovative pooled funding models, such as the Sahel Regional Fund, demonstrate that mandating equal overhead sharing between international and local partners can enhance self-sufficiency while building local capacity (ICVA, 2023). These innovative financing approaches directly enable the broader transformation toward locally led humanitarian responses that are reshaping the sector.

The humanitarian space is undergoing a revolution, with localization the primary theme in strategic guidelines and operational strategies. This focuses on strengthening local actors, enhancing community resilience, and tailoring aid to be contextually meaningful and sustainable. The Global WASH Cluster (GWC) Strategy 2025 is in line with the spirit of localization in its support for strengthening regional capacity and leadership in humanitarian response (GWC, 2022). It requires a paradigm shift in which local institutions are not only implementing partners but also stakeholders in decision-making, resource mobilization, and intervention planning. The GWC Inter Cluster Collaboration-Coordination Matrix-Guidance is a tool designed to help actors map collaboration across humanitarian clusters (GWC, 2025). It therefore seeks to ensure interventions are more responsive to the needs and dynamics of the affected communities, resulting in effective and sustainable impacts (GWC, 2022). The 2025 Global Report on Internal Displacement records a high of 75.9 million individuals internally displaced due to conflicts and disasters that triggered these record numbers (iDMC, 2025).

The localization of humanitarian operations and approaches is a significant trend, not an exception, but a paradigm shift towards improved, equitable, and sustainable assistance. Through local support and interventions tailored to local needs, the humanitarian community can serve affected populations more effectively and promote sustainable solutions. Local stakeholders are often the first to respond in crisis settings, playing a critical role in delivering early relief and assistance. However, persistent challenges, including coordination, capacity development, and sustained support for local organizations, continue to hinder the effectiveness of localized responses, particularly in protracted displacement contexts. Strengthening local institutions is crucial to ensure timely and culturally sensitive aid, as well as to support pathways toward sustainable solutions.

This localization imperative is particularly critical given that 32 countries receive health official development assistance equivalent to more than 25 per cent of their total health expenditure (Sabow et al., 2025). In these contexts, pooled funds with majority NGO governance provide 'valuable expertise and practical assessments of issues such as access limitation and target selection', ensuring that funding decisions reflect ground-level realities (ICVA, 2023: 4). Models like the Sahel Regional Fund, which is primarily governed by NGOs at the regional level, demonstrate how localized decision-making can address cross-border dynamics while maintaining accountability to affected populations (ICVA, 2023).

UNICEF's Strategic Plan 2022–2025 identifies localization as a key to its success in reaching children, particularly in humanitarian situations (UNICEF, 2022). Similarly, Save the Children's Strategic Plan 2025–2027 emphasizes reaching children, with particular focus on conflict, climate change, inequality, and gender injustice (Save the Children, 2025). It highlights a more substantial commitment to a locally led yet globally connected approach, partnering closely with local actors while leveraging the full strength of Save the Children International's global movement to maximize impact for and with children. By focusing on local ownership and capacity building, key international NGOs aim to enhance the effectiveness and sustainability of their programmes, enabling children and families to receive support in a timely and culturally responsive manner.

To make the concepts of localization work as effectively as possible, some practical steps need to be taken:

- *Capacity building*: This includes investment and expenditure on training and support for local agencies, enabling them to become more technically, managerially, and financially capable.
- *Inclusive participation*: Facilitating local stakeholders to be involved in every phase of the humanitarian programme cycle, ranging from planning through to evaluation.
- *Resource allocation*: Ensuring a high percentage of humanitarian resources is allocated to local organizations, allowing them to drive and coordinate action.
- *Contextual understanding*: Creating interventions that are locally appropriate to the unique cultural, social, and political context of affected communities.
- *Sustainability planning*: Long-term programme planning, with a focus on local capacity building and the sustaining of services beyond the immediate response phase.

These diverse skill requirements reflect a fundamental shift in how WASH programming must operate in an era of reduced traditional funding. As Sabow et al. (2025) outline, the sector must pursue four strategic levers: capturing efficiencies in programme design, mobilizing new resources, reprioritizing high-impact investments, and restructuring the development ecosystem. The emergence of innovative pooled funding mechanisms offers a pathway forward, with evidence showing that 'diverse funding mechanisms should foster exchange and collaboration, facilitating an environment where stakeholders can learn from different experiences' (ICVA, 2023: 25). By combining technological innovation, private sector engagement, and locally led governance structures, the WASH sector can navigate the transition from dependency on traditional aid to a more resilient and diversified funding future.

Financing innovation and governance reform

Public–private partnerships are now becoming central to overcoming WASH challenges. In Pune, India, for example, SWaCH, a cooperative of waste pickers, has integrated informal waste pickers into the formalized waste management process, training them and providing them with predictable incomes (Express News Service, 2021). This type of public–private partnership between the government and the poor is an example of how private sector engagement can enhance service delivery and promote social inclusivity (Gawade, 2025). These partnerships reflect a broader trend toward restructuring the global development ecosystem. As traditional funding declines, hybrid governance models are emerging in which private companies act as fund management agents in pooled funds, such as the Aid Fund for Northern Syria (AFNS), bringing professional expertise while upholding humanitarian principles (ICVA, 2023). This illustrates how public–private collaboration can mobilize resources from 'nontraditional donors' while ensuring accountability (Sabow et al., 2025).

The private sector plays a complex and evolving role in WASH, contributing both progress and setbacks. While private enterprises can drive innovation and improve service delivery, challenges such as the commodification of water and the need for ethical safeguards persist. Balancing profitability with social responsibility remains essential to effective private sector engagement (Rieiro et al., 2020). Yet, these same actors often operate within profit-driven models that commodify essential services, exacerbate inequities, and marginalize the most vulnerable. The Ground Truth Solutions 2025 report highlights that as international assistance wanes, communities are organizing their own mutual aid efforts and informal service systems, reflecting a deep understanding of their context and resilience (GTS, 2025). Private actors must recognize that effectiveness in this space is not just about delivery speed or scale, but about aligning with and supporting community priorities, ownership, and long-term sustainability. This community-driven momentum creates both opportunities and challenges for private sector engagement, requiring a fundamental rethinking of how businesses interact with humanitarian systems.

As global aid systems are reshaped by budget reductions and shifting geopolitical interests, the humanitarian sector faces a crossroads. The question is no longer how to do more with less, but how to do differently. This requires moving beyond a transactional view of the private sector as merely a supplier of services and toward a model in which private actors are held accountable for advancing equity, ethics, and social outcomes. This involves reorienting investment strategies to prioritize long-term impact over short-term returns, fostering new forms of partnerships that value community knowledge as much as technical expertise, and integrating flexibility and transparency into business models (Sabow et al., 2025). In this moment of contraction and realignment, the private sector must evolve not only in function but in purpose, becoming part of a broader transformation that reclaims WASH as a public good grounded in dignity, justice, and shared responsibility.

The transformation of funding mechanisms extends beyond technological solutions to include innovative governance structures. A comparative analysis of emerging pooled funding models reveals how NGO-led governance can enhance local ownership and operational efficiency (ICVA, 2023). The Start Fund's rapid response mechanism, collectively managed by NGO members, demonstrates how humanitarian actors can make swift funding decisions within 72 hours of a crisis onset. Similarly, the AFNS employs a tiered eligibility system that allows local NGOs to progress through different funding levels based on capacity assessments (ICVA, 2023). These models exemplify how restructured governance can mobilize resources from diverse sources while maintaining focus on localization and efficiency. These governance innovations, combined with emerging technologies, offer unprecedented opportunities to accelerate local capacity building and reduce dependency on traditional humanitarian systems.

Leveraging artificial intelligence to reduce dependency

Artificial intelligence (AI) is rapidly becoming a transformative tool in the WASH sector, particularly for reducing dependency on overstretched humanitarian systems and improving service sustainability. Platforms such as SmartTerra (https://www.smartterra.io/) and WASH AI (https://www.washai.org/) exemplify the growing potential for digital tools to reduce leakages, enhance revenue collection, and deliver real-time, context-specific technical knowledge directly into the hands of WASH practitioners. These systems not only drive efficiency but also empower local actors to maintain and optimize services independently (Prakash, 2025).

In humanitarian contexts, the value of AI extends well beyond automation to directly support localization goals. By providing real-time, context-specific technical knowledge in local languages, AI platforms empower community water committees, local technicians, and municipal authorities to diagnose problems, implement solutions, and maintain services without waiting for external experts. For example, AI-powered diagnostic tools can help local operators identify pump failures or water quality issues. At the same time, predictive analytics enable communities to anticipate and prevent infrastructure breakdowns before they occur. This democratization of technical expertise is crucial in contexts where international support is diminishing, transforming local actors from aid recipients into empowered service providers who can sustain WASH systems independently (Mikhaylov et al., 2018).

To fully unlock these benefits, AI must be embedded through collaborative models that involve local governments, humanitarian actors, the private sector, and academia. These partnerships must prioritize building local AI literacy and ensuring that communities not only use but also shape these tools to meet their specific needs. The development of centres of excellence and policy labs in the public sector shows how such cooperation can transform public service delivery, even under the most uncertain conditions (Mikhaylov et al., 2018).

By applying similar strategies to WASH in emergencies, AI can become a cornerstone of anticipatory, locally driven, and resilient humanitarian programming that reduces long-term dependency on international assistance while building sustainable local capacity.

Diverse role of WASH professionals moving forward

The transforming face of the WASH sector requires widening the expertise and skill sets of sector professionals. Experts now recommend integrating research, evidence-based policy formulation, and sustainable interventions into WASH interventions. Coordination among academia, civil society, and the private sector is crucial for developing cost-effective and sustainable solutions to address the diverse challenges in the sector (SDPI, 2024).

Over the next 5–10 years, WASH professionals will need to acquire a range of skills to address increasingly complex issues. Digital and data science capacities, such as geographic information systems (GIS), Internet of Things (IoT), and big data analysis, will be critical in maximizing real-time water quality monitoring and service delivery (Martinez et al., 2021). Knowledge of the impact of climate change and having water and sanitation systems that are resilient will be essential as more frequent extreme climate events occur (WEF, 2025a, 2025b). Additionally, the capability of behavioural science to promote effective hygiene, along with community engagement strategies that facilitate inclusive and gender-sensitive programming, will be crucial (Needham, 2024). Practical, sound project management skills, such as systems thinking and coordination of stakeholders, will enable experts to solve intricate, interconnected problems in the areas of water, health, and the environment (WEF, 2025a, 2025b).

WASH experts also need to strengthen their policy-influencing and governance skills to shape policy, secure funding, and establish public–private partnerships (Mikhaylov et al., 2018). Emerging technologies, ranging from intelligent sanitation to renewable energy-driven systems, will propel innovation and scalability of solutions across various contexts (Castrillon, 2025). Mainstreaming WASH into more universal public health policy, specifically for infection prevention and pandemic preparedness, will become increasingly significant (Mirin et al., 2022). Ultimately, cultural competencies, ethical awareness, and conflict resolution capacity will be essential for working effectively across communities and ensuring equal access to safe water and sanitation for all (WEF, 2025a, 2025b).

Key skill sets for WASH professionals in the next 5 to 10 years

Skill set area	*Key competencies*
Data science and digital tools	Data analysis, GIS, IoT, big data
Climate change and resilience	Climate adaptation, resilience system design
Behavioural science	Behaviour change, community engagement

(*Continues*)

(Continued)

Skill set area	*Key competencies*
Project and system management	Multi-stakeholder coordination, system thinking
Policy and governance	Advocacy, regulation, and financing
Innovation and technology	Emerging technology, piloting, scaling innovations
Health response	IPC, outbreak management, cross-sector collaboration
Cultural competency and ethics	Cultural sensitivity, ethics, and conflict resolution

Conclusion: From crisis response to sustainable transformation

The convergence of funding constraints, technological innovation, and localization imperatives presents both an unprecedented challenge and a transformative opportunity for the WASH sector. The coordination guidelines in this compendium not only detail emergency protocols but also serve as a practical roadmap for managing this transition. By integrating WASH with health and nutrition from the onset of emergencies, fostering genuine community leadership, and leveraging both traditional and innovative financing mechanisms, these guidelines enable practitioners to build resilient systems even in crisis contexts.

Success in this new paradigm requires simultaneous action across multiple fronts. Financial sustainability demands creative partnerships that blend public, private, and community resources. Technological adoption must prioritize local empowerment over external dependency. Professional development must equip WASH practitioners with skills that span technical expertise, cultural competency, and systems thinking. Most critically, all interventions must be grounded in the recognition that affected communities possess the knowledge, capacity, and agency to lead their own development, requiring humanitarian actors to shift from implementers to facilitators and partners. This means embracing integrated approaches that address root causes rather than symptoms, building upon existing community strengths rather than importing external solutions, and creating sustainable systems from day one rather than transitioning from relief to development. As the sector navigates this fundamental transformation, these coordination guidelines serve as both a practical guide and a vision for building inclusive, adaptive, and sustainable WASH solutions that are rooted in community leadership and long-term impact.

Bibliography

Aqua for All. 2024. 'Blended Finance: Paving the Way to Climate-Smart Water and Sanitation Investments'. Aqua for All, 21 November. https://aquaforall.org/news/blended-finance-paving-the-way-to-climate-smart-water-and-sanitation-investments/

Castrillon, Caroline. 2025. 'LinkedIn Reveals the Most In-Demand Skills on the Rise for 2025', Forbes, 19 March. https://www.forbes.com/sites/carolinecastrillon/2025/03/19/linkedin-reveals-the-most-in-demand-skills-on-the-rise-for-2025/

Dietvorst, Cor. 2018. 'Blended Finance: Is It All in a Mix?' IRC, 14 December. https://www.ircwash.org/blog/blended-finance-it-all-mix

Express News Service. 2021. 'Waste Pickers' Cooperative SWaCH Warns PMC against Hiring Private Contractors'. *The Indian Express*, 11 January. https://indianexpress.com/article/cities/pune/waste-pickers-cooperative-swach-warns-pmc-against-hiring-private-contractors-7142321/

Gawade, Shatakshi. 2025. '"Waste Collection Is Green Work": How a pro-Poor Partnership Created Jobs and Cleaned a City.' *The Guardian*, Environment, 22 May. https://www.theguardian.com/environment/2025/may/22/waste-collection-green-work-pro-poor-partnership-pune-india

Global WASH Cluster (GWC). 2022. *Global WASH Cluster, Strategic Plan 2022–2025*. Geneva: United Nations Children's Fund (UNICEF). https://www.washcluster.net/sites/gwc.com/files/inline-files/Global_WASH_Cluster_Strategic%20Plan_2022_2025_FINAL_lowres.pdf

GWC. 2025. "GWC Inter Cluster Collaboration-Coordination Matrix-Guidance Note." Global WASH Cluster. https://www.washcluster.net/node/32296.

Ground Truth Solutions (GTS). 2025. *What Crisis Affected Communities Need from a Humanitarian Reset: A Guide Based on Two Years of Conversations with People on the Front Lines of Crisis*. GTS. https://static1.squarespace.com/static/62e895bdf6085938506cc492/t/67e16a99990a7169d380c883/1742826139841/GTS_Global+analysis+report_March+2025_EN.pdf

ICVA. 2023. *Pooled Funding Models: Governance Systems*. ICVA. https://www.icvanetwork.org/uploads/2023/12/ICVA-Pooled-Funding-Models-Governance-Systems.pdf

Internal Displacement Monitoring Centre (iDMC). 2025. *Global Report on Internal Displacement (GRID)*. iDMC. https://www.internal-displacement.org/global-report/

Jurji, Zaid, and Bioye Ogunjobi. 2023. 'Leveraging the Power of the Private Sector to Tackle Poverty and WASH Challenges in Nigeria'. UNICEF Nigeria. https://www.unicef.org/nigeria/stories/leveraging-power-private-sector-tackle-poverty-and-wash-challenges-nigeria

Martinez, Iñigo, Elisabeth Viles, and Igor G. Olaizola. 2021. 'Data Science Methodologies: Current Challenges and Future Approaches'. *Big Data Research* 24: 100183. https://doi.org/10.1016/j.bdr.2020.100183

Mikhaylov, Slava Jankin, Marc Esteve, and Averill Campion. 2018. 'Artificial Intelligence for the Public Sector: Opportunities and Challenges of Cross-Sector Collaboration.' *Philosophical Transactions of the Royal Society A* 376 (2128). https://doi.org/10.1098/rsta.2017.0357

Mirin, Nicholas, Heather Mattie, Latifa Jackson, Zainab Samad, and Rumi Chunara. 2022. 'Data Science in Public Health: Building Next Generation Capacity'. *Harvard Data Science Review* 4 (4). https://hdsr.mitpress.mit.edu/pub/pjhqev7u/release/2

Needham, Amber. 2024. 'Professional Development Skills Trending for 2025'. SPD, 15 August. https://www.salford.ac.uk/spd/professional-development-skills-trending-2025.

Prakash, Bhawna. 2025. 'Accelerating Private Sector Engagement for Urban Water Security'. CSIS, 6 January. https://www.csis.org/analysis/accelerating-private-sector-engagement-urban-water-security

Rieiro, Maria, Sue Cavill, Maya Wood, Agnes Makanyi, and Andrew Trevett. 2020. 'A Global Assessment of Budgeting and Financing for WASH in Schools'. *Waterlines* 39 (4): 293–312. https://doi.org/10.3362/1756-3488.19-00019

Sabow, Adam, Matt Craven, Matt Wilson, Michael Conway, Tina Holt, Connor Rochford, and Sarah Anderson. 2025. 'The Future of Foreign Aid: A Generational Shift'. McKinsey & Company, 6 May. https://www.mckinsey.com/industries/social-sector/our-insights/a-generational-shift-the-future-of-foreign-aid#/

Save the Children. 2025. *Partnering with Children to Change the World: Save the Children's Global Strategy 2025–2027*. Save the Children. https://resourcecentre.savethechildren.net/document/partnering-with-children-to-change-the-world-save-the-childrens-global-strategy-2025-2027

Sustainable Development Policy Institute (SDPI). 2024. 'Experts Call for Private Sector Action on WASH'. SDPI, 22 January. https://sdpi.org/8873/news_detail

UNICEF. 2022. *UNICEF Strategic Plan 2022–2025: Renewed Ambition toward 2030*. New York: United Nations Children's Fund (UNICEF). https://www.unicef.org/reports/unicef-strategic-plan-2022-2025

World Economic Forum (WEF). 2025a. 'Skills Outlook', in *The Future of Jobs Report 2025*. WEF. https://www.weforum.org/publications/the-future-of-jobs-report-2025/in-full/3-skills-outlook/

WEF. 2025b. 'Future of Jobs Report 2025: 78 Million New Job Opportunities by 2030 but Urgent Upskilling Needed to Prepare Workforces'. WEF, 7 January. https://www.weforum.org/press/2025/01/future-of-jobs-report-2025-78-million-new-job-opportunities-by-2030-but-urgent-upskilling-needed-to-prepare-workforces/

ANNEX 1
Practitioners' Toolkit for Integrated WASH in Emergencies

Summary

Purpose and scope

The Practitioners' Toolkit for Integrated Water, Sanitation, and Hygiene (WASH) in Emergencies provides practical guidance, tools, and templates to support the implementation of integrated WASH interventions in humanitarian crises. It complements the coordination guidelines for WASH with health and WASH with nutrition integration with resources for operationalizing coordination, assessment, planning, delivery, and monitoring of joint activities at national and subnational levels.

The Toolkit draws upon established best practices and innovations from the field to propose a more systematic and accountable approach to WASH emergency response. It is intended for use by WASH programme managers, coordinators, and implementing partners across the humanitarian programme cycle, from preparedness and contingency planning through to post-emergency transition and recovery.

Contents and organization

The Toolkit is organized into five key sections spanning the humanitarian programme cycle:

1. *Coordination tools*: Resources for mapping stakeholders, establishing coordination platforms, harmonizing ways of working, and managing multi-stakeholder initiatives.
2. *Assessment tools*: Methods and instruments for joint rapid assessments, in-depth surveys, and participatory analysis of WASH-related public health strengths, capabilities, risks, and vulnerabilities.
3. *Planning and strategy tools*: Templates for multi-sector response planning, development of context-specific and evidence-based WASH strategies, and participatory design with communities.

4. *Implementation tools*: Guidance for integrated hygiene promotion campaigns, capacity building of frontline workers, and quality assurance of service delivery.
5. *Monitoring and evaluation tools*: Frameworks and methods for process and performance monitoring, real-time course correction, and documentation of learning and impact.

Within each section, specific tools are provided with step-by-step instructions, key considerations for application, and links to further resources. These range from editable planning templates to mobile data collection forms to participatory facilitation guides.

What's different?

The Toolkit places particular emphasis on:

- *Integration*: Joint analysis, planning, and monitoring across the WASH, health, and nutrition sectors to identify and respond to shared priorities and risks.
- *User-centred design*: Practical tools for engaging affected communities throughout the programme cycle to enhance the relevance, quality, and sustainability of interventions.
- *Localization*: Resources for assessing and strengthening the capacity of local WASH actors to take on greater leadership and decision-making roles.
- *Evidence-based action*: Methods for rapid generation, synthesis, and utilization of public health data to inform targeting and adaptation of WASH strategies.
- *Accountability and learning*: Mechanisms for transparently tracking and communicating results and promoting a culture of continuous improvement and knowledge sharing.

How to use

The Toolkit is designed to be modular and adaptable to different operational contexts and information needs. Users are encouraged to review the tools in each section and determine which resources are most applicable for their specific coordination and implementation needs.

Each tool is presented as an independent resource that can be extracted and adapted. However, there are interconnections and shared principles among the tools that justify a thorough review.

Effective use of the Toolkit will require:

- *Institutional uptake*: Socialization and endorsement of tools as common approaches by WASH coordination platforms and sector lead agencies.
- *Capacity strengthening*: Orientation and ongoing support for field teams to meaningfully apply the tools as part of their day-to-day work.

- *Adequate resourcing*: Budgeting of time and funds to enable high-quality and participatory analysis, planning, and monitoring.
- *User feedback*: Ongoing input from practitioners to document their experiences and continually refine the tools based on field realities and emerging needs.

Way forward

This Toolkit represents a starting point for a shared, field-driven approach to integrated WASH in emergencies. Its development has drawn upon the collective wisdom of seasoned practitioners, but its impact will depend on continued learning and localization.

Priority next steps include:

1. Dissemination of the Toolkit through global and regional WASH coordination platforms and communities of practice.
2. Mobilization of resources for capacity building and field testing of tools in diverse operational settings.
3. Documentation of case studies and user feedback to chronicle the application of the Toolkit and inform future iterations.
4. Identification of gaps and development of additional tools based on field demand and evolving best practices.

Ultimately, the Toolkit's success will be measured by its contribution to more timely, effective, and accountable WASH responses that measurably improve the health and dignity of crisis-affected populations.

Sections

Section 1: Coordination tools

1.1 Stakeholder identification checklist
1.2 Coordination committee terms of reference (TOR) template
1.3 Stakeholder analysis and mapping tools
1.4 Social network analysis guide
1.5 Stakeholder roles and responsibilities matrix
1.6 Coordination performance scorecard
1.7 Coordination timeline (first 45 days)

Section 2: Assessment tools

2.1 Participatory community mapping guide
2.2 Household WASH and health survey
2.3 Nutrition-sensitive WASH risk assessment checklist
2.4 Health facility WASH assessment checklist
2.5 Committee setup checklist
2.6 WASH-IPC monitoring checklist

Section 3: Planning and strategy tools

3.1 Integrated WASH-nutrition-health response planning template
3.2 Nutrition-sensitive WASH strategy development guide
3.3 Community engagement planning framework
3.4 Capacity assessment and building tools
3.5 Health system capacity mapping tool
3.6 Joint capacity building plan
3.7 Community-level joint action plan template

Section 4: Implementation tools

4.1 Joint workplan and budget template
4.2 Training and staff development guides
4.3 Integrated outreach and campaign planning tools
4.4 WASH and nutrition behaviour change communication toolkit
4.5 WASH in healthcare facility improvement planning template
4.6 Integrated outreach strategy template
4.7 Integrated risk communication and community engagement plan
4.8 Community WASH and nutrition committee terms of reference (TOR) template
4.9 Community coordination timeline and task checklist
4.10 Outreach worker training package on WASH and nutrition

Section 5: Monitoring and feedback tools

5.1 Integrated monitoring framework
5.2 Outbreak investigation and response checklist
5.3 Community feedback mechanism checklist
5.4 Supportive supervision checklist
5.5 Performance review and learning tools
5.6 Monthly reporting format for community committees

Section 1: Coordination tools

1.1 Stakeholder identification checklist

Purpose: To identify and engage the full range of stakeholders needed for effective integrated WASH coordination in emergency response.

When to use: At the outset of an emergency, during preparedness planning, and at regular intervals, to track stakeholder landscape changes.

Government authorities:

- Relevant ministries (Health/Nutrition, Water/Sanitation/Hygiene, Finance, Planning, Environment, Local Government, Public Works, Education, Agriculture, Housing)
- National Statistics Office

- Subnational and local government authorities
- District/provincial health management teams
- Water and sanitation utilities
- Infection prevention and control (IPC) focal points at the district level
- Local municipal councils (representatives responsible for health facility infrastructure)
- Village development committees
- Agriculture and food security officers
- Government social welfare systems
- Public safety officials (police, customs officials)
- Environmental health officers

Humanitarian and development organizations:

- Global coordination mechanisms (Global WASH and Nutrition Clusters)
- International NGOs, including those specializing in assessment (e.g. REACH, ACAPS)
- Local NGOs and community based-organizations, including those specializing in assessment
- Organizations of persons with disabilities and older people's associations
- Red Cross/Red Crescent Societies
- Hygiene promotion working groups
- International NGOs with local presence
- Nurses and midwives
- Nutrition specialists
- Cleaners and waste handlers
- IPC professionals and IPC committees
- Health facility management committees
- Medical and administrative staff

Community representatives:

- Community leaders, including traditional, religious, and elected representatives
- Women's groups and representatives
- Youth organizations
- Faith-based organizations
- Organizations representing marginalized populations, including people living with disabilities
- Existing community-based structures (e.g. care groups, community health workers, village WASH and nutrition committees)
- Village leaders and traditional authorities (both male and female)
- School representatives (administrators, teachers, parent-teacher associations)
- Disabled persons organizations
- Care groups and mother-to-mother support groups

- Informal community leaders, such as elders
- Local WASH and nutrition committees
- Community health workers and nutrition promoters
- Associations of community health workers
- Traditional healer and midwife networks

Private sector:

- Local water and sanitation service providers
- Food producers, processors, and distributors
- Hygiene and nutrition product suppliers and retailers
- Financial service providers and microfinance institutions
- Major utilities and private sector WASH and nutrition companies
- Tradespeople (plumbers, waste collectors, masons)
- Savings groups
- Media outlets (radio, newspapers, television)

Academic and research institutions:

- Universities with relevant WASH, nutrition, public health, and social science programmes
- Research centres and institutes focused on public health, WASH, and emergency response
- Training and capacity building institutes in WASH and nutrition fields
- Local colleges and universities
- Vocational training institutes
- Local public health professional associations
- Farmer cooperatives and agriculture extension networks

UN agencies and donors:

- United Nations Children's Fund (UNICEF)
- World Health Organization (WHO)
- World Food Programme (WFP)
- Food and Agriculture Organization of the United Nations (FAO)
- United Nations High Commissioner for Refugees (UNHCR) (refugee settings)
- Major donors supporting WASH, nutrition, and health system strengthening initiatives

Inter-cluster coordination:

- Office for the Coordination of Humanitarian Affairs (OCHA) and the Humanitarian Country Team
- Inter-Cluster Coordination Group (ICCG) and relevant clusters

Process:

- Convene a stakeholder identification session with diverse participants.
- Using the checklist, brainstorm all relevant stakeholders for each category.
- Prioritize those with the most direct influence and interest in integrated WASH.
- Map the key relationships and information flows between stakeholder groups.
- Identify any gaps or imbalances in representation across categories.
- Develop a contact list of focal points and decision-makers for each priority stakeholder.
- Update the stakeholder list on a quarterly basis and before major planning milestones.

Key considerations:

- Ensure balance between WASH, health and nutrition sector stakeholders.
- Include representatives of both affected and host communities.
- Engage stakeholders at national, subnational, and community levels.
- Don't forget stakeholders who may be outside established coordination structures.
- Assess power dynamics and potential conflicts between stakeholder interests.
- Be sensitive to pre-existing tensions or mistrust between stakeholder groups.

1.2 Coordination committee terms of reference (TOR) template

Purpose: To clarify the roles, responsibilities, and operating procedures for integrated WASH coordination platforms at national and subnational levels.

When to use: When establishing new or strengthening existing coordination platforms for integrated emergency WASH response.

Key components

Background and rationale:

- Brief overview of emergency context
- Need for integrated WASH approach
- Global standards and guidelines underpinning TOR

Purpose/objectives:

- Overall aim of the committee
- Specific objectives for coordination, information sharing, and integrated action

Chair and secretariat:

- Designated lead agency and supporting agencies
- Roles of the chair and secretariat
- Criteria and process for rotating chair

Membership:

- Composition of the committee by stakeholder groups
- Criteria and process for membership selection
- Expectations for participation

Structure and frequency:

- Meeting frequency and location
- Alternative modes for remote participation
- Linkages with other coordination platforms (e.g. ICCG)

Roles and responsibilities:

- Key functions: information sharing, joint analysis, strategic planning, standards/guideline development, capacity building, monitoring and evaluation
- Specific deliverables under each function
- Division of responsibilities between members

Procedures:

- Agenda setting and circulation
- Minute-taking and distribution
- Decision-making processes (consensus, voting)
- Conflict resolution mechanisms

Communications:

- Information sharing protocols within and outside the committee
- Communication channels for engaging other stakeholders
- Branding and visibility guidelines for joint products

Resources:

- Human resource commitments from member agencies
- Financial contributions for committee operations
- In-kind logistical support

Monitoring and reporting:

- Progress tracking against work plan
- Monitoring of member participation and follow-through on action points
- Reporting requirements to other platforms

Process:

1. Designate a multi-stakeholder task team to draft the TOR.
2. Review examples from previous emergencies and global templates.
3. Consult bilaterally with key stakeholder groups to understand their expectations.
4. Circulate a first draft for written feedback from prospective members.
5. Convene a face-to-face or virtual workshop to validate the TOR.
6. Finalize TOR with clear responsibilities and resource commitments.
7. Disseminate TOR to all members and other relevant stakeholders.
8. Review TOR after three months and adjust as needed based on experience.

Key considerations:

- Balance inclusivity of membership with efficiency of decision-making.
- Tailor language to be contextually and culturally appropriate.
- Ensure TOR aligns with government emergency coordination architecture.
- Specify how the committee relates to sector-specific coordination groups.
- Develop a compact TOR summary that can be readily shared.
- Translate the TOR into local languages to enable wide dissemination.

Terms of reference template:

1. *Title*: [Community Name] WASH and Nutrition Committee
2. *Purpose*: To coordinate and lead the implementation of integrated WASH and nutrition activities at the community level
3. *Scope*: Oversee planning, implementation, monitoring, and coordination with local stakeholders
4. Membership criteria:
   a. Balanced gender representation
   b. Inclusive of youth, elderly, and marginalized groups
   c. Sectoral representation from health, WASH, education, agriculture
5. Roles and responsibilities:
   a. Coordinate integrated WASH and nutrition interventions
   b. Liaise with government and humanitarian actors
   c. Monitor implementation and collect community feedback
   d. Facilitate participatory assessments and planning
   e. Mobilize resources and organize campaigns
6. Meeting schedule:
   a. Weekly meetings during emergencies, biweekly otherwise
   b. Minutes documented and shared with stakeholders
7. Decision-making:
   a. By consensus or majority vote
   b. Quorum defined as at least 60 per cent of members

8. Accountability and transparency:
   a. Reports shared in public community forums
   b. Complaints and feedback mechanisms operational
9. Linkages:
   a. Connected to subnational WASH and nutrition platforms
   b. Reports upwards to local government

1.3 Stakeholder analysis and mapping tools

Purpose: To visualize and analyse the key relationships, influence dynamics, and engagement opportunities among stakeholders in integrated WASH programming.

When to use: During preparedness and emergency actions to identify coordination entry points, throughout response to monitor changing stakeholder landscape.

Stakeholder matrix:

1. List all identified stakeholders
2. Assess level of interest (low to high) in integrated WASH outcomes
3. Assess level of influence (low to high) over WASH policies, resources, and implementation
4. Plot stakeholders on a quadrant matrix:
   a. High interest/high influence: Key players – closely involve and engage
   b. High interest/low influence: Promoters – keep informed and build capacity
   c. Low interest/high influence: Gatekeepers – analyse interests and convince
   d. Low interest/low influence: Bystanders – monitor and engage selectively
5. Develop tailored engagement strategies for each quadrant
6. Update matrix regularly as stakeholder positions change

Social network mapping:

1. Identify key connectors, hubs, and influencers through stakeholder discussions
2. Map relational flows of information, resources, and decisions among actors
3. Analyse network for:
   a. *Density*: Level of interconnectivity and cohesion in the network
   b. *Centrality*: Importance/influence of individual actors based on their number and quality of connections
   c. *Bridges*: Actors that connect disparate subgroups in the network
   d. *Isolates*: Actors that are disconnected from the main network components

4. Identify opportunities to:
   a. Strengthen connections between WASH and other sector actors
   b. Engage influential champions to promote integrated approaches
   c. Bridge silos and disconnects in dialogue and decision-making
   d. Expand reach to isolated or marginalized stakeholders
5. Track changes in network structure over time as relationships evolve

Venn diagram:

1. Group stakeholders into main categories (e.g. government, UN, NGO, private sector)
2. Draw proportional circles for each category – size determined by relative importance
3. Arrange circles with overlapping areas indicating degree of mutual involvement
4. Annotate diagram with key resources, responsibilities or capacities that each group brings
5. Identify opportunities for greater collaboration and synergy in the overlapping spaces
6. Discuss implications of stakeholder separation and interdependencies

Tips:

- Involve stakeholders themselves in mapping their connections and relationships
- Analyse both formal and informal interactions and influences
- Consider mapping at multiple scales – national strategic level to local operational level
- Use network data to inform partnership agreements, steering committee setup, reporting lines
- Pair relational mapping with institutional capacity assessments for robust analysis

1.4 Social network analysis guide

Purpose: To map the informal social and community relationships that influence WASH behaviours, social norms, and information flows.

When to use: To inform behaviour change strategies, identify influential champions, track diffusion of ideas and practices through a community.

Step 1: Define scope and purpose:

- Clearly state target group and WASH behaviours/norms of interest.
- Assemble team with local cultural knowledge and language skills.
- Select sites to provide cross-section of target group.

Step 2: Design network survey:

- Determine appropriate question types to elicit network data:
  - *Name generator*: Ask respondents to freely list people they interact with on a topic
  - *Roster*: Ask about interactions with a pre-selected list of people/organizations
  - *Affiliation*: Ask about membership/participation in community groups or events
- Design questionnaire with mix of close-ended and open-ended formats.
- Pretest and refine questions to ensure comprehension and validity.

Step 3: Map personal networks:

- Randomly select 10–15 initial seed respondents.
- Conduct personal network interviews with each seed.
- Use name generators to elicit 10–20 alters (contacts) from each seed:
  - Alters can be individuals, influencers, groups, service providers
- Ask seeds about nature of relationship and WASH interactions with each alter.
- Expand network map by conducting interviews with named alters.
- Continue snowball sampling 2–3 steps beyond seeds until saturation.

Step 4: Analyse network structure:

- Enter network data into analysis software (e.g. UCINET, Gephi).
- Visualize networks with nodes (individuals) and ties (relationships).
- Calculate key network metrics:
  - *Size*: Number of nodes in the network
  - *Density*: Proportion of actual ties to all possible ties
  - *Degree centrality*: Number of ties held by each node
  - *Betweenness centrality*: Frequency that a node lies on paths between others
  - *Bridges*: Nodes that connect otherwise disconnected parts of the network
- Examine metrics visually and statistically to identify patterns.
- Compare network structures across sites or subgroups.

Step 5: Map network content:

- Use survey responses to map content of ties in the network.
- Code relationships by frequency, direction, type of support (e.g. information, resources, advice).
- Differentiate strong and weak ties based on frequency, depth, reciprocity.

- Identify ties that specifically convey WASH information and influence.
- Analyse which types of ties are correlated with target WASH behaviours.
- Examine the role of influencers in promoting or blocking behaviours.

Step 6: Apply findings to WASH strategies:

- Engage network hubs and influencers as hygiene promoters and early adopters.
- Recruit bridging actors to carry messages across subgroups.
- Target strong-tie relationships for social reinforcement of behaviour change.
- Tailor behaviour change approaches to fit network patterns across sites.
- Monitor behaviour diffusion from early adopters through their networks.
- Evaluate how network structures change in response to interventions.

Tips:

- Triangulate network data with qualitative contextual data to interpret findings.
- Consider power dynamics that affect individuals' network positions and influence.
- Stratify analysis by gender, age, class or other salient social categories.
- Ensure confidentiality and manage disclosure risks from network participation.
- Validate insights with community interpretations before acting on them.

1.5 Stakeholder roles and responsibilities matrix

Stakeholder	*Coordination roles*	*Implementation roles*
Ministry of Health	Co-lead national coordination platform	WASH in health facility standards and guidelines
	Chair health sector meetings	Health staff training and supervision on WASH-IPC
	Ensure integration of WASH in nutrition policies and guidelines	Integrate WASH into nutrition programmes
Ministry of Water and Sanitation	Co-lead national coordination platform	WASH infrastructure and service provision
	Chair WASH sector meetings	Support WASH assessments and improvements in health and nutrition facilities

(*Continues*)

(Continued)

Stakeholder	*Coordination roles*	*Implementation roles*
Ministry of Nutrition (or relevant department)	Participate in national coordination platform Ensure integration of WASH in nutrition policies and guidelines	Develop and implement nutrition-sensitive WASH strategies Coordinate with WASH sector on nutrition-specific interventions
WHO	Provide technical guidance on WASH standards Support coordination with global health and nutrition clusters	Support implementation of WASH FIT and other tools Provide guidance on WASH in nutrition in emergencies
UNICEF	Support coordination of WASH sector response Information management and analysis Support coordination with global nutrition clusters	WASH in health and nutrition facility assessments and improvements Hygiene kit distribution and promotion Support integration of WASH into nutrition programmes
Other UN agencies (UNHCR, UNDP, WFP)	Ensure integration of WASH in other sectors, including nutrition	Support based on mandate and capacities, including nutrition-sensitive WASH interventions
Health, nutrition and WASH NGOs and Red Cross	Active participation in coordination forums Share information and provide surge capacity	WASH service delivery and facility repairs Social and behaviour change for hygiene and nutrition Integrate WASH into community-based nutrition programmes
Health and nutrition facility management	Represent facility-level needs and capacities Coordinate with district health and nutrition authorities	Oversee day-to-day O&M of WASH services Orient and supervise staff on WASH-IPC and nutrition-sensitive WASH practices
Donors	Allocate resources to support joint priorities, including nutrition-sensitive WASH Advocate for integration in funding mechanisms	Monitor implementation and report to constituents Provide technical assistance where needed, including on integrated WASH-nutrition programming

Note: WASH FIT, water and sanitation for health facility improvement tool; UNHCR, United Nations High Commissioner for Refugees; UNDP, United Nations Development Programme; WFP, World Food Programme; O&M, operation and maintenance

1.6 Coordination performance scorecard

Performance area	*Indicator*	*Quarter 1*	*Quarter 2*	*Quarter 3*	*Quarter 4*
Coordination structure and regularity	Existence of joint WASH-health-nutrition coordination mechanism (Y/N)				
	% of planned meetings held				
	Attendance rate of key ministries and partners				
Strategic planning and resource mobilization	Existence of joint WASH-health-nutrition strategy (Y/N)				
	% of HRP WASH-health-nutrition projects funded				
	% of funded projects with joint targeting				
Capacity building of national and subnational actors	# of joint WASH-health-nutrition trainings held				
	# of national actors trained on integrated approach				
	% of subnational platforms replicating approach				
Integrated programming and geographic convergence	% of priority districts with joint WASH-health-nutrition interventions				
	% of health facilities and nutrition sites with minimum WASH standards				
	# of joint social behaviour change campaigns for health and nutrition outcomes				
Monitoring and knowledge management	Existence of common WASH-health-nutrition indicators (Y/N)				
	Regularity of joint monitoring visits to health facilities and nutrition sites				
	# of learning events and products disseminated on integrated programming				

Note: HRP refers to humanitarian response plan

How to use the scorecard:

- Assess the status of each indicator using a traffic light system (red/yellow/green) for both health and nutrition integration.
- Set quarterly targets for improving WASH-health-nutrition coordination and track progress over time.
- Discuss results in joint coordination meetings and identify bottlenecks and opportunities for strengthening integration.
- Develop remedial action plans for underperforming areas, considering both health and nutrition aspects.
- Document and disseminate success stories, innovations, and lessons learned on integrated WASH with health and nutrition programming.

1.7 Coordination timeline (first 45 days)

Days 1-10: Initial coordination and assessment:

1. Activate national WASH and health/nutrition coordination platform.
2. Convene initial stakeholder meeting to agree on joint objectives, roles, and responsibilities.
3. Conduct rapid assessments of WASH in health facilities and nutrition centres using relevant checklists.
4. Map existing capacities and gaps across WASH, health, and nutrition sectors.
5. Issue initial situation report and joint flash appeal.

Days 11-30: Response strategy and planning:

1. Establish technical working groups on priority issues (e.g. WASH in health facilities, WASH in nutrition centres, hygiene promotion, water quality surveillance).
2. Develop joint WASH-health-nutrition response strategy based on assessment findings.
3. Draft and circulate standard operating procedures for WASH in health facilities and nutrition centres.
4. Develop costed improvement plans for priority health facilities and nutrition centres.
5. Launch joint hygiene promotion and community engagement activities, targeting key behaviours relevant to both health and nutrition outcomes.

Days 31-45: Implementation and monitoring:

1. Train health and nutrition staff on WASH protocols, infection prevention, and control.
2. Distribute critical WASH supplies to health facilities, nutrition centres, and affected communities.

3. Conduct joint supportive supervision visits to monitor implementation of WASH in health and nutrition settings.
4. Convene coordination meetings to review progress against plans, covering both health and nutrition aspects.
5. Document and disseminate lessons learned and good practices in integrated WASH-health-nutrition programming.

Section 2: Assessment tools

2.1 Participatory community mapping guide

Purpose: To rapidly gather community insights on WASH and health risks, vulnerabilities, capacities, and priorities to inform integrated emergency programming.

When to use: During the initial rapid assessment phase, within the first two weeks of sudden onset emergencies or when expanding to new areas in protracted crises.

Participants:

- Diverse cross-section of affected community (women, men, elderly, youth, people with disabilities)
- Community leaders and influencers
- Local health workers, teachers, and WASH technicians
- Community volunteers and mobilizers

Materials:

- Large sheets of paper or plastic
- Marker pens, sticky notes, stickers
- Voting tokens (pebbles, beans)
- Camera to record the maps
- Notebook and pen for documenting discussion

Process:

Step 1: Opening and introductions (10 min):

- Welcome participants and do a quick round of introductions.
- Explain the purpose of the exercise and how the maps will be used.
- Agree on ground rules for participation.

Step 2: Drawing the base map (20 min):

- Ask participants to sketch key community landmarks (roads, facilities, markets, schools).
- Encourage participants to lead the mapping and decide the symbols to use.

- Probe locations of WASH infrastructure (water points, toilets, waste sites).
- Check for any major omissions in the base map.

Step 3: Identifying problems and hazards (30 min):

- Ask participants to mark on the map:
  - damaged or non-functional WASH infrastructure
  - open defecation and waste dumping areas
  - stagnant water and flooding zones
  - overcrowded areas lacking WASH services
  - underserved areas and households
- Use different coloured markers or stickers to categorize issues.
- Discuss the impacts of the identified hazards on health and nutrition.

Step 4: Mapping vulnerabilities and capacities (30 min):

- Have participants identify on the map:
  - households with pregnant women, children under five, people with disabilities or chronic illnesses
  - high-risk livelihood groups (e.g. farmers in a drought)
  - WASH and health skills/assets that can be leveraged
  - active community structures for potential mobilization
  - evacuation sites and routes
- Discuss how vulnerability factors may influence WASH and health risks.

Step 5: Ranking priorities (20 min):

- Ask participants to list the top five WASH and health issues affecting the community.
- Have them vote on the top three priorities using tokens.
- Facilitate a discussion on the root causes of the prioritized issues.
- Document the ranking results and rationale.

Step 6: Action planning (30 min):

- Brainstorm potential solutions and coping mechanisms for the prioritized issues.
- Identify what capacities need to be strengthened to implement solutions.
- Discuss community contributions and external support needed.
- Agree on immediate next steps and follow-up actions.

Step 7: Wrap up and next steps (10 min):

- Summarize the key findings and decisions from the mapping exercise.
- Take photos of the final maps for digitization and analysis.
- Explain how the results will be shared back with the community for validation.
- Thank participants for their active engagement.

Key considerations:

- Conduct mapping with separate groups if needed to ensure active participation of women and marginalized individuals.
- Allocate enough time for in-depth discussions; the mapping may require several hours.
- Have a clear plan for how to process and operationalize the mapping data.
- Be aware of sensitive protection issues that may arise during the mapping.
- Coordinate with other sectors to maximize coverage and minimize assessment fatigue.
- Adapt the tools for low-literacy participants or people with visual impairments.

2.2 Household WASH and health survey

Purpose: To collect standardized household-level data on WASH conditions, practices, and health outcomes to inform targeting, programme design, and monitoring of integrated interventions.

Survey sections

Household profile:

- Demographics (age, gender, disability)
- Education and livelihoods
- Displacement status

Water supply:

- Primary drinking water source
- Distance and time to source
- Quantity of water collected
- Water treatment and storage
- Water point accessibility and safety

Sanitation:

- Household toilet access and type
- Shared or communal toilet usage
- Handwashing facility near toilet
- Child feces disposal methods
- Menstrual hygiene practices

Hygiene:

- Handwashing knowledge and behaviour
- Soap and water availability

- Bathing practices
- Food hygiene behaviours

Waste management:

- Household waste disposal methods
- Animal waste management
- Community waste collection services

Vector control:

- Presence of vectors (flies, mosquitoes, rats)
- Bed net usage
- Indoor residual spraying

WASH-related disease:

- Diarrhea prevalence in past two weeks
- Acute respiratory infection prevalence
- Proxy indicators of undernutrition (mid-upper arm circumference, MUAC)
- Healthcare-seeking behaviours

Menstrual hygiene management:

- Access to menstrual materials
- Privacy for changing and washing
- Disposal facilities

WASH in institutions:

- School WASH conditions for children
- WASH in health facilities used

Accountability and feedback:

- Participation in WASH decisions
- Feedback/complaint mechanisms
- Satisfaction with WASH services

Sampling:

- Determine sampling frame and approach based on population size, geographic spread, and sub-population analysis needs.
- Use two-stage cluster sampling if household lists are not available.
- Consider stratifying the sample based on different living situations.
- Aim for a 95 per cent confidence level and 5 per cent margin of error.
- Factor in non-response rate into sample size.

Implementation:

- Design a survey collaboratively with WASH and health and nutrition actors.
- Contextualize questions while maintaining comparability across settings.

- Pretest survey tools and provide enumerator training.
- Use electronic data collection with tablets where feasible.
- Coordinate timing with other household assessments to minimize duplication.
- Analyse data disaggregated by sex, age, and disability.
- Share findings in accessible formats with communities and decision-makers.

Ethics and safeguarding:

- Secure informed consent and protect confidentiality.
- Train teams on how to safely handle sensitive issues.
- Be prepared to refer protection cases.
- Adhere to data protection protocols.

Resources

UNHCR Standardized WASH KAP Survey, for example:

- UNHCR. 2019. 'Uganda – WASH KAP Survey Palabek Settlement (Refugees & Host Community), October 2019'. https://microdata.unhcr.org/index.php/catalog/253/study-description

WHO and UNICEF JMP Core Questions on Water, Sanitation, and Hygiene for Household Surveys, for example:

- WHO and UNICEF. 2018. 'Core Questions on Water, Sanitation and Hygiene for Household Surveys: 2018 Update'. United Nations Children's Fund (UNICEF) and World Health Organization (WHO). https://washdata.org/sites/default/files/documents/reports/2019-03/JMP-2018-core-questions-for-household-surveys.pdf

2.3 Nutrition-sensitive WASH risk assessment checklist

Purpose: To identify community-level nutrition and health-related factors that can increase vulnerability to WASH-related disease and malnutrition.

When to use: As a complement to initial rapid WASH assessments or as part of a more in-depth situational analysis.

Key risk categories and indicators

Health status and disease:

- Prevalence of undernutrition among children under five (stunting, wasting, underweight)
- Prevalence of anaemia among children and women of reproductive age

- Incidence of diarrheal disease, cholera, hepatitis E
- Incidence of acute respiratory infections, measles, malaria

Health care and referral:

- Coverage of measles and rotavirus vaccination
- Availability of oral rehydration solution and zinc supplementation
- Availability of malnutrition screening and treatment services
- Functionality of community health worker and referral systems

Infant and young child feeding:

- Exclusive breastfeeding rate for infants under six months
- Minimum acceptable diet for children 6–23 months
- Safe preparation and storage of complementary foods
- Coverage of micronutrient powders or fortified complementary foods

Food security and livelihoods:

- Household food insecurity experience scale
- Household dietary diversity score
- Proportion of expenditures on food
- Availability and price of nutritious food groups in local markets

Care environment:

- Women's decision-making power over household resources
- Prevalence of child marriage and adolescent pregnancy
- Traditional beliefs and taboos related to feeding and care practices
- Time and workload constraints for women and girls

Methodology:

1. Conduct a desk review of existing health and nutrition data from facility records, previous surveys, and early warning systems.
2. Convene a multi-stakeholder workshop to map nutrition-sensitive risk factors and indicators to include in the assessment.
3. Define the assessment area based on health system catchment areas and WASH service zones.
4. Design data collection tools, including:
   a. Community focus group discussion guides
   b. Semi-structured interview questionnaires for health workers and mothers
   c. Market price and food availability checklists
   d. Health facility infrastructure and service availability assessment
5. Train assessment teams on nutrition concepts, interview skills, and data collection tools.
6. Randomly select a representative sample of health facilities, communities, and markets.

7. Triangulate data to validate findings across different sources and methods.
8. Conduct a joint analysis workshop with WASH, health, and nutrition stakeholders.
9. Identify priority risk factors to address through integrated WASH and nutrition interventions.
10. Develop a dissemination plan to share assessment findings and recommendations.

Key considerations:

- Coordinate with food security and livelihoods actors on market and household economy analysis.
- Collect data disaggregated by sex, age, and disability to understand differential risks.
- Consider seasonal variations in food security, disease, and care practices.
- Assess both the availability and quality of nutrition and health services.
- Analyse power dynamics and sociocultural factors affecting nutrition behaviours.
- Engage communities in validating risk analysis and prioritizing actions.

Resources

SMART Methodology for Nutrition Surveys:

- ACF and SMART. 2014. 'Guidelines: Rapid SMART Surveys for Emergencies'. SMART. https://smartmethodology.org/survey-planning-tools/smart-methodology/rapid-smart-methodology/
- FHI 360. 2024. IYCF-E Assessment Guide. Durham, NC: FHI 360. https://www.nutritioncluster.net/sites/nutritioncluster.com/files/2024-12/IYCF-E-Assessment-Guide-v6.pdf
- SMART. 2017. 'Measuring Mortality, Nutritional Status, and Food Security in Crisis Situations: SMART Methodology'. SMART. https://smartmethodology.org/survey-planning-tools/smart-methodology/

2.4 Health facility WASH assessment checklist

Purpose: To rapidly assess WASH infrastructure and practices in health facilities to identify gaps, inform response planning, and monitor improvements.

When to use: Initial needs assessment for facilities serving affected populations, ongoing monitoring and evaluation visits, and disease outbreak investigations.

Key areas to assess

Water supply:

- Presence and location of water points
- Quantity of water available per day per patient/staff (target 50–100 L)
- Drinking water quality (at points of delivery and consumption)
- Water treatment and safe storage practices
- Operation and maintenance arrangements, responsibilities

Sanitation:

- Number of functional, accessible toilets for staff, patients, and visitors (target 1:20)
- Gender segregation and menstrual hygiene facilities
- Cleanliness, privacy, and security of facilities
- Availability of anal cleansing and handwashing materials
- Safe containment and disposal of sewage and fecal waste

Hygiene:

- Handwashing stations in key locations (target within 5 m of toilets, points of care)
- Soap and water or alcohol rub is consistently available
- Hygiene promotion materials and activities for staff, patients, carers
- Facility cleaning protocols, supplies, and compliance
- Disinfection of reusable medical equipment

Environmental cleaning:

- Protocols for cleaning high-risk surfaces, spills, laundry
- Availability and use of appropriate detergents and disinfectants
- Staff training and performance monitoring
- Cleaning equipment storage and maintenance

Healthcare waste management:

- Segregation of waste at the point of generation (minimum three bins)
- Use of colour-coded bins and bag labelling
- Sharps handling and storage practices
- Treatment and disposal methods (on- or off-site)
- Clearly demarcated and controlled waste zones

Infection prevention and control (IPC):

- Availability and use of personal protective equipment
- Isolation and spacing of patients
- Visitor instructions and management
- Laboratory biosafety measures
- Staff IPC training and compliance monitoring

Assessment process:

1. Select a sample of facilities covering a range of levels and types.
2. Adapt checklist to local context, disease profile, guidelines.
3. Train assessment teams on observation, testing, and interview methods.
4. Collect data through facility walkthroughs, document reviews, discussions.
5. Conduct quick analyses to identify major gaps and resource needs.
6. Present findings and recommendations to facility managers and health authorities.
7. Agree on improvement plans and monitoring milestones.
8. Share summary results with WASH and health coordination platforms.

Tips:

- Partner an engineer and health professional for holistic assessment.
- Engage facility staff and patients in identifying solutions, not just problems.
- Prioritize low-cost, rapidly implementable actions in emergencies.
- Coordinate with other facility assessments to reduce duplication.
- Include WASH questions in wider health facility readiness checklists.
- Promote WASH FIT or other national survey tools for standardized monitoring.

Resources

WASH in healthcare facilities (HCF) evaluation and reporting tools:

- WASH in HCF. no date. 'WASH in HCF Evaluation and Reporting Tools'. WASH in Health Care Facilities. Accessed 9 April 2025. https://washinhcf.org/resource/wash-in-hcf-evaluation-and-reporting-tools/

WHO/UNICEF WASH FIT guide and tools:

- WHO and UNICEF. 2022. *Water and Sanitation for Health Facility Improvement Tool (WASH FIT): A Practical Guide for Improving Quality of Care through Water, Sanitation and Hygiene in Health Care Facilities*, 2nd edn. Geneva: World Health Organization (WHO).

2.5 Committee setup checklist

Refer to Annex 1 Section 1.2 for a sample terms of reference for community WASH committees.

- Agree on mandate and scope of work for the committee.
- Define composition with balanced representation across key groups.
- Outline clear roles and responsibilities of members.
- Establish leadership structure and main focal point.
- Agree on meeting frequency, venue, and secretariat support.
- Put documentation and reporting procedures in place.
- Orient members on WASH and health linkages and ways of working.
- Develop annual work plan with priority activities and timeline.

- Clarify decision-making processes and quorum requirements.
- Set up coordination and communication protocols with other local structures.

2.6 WASH-IPC monitoring checklist

Refer to the Sphere Handbook and WHO/UNICEF guidance for additional WASH-IPC monitoring considerations in community settings.

- Rapid assessment conducted on WASH conditions in community
- Soap and water available at all communal handwashing facilities
- Community toilets/latrines clean and functional with handwashing
- Waste regularly collected and safely disposed in designated site
- Water sources protected from contamination and tested for quality
- Isolation spaces have adequate WASH facilities for patients and staff
- Social distancing maintained in communal water collection points
- High-touch public surfaces disinfected at least daily
- WASH/IPC supplies pre-positioned for outbreak response
- Community health workers have PPE and training on IPC protocols

Section 3: Planning and strategy tools

3.1 Integrated WASH-nutrition-health response planning template

Purpose: To develop a coherent and aligned operational plan for multi-sector actors to address priority public health risks through integrated WASH, health, and nutrition interventions.

When to use: Within the first 30 days of response after initial rapid assessments and continuously updated based on situational changes and community feedback.

Key components

Situation analysis:

- Public health risk and capacity assessment findings
- Humanitarian needs overview and key indicators
- Response gaps and lessons from previous interventions

Target population and geographic scope:

- Population numbers, characteristics, and trends
- Priority geographic areas based on health and nutrition status
- Vulnerability criteria for beneficiary targeting

Strategic objectives and indicators:

- Public health and nutrition goals with timeframes
- Primary outcome indicators and targets
- Risks and assumptions underpinning the response logic

Sector-specific and integrated activities:

- WASH infrastructure and service delivery
- Health and nutrition facility-based interventions
- Community-based disease prevention and health promotion
- Integrated outreach and mobile services
- Cross-cutting activities (e.g. WASH in schools, menstrual hygiene management, MHM)

Coordination and partnership arrangements:

- Roles and responsibilities of sector lead agencies
- Inter-sector coordination platforms and meeting schedules
- Linkages with government and development actors
- Opportunities for multi-stakeholder initiatives

Supplies and logistics:

- Critical supply needs and gaps by sector
- Common procurement and transportation mechanisms
- Storage and distribution strategies
- Contingency plans for supply chain risks

Human resources and capacity building:

- Staffing requirements and availability by sector
- Surge support and standby partnership arrangements
- Training and capacity building priorities
- Duty of care and well-being support for frontline workers

Community engagement and accountability:

- Approaches for community participation in planning and delivery
- Localized communication and feedback channels
- Complaint and response mechanisms
- Inclusion strategies for marginalized groups

Monitoring and evaluation:

- Multi-sector outcome and process indicators
- Integrated survey and surveillance methodologies
- Roles and timelines for joint monitoring
- Learning and knowledge management strategies

Budgets and resource mobilization:

- Sector and agency-specific funding requirements
- Complementarity of funding sources and timelines
- Advocacy and resource mobilization strategies
- Financial tracking and reporting protocols

Activity matrix

Sector	*WASH*	*Health*	*Nutrition*	*WASH-health-nutrition*
Activity	Rehabilitation of water points	Oral Cholera Vaccination campaign	Infant and Young Child Feeding (IYCF) counselling	Hygiene promotion and soap distribution
Output indicator	# of water points restored	% of high-risk population vaccinated	% of mothers receiving IYCF counselling	# of households receiving hygiene kits
Timeframe	Month 1–3	Month 2	Month 1–6	Month 1–3
Target population	5,000 households	20,000 people	2,000 PLW	5,000 households
Geographic area	District A	District A, B	District B	District A, B
Lead agency	UNICEF	WHO	UNICEF	NGO Y
Implementing partners	NGO X, Y	MoH, NGO Z	NGO X, District Health Office	Community health workers
Funding source	CERF	GAVI	OFDA	ECHO

Note: PLW, pregnant and lactating women; MoH, Ministry of Health; CERF, Central Emergency Response Fund; GAVI, Global Alliance for Vaccines and Immunization; OFDA, Office of US Foreign Disaster Assistance; ECHO, European Civil Protection and Humanitarian Aid Operations

Monitoring framework

Objective	*Indicator*	*Definition and measurement*	*Target*	*Data source and frequency*
Reduce morbidity and mortality from diarrheal disease	% of children under five with diarrhea in last two weeks	Caregiver report of three or more loose stools per day	<10%	Household survey (baseline, midline, endline)
	Incidence of cholera cases	Health facility admissions for AWD per 1,000 population	<1/1,000	Early warning alert and response system
Improve the nutritional status of children under five	Prevalence of global acute malnutrition (GAM)	% of children 6–59 m with MUAC <12.5 cm or bilateral pitting oedema	<5%	SMART nutrition survey (quarterly)
	% of children 6-23m meeting minimum acceptable diet	Breastfed children receiving minimum dietary diversity and meal frequency, non-breastfed children fed minimum milk and dietary diversity	>70%	IYCF survey (quarterly)

Note: AWD, acute watery diarrhea

Resources

Global WASH Cluster Response Planning Toolkit:

- GWC. no date. 'GWC Coordination Tool Kit (CTK) – Confluence'. Accessed 9 April 2025. https://washcluster.atlassian.net/wiki/spaces/CTK/overview

Health Cluster Guide:

- WHO. 2020. *Health Cluster Guide: A Practical Handbook*. World Health Organization (WHO). https://healthcluster.who.int/publications/i/item/9789240004726

UNICEF Nutrition-WASH Toolkit:

- UNICEF. 2016. *Nutrition-WASH Toolkits: Guide for Practical Joint Actions Nutrition-Water, Sanitation and Hygiene (WASH)*. https://www.unicef.org/eap/reports/nutrition-wash-toolkit-guide-practical-joint-actions

Key considerations:

- Involve multi-sector field teams in the response planning process from the outset.
- Harmonize planning cycles and templates across sectors to the extent possible.
- Sequence and layer WASH, health, and nutrition inputs to maximize synergies.
- Include process milestones to track implementation quality, not just outputs.
- Balance quick wins and community priorities with evidence-based impact.
- Develop costed contingency plans for most likely outbreak and natural hazard scenarios.
- Promote early recovery and sustainability strategies, not just temporary fixes.
- Regularly monitor and adapt plans based on changes in needs, capacities, and funding.

3.2 Nutrition-sensitive WASH strategy development guide

Purpose: To provide a step-by-step process for designing integrated, nutrition-sensitive WASH strategies and interventions in humanitarian crises.

When to use: During preparedness contingency planning, at the onset of acute emergency response, as part of routine programme design cycles.

Step 1: Assess nutrition-WASH linkages:

- Consult existing data on nutritional status, disease burden, WASH coverage in affected areas.
- Conduct rapid assessments using the Nutrition-sensitive WASH risk assessment checklist (tool 2.3).

- Identify key pathways linking poor WASH conditions to nutritional outcomes in the local context:
  - diarrheal disease and environmental enteropathy
  - geohelminth and other parasitic infections
  - food and water safety from farm to plate
  - maternal and caregiver WASH practices
  - environmental hygiene in homes, schools, and health facilities
- Analyse the relative contribution of WASH-related causes to the local malnutrition burden.

Step 2: Set nutrition-sensitive objectives and outcomes:

- Consult nutrition sector to understand priority at-risk groups, targets, timelines.
- Set strategic WASH objectives and outcomes that directly support nutrition goals, e.g.
  - reduced diarrhea and enteric infection incidence among children under two
  - improved access to safe water and hygiene for formula-feeding infants
  - decreased open defecation and environmental contamination in settlements
  - increased caregiver handwashing at critical times for food preparation and child feeding
- Ensure WASH objectives are time-bound, specific, measurable, and achievable within response capacity.
- Include both prevention and treatment components: e.g. WASH in outpatient malnutrition centres.

Step 3: Design integrated WASH and nutrition packages:

- Coordinate selection of target areas and households with nutrition counterparts.
- Plan joint targeting, timing, and delivery of services when possible to reinforce impact.
- Develop integrated packages tailored to the needs of specific groups:
  - pregnant and lactating women
  - children under two or five years of age
  - severely and moderately acute malnourished cases
  - people living with HIV/AIDS and chronic illnesses
- Consider age-appropriate technologies and designs: e.g. child-sized potties, handwashing devices.
- Layer hygiene behaviour change with food and health interventions along the continuum of care.
- Identify mechanisms to transition households from temporary to more durable WASH solutions.

Step 4: Engage communities in planning and delivery:

- Understand traditional practices and perceptions around WASH and nutrition through participatory discussions.
- Explore existing coping strategies, positive behaviours to build on, and barriers to change.
- Engage mothers, fathers, grandparents, siblings, and other key influencers in designing household solutions.
- Mobilize champions from care groups, mother-to-mother support groups, village health teams, etc.
- Co-design communication campaigns that resonate with motivators and social norms.
- Build the capacity of community outreach workers to negotiate improved practices.

Step 5: Establish joint monitoring processes:

- Identify a few high-priority, sensitive indicators to track WASH and nutrition interactions.
- Integrate key nutrition-sensitive metrics into WASH monitoring systems: e.g. diarrhea rates, food hygiene scores.
- Coordinate baselines and re-assessments with nutrition surveys when feasible.
- Monitor distribution and uptake of household WASH supplies: e.g. soap, water treatment.
- Conduct joint analysis to explore trends between WASH exposures and nutrition outcomes.
- Establish feedback loops to inform adaptations in targeting, messaging, distribution.
- Document and disseminate learning on nutrition-sensitive WASH programming.

Resources

UNICEF Nutrition-WASH Toolkit:

- UNICEF. 2016. *Nutrition-WASH Toolkits: Guide for Practical Joint Actions Nutrition-Water, Sanitation and Hygiene (WASH).* https://www.unicef.org/eap/reports/nutrition-wash-toolkit-guide-practical-joint-actions

WHO Guidelines on Sanitation and Health:

- WHO. 2018. *Guidelines on Sanitation and Health.* Geneva: World Health Organization. https://www.who.int/publications/i/item/9789241514705

3.3 Community engagement planning framework

Purpose: To provide a structured approach for engaging affected communities as active partners in all phases of the humanitarian programme cycle for WASH interventions.

When to use: From earliest stages of response planning through to transition and recovery.

Key principles:

- Enable communities to take a leadership role in assessing, designing, implementing, and monitoring WASH activities.
- Listen to and act on the needs and concerns voiced by diverse community members.
- Build on existing community capacities and coping strategies before introducing new approaches.
- Ensure engagement approaches are culturally acceptable and conflict-sensitive.
- Maintain transparency and accountability to affected people in all interactions.

Phase 1: Needs assessment and risk analysis:

- Support community representatives to participate in multisectoral needs assessments.
- Conduct focus group discussions with diverse community members to understand WASH practices, vulnerabilities, and priorities.
- Use participatory mapping to identify high-risk areas, access barriers, and local resources.
- Analyse power dynamics and social tensions that may affect safe and equitable participation.
- Engage local leaders to validate assessment findings and build trust.

Phase 2: Strategic planning and capacity mapping:

- Facilitate community visioning exercises to define success for WASH interventions.
- Conduct participatory barrier analysis to identify blockers and enablers of desired WASH behaviours.
- Map formal and informal community structures that can be leveraged for mobilization.
- Establish WASH committees with inclusive representation (gender, age, disability, ethnicity).
- Assess community capacity and training needs to take on increasing WASH roles.
- Develop communication and feedback channels appropriate to local preferences and literacy.

Phase 3: Implementation and monitoring:

- Engage community volunteers in the construction, operation, and maintenance of WASH facilities.
- Partner with community health workers, teachers, and religious leaders as WASH promoters.
- Train and mentor WASH entrepreneurs to support local livelihoods and market solutions.
- Foster community-led monitoring systems, e.g. water and sanitation for health facility improvement tool (WASH FIT), community scorecards, citizen report cards.
- Establish accessible, safe, and responsive feedback and complaint mechanisms.
- Discuss monitoring results in public meetings and agree on remedial actions with the community.

Phase 4: Transition and sustainability:

- Develop community capacity to take on management of WASH facilities and services.
- Facilitate links between WASH committees and formal governance structures for ongoing support.
- Explore cost-recovery and financing models to fund WASH operations and maintenance.
- Transition WASH data collection and analysis to permanent local systems.
- Conduct participatory evaluations and after action reviews to identify lessons learned.
- Celebrate community achievements and recognize volunteer contributions.

Planning considerations:

- Start community engagement from day one and sustain it throughout the implementation.
- Set clear expectations and success metrics for community participation at each phase.
- Budget adequately for community capacity building, volunteer support, local materials.
- Allow sufficient time and iteration for participatory processes amidst response pressures.
- Manage community fatigue from multiple disjointed engagement efforts across agencies.
- Consider safety, security, and power dimensions that enable or constrain inclusive participation.
- Monitor community participation by different groups and course-correct exclusionary practices.
- Document and share good practices and lessons in community engagement for WASH.

Community engagement toolbox:

- *Context analysis*: Social mapping, power analysis, conflict assessment.
- *Needs assessment*: Participatory rural appraisal, focus group discussions, transect walks.
- *Planning*: Community action planning, participatory hygiene and sanitation transformation (PHAST), barrier analysis, community-led total sanitation (CLTS) triggering.
- *Capacity building*: Training of trainers, on-the-job coaching, learning exchanges.
- *Mobilization*: Care groups, WASH clubs in schools, village savings and loans.
- Outreach: Household counselling, community theatre, local media campaigns.
- *Monitoring*: Community scorecards, citizen report cards, WASH FIT, most significant change.
- *Feedback*: Suggestion boxes, helpdesks, SMS/phone hotlines, community consultations.
- *Governance*: WASH committee by-laws, conflict resolution, links to local authorities.
- *Livelihoods*: Sanitation marketing, WASH enterprises, vocational skills training.

Resources

Oxfam Guide to Community Engagement in WASH:

- Oxfam. 2016. *Guide to Community Engagement in WaSH: A Practitioners' Guide, Based on Lessons from Ebola*. Oxfam. https://policy-practice.oxfam.org/resources/guide-to-community-engagement-in-wash-a-practitioners-guide-based-on-lessons-fr-620139/

IFRC Guide on Hygiene Promotion in Emergencies:

- IFRC. 2017. *WASH Guidelines for Hygiene Promotion in Emergency Operations*. Geneva: International Federation of Red Cross and Red Crescent Societies.

Global WASH Cluster Accountability Toolkit:

- GWC. no date. 'GWC Coordination Tool Kit (CTK) – Confluence'. Accessed 9 April 2025. https://washcluster.atlassian.net/wiki/spaces/CTK/overview

3.4 Capacity assessment and building tools

Purpose: To systematically assess and strengthen the capacity of local WASH actors to prepare for, respond to, and recover from emergencies.

When to use: During preparedness and contingency planning, at the early stages of response, identify delivery partners, and monitor progress and address gaps throughout response.

Step 1: Define capacity assessment objectives:

- Identify the target organizations or individuals whose capacity will be assessed.
- Agree on domains of capacity to focus on (e.g. technical, organizational, financial).
- Determine how assessment data will inform project design, partnership agreements, and training plans.
- Clarify the timeline and resources available for the capacity assessment.

Step 2: Review existing capacity information:

- Gather organizational profiles, staffing data, and policies from HR departments.
- Compile past capacity assessment reports from coordination platforms.
- Review training records, workshop attendance, drill participation.
- Analyse past response evaluations for performance strengths and gaps.
- Consult national capacity benchmarks and standards where available.

Step 3: Select appropriate assessment tools:

- Tailor tools to context, purpose, and organizational level (system, organization, individual).
- Consider a mix of self-assessment questionnaires, interviews, focus groups, observations.
- Examples of common capacity assessment tools:
  - WASH Cluster Competency Framework:
    - GWC. 2023. *Competency Framework for Cluster Coordination.* Global WASH Cluster. https://www.washcluster.net/file-download/download/public/52856
- Prioritize tools that build in action planning and tracking.

Step 4: Conduct capacity assessments:

- Train assessment facilitators on objectives, tools, participatory approaches.
- Schedule assessments at convenient times and in accessible locations.
- Explain purpose and confidentiality measures, gain informed consent.
- Facilitate self-reflection and constructive peer feedback – avoid external judgement.
- Probe reasons behind capacity strengths and weaknesses.
- Triangulate self-reported data with document review and observation.
- Provide immediate verbal feedback and validate key findings with participants.

Step 5: Analyse and apply assessment findings:

- Consolidate data across tools and identify common capacity themes.
- Map findings against relevant capacity frameworks to spot gaps and assets.
- Highlight priorities for capacity building based on risk analysis and response needs.
- Present findings to coordination platforms and advocate for collective gap-filling.
- Use results to match roles and responsibilities to organizational capacities.
- Develop phased capacity-strengthening plans linked to preparedness and response.
- Discuss sensitive organizational development issues bilaterally and confidentially.

Step 6: Design and deliver capacity building programme:

- Jointly define capacity building objectives and success indicators with participants.
- Tailor mix of training modalities to learning objectives, audience, and feasibility:
  - classroom-based training
  - on-the-job coaching and shadowing
  - simulations and drills
  - peer-to-peer learning exchanges
  - online and mobile training courses
  - blended learning programmes
- Develop practical exercises and case studies grounded in local response scenarios.
- Incorporate training follow-up and application assignments to reinforce learning.
- Provide ongoing mentoring, supervision, and refresher training to sustain skills.
- Re-assess capacity at regular intervals to demonstrate improvement and update plans.

Illustrative WASH capacity building topics:

- WASH sector coordination and humanitarian architecture
- WASH needs assessments and response analysis
- WASH minimum standards and indicators
- Water supply and quality in emergencies
- Excreta disposal and fecal sludge management
- Vector control and solid waste management
- Hygiene promotion and community engagement

- WASH non-food item selection and distribution
- WASH facility operation and maintenance
- WASH data collection, analysis, and reporting
- WASH preparedness and contingency planning
- WASH strategy development and transition planning
- WASH technical trainings (e.g. pipe fitting, latrine construction, water testing)

Tips for effective capacity building:

- Base capacity plans on systematic needs assessments, not ad hoc requests.
- Engage participants in designing their own learning journey.
- Start with function (what needs to get done), then form (how to structure learning).
- Promote holistic capacity building that integrates knowledge, skills, and attitudes.
- Balance short-term skill needs with longer-term organizational development.
- Leverage existing training resources and platforms to avoid duplication.
- Adapt generic training materials with local case studies, photos, vocabulary.
- Create space for criticism of poor practices and discussion of unintended consequences.
- Build coaching and mentoring skills of managers to provide ongoing support.
- Monitor learning outcomes at individual, organizational, and sector levels.

3.5 Health system capacity mapping tool

Refer to Annex 1 Sections 1.3 and 3.4 for guidance on stakeholder capacity mapping and capacity building. Key domains to assess health system capacity for WASH include:

- Dedicated budget line and funding flows for WASH in healthcare facilities
- Existence and implementation of national policies, standards, and protocols
- Sufficient WASH-IPC trained health workforce in place
- Availability of critical WASH infrastructure, supplies, and equipment
- Clearly defined O&M responsibilities and sufficient budget
- Regular monitoring and remedial action on WASH indicators
- Capacity for medical waste management and environmental cleaning

Based on the mapping, develop capacity building plans outlining training, mentoring, and system strengthening priorities.

3.6 Joint capacity building plan

Refer to Annex 1 Section 3.4 for more guidance on assessing capacity gaps and developing joint capacity building plans.

Training topic	*WASH-nutrition linkages and integrated programming*	*Nutrition-sensitive WASH assessment and analysis*	*Social behaviour change for key WASH-nutrition practices*	*Joint supportive supervision for community platforms*
Target group	WASH and nutrition managers	Subnational officials	Outreach workers	District authorities
Timeline	Q1	Q2	Q2/Q3	Q3
Training modality	Three-day workshop	Mentoring	Hands-on training	On-the-job
Facility / location	National level	Three priority districts	District level	Six target communities
Lead trainers	UNICEF/MOH	Consultants	MOH/NGOs	UNICEF
Resources	$$	$	$$	$
Monitoring	Pre/post test	Quality of analysis	Observation of skills	Supervision reports

3.7 Community-level joint action plan template

Refer to Annex 1 Section 3.1 for a template joint operational action plan. Key components:

- Shared objectives and indicators across WASH and health
- Community-level targets and timeline for each activity
- Responsibility assignment to community structures and partners
- Resource requirements and community contributions
- Coordination mechanisms and information sharing protocols
- Monitoring system for tracking progress and resolving bottlenecks

Section 4: Implementation tools

4.1 Joint workplan and budget template

Purpose: To collaboratively plan and track the implementation of integrated WASH activities across agencies and sectors.

When to use: After initial rapid assessment and periodically through response to modify plans based on monitoring data and evolving needs.

Key components

Shared objectives and indicators:

- Clearly state joint WASH objectives linked to public health, nutrition, and other sector outcomes.

- Specify SMART (Standardized Monitoring and Assessment of Relief and Transitions) indicators with targets and timeframes.
- Outline key assumptions and risks that may affect the achievement of objectives.

Planned activities:

- Logically sequence WASH activities needed to achieve each objective.
- Specify what inputs and tasks are required under each activity.
- Estimate a realistic implementation timeline and indicate any dependencies between activities.
- Designate lead agency and supporting partners accountable for each activity.
- Define target locations and populations for service delivery and behaviour change.

Resource requirements:

- Quantify human resources needed by function, competency level, and time period.
- Detail material resources, supplies, and equipment requirements.
- Specify logistical and operational support needs: e.g. transportation, storage, security.
- Estimate total financial costs disaggregated by activity, agency, and funding source.
- Indicate confirmed funds and gaps to inform resource mobilization.

Coordination and quality assurance:

- Plan joint assessments and monitoring visits at key milestones.
- Harmonize data collection, analysis, and reporting across agencies and sectors.
- Agree on common technical standards, behaviour change approaches, and beneficiary selection criteria.
- Establish communication and problem-solving protocols between partners.
- Budget for coordination functions, including information management and meeting costs.

Flexibility and risk management:

- Build in contingency plans and pre-positioned resources for likely scenarios.
- Maintain flexibility to adapt plans based on monitoring data and community feedback.
- Identify potential internal and external risks and appropriate mitigation measures.
- Develop clear triggers and decision points for scaling up or phasing out assistance.
- Plan progressive handover to local actors as capacity allows.

Tips for joint work planning:

- Use participatory methods to engage implementation teams in work planning.
- Leverage seasonal calendars and market data to optimize the timing of activities.
- Ensure WASH plans are synchronized with health, nutrition, and other sector priorities.
- Specify which costs are shared across agencies to avoid double-counting.
- Allow flexibility in format – Gantt charts may be too rigid for uncertain contexts.
- Keep plans realistic but ambitious enough to encourage innovation and surge capacity.
- Include quick impact actions to demonstrate early results while setting longer-term goals.
- Stress-test draft plans with key informants to validate assumptions and feasibility.
- Disseminate final work plans widely and train staff and partners on their use.
- Review and update work plans frequently based on progress monitoring and context changes.

4.2 Training and staff development guides

Purpose: To enhance the capacity of WASH staff and partners to deliver quality, accountable, and sustainable services in emergency contexts.

When to use: During preparedness to establish foundational skills, at response onset to build surge capacity, and throughout implementation to address performance gaps and staff turnover.

Step 1: Conduct training needs assessment:

- Review job descriptions and performance management data to identify competency gaps.
- Assess the readiness of staff to take on new functions under revised WASH strategies.
- Analyse past response evaluations and incident reports for areas of underperformance.
- Consult supervisors on observed skill and knowledge deficits among teams.
- Survey staff on perceived training needs and learning preferences.
- Triangulate needs assessment data to prioritize training topics and audiences.

Step 2: Define training objectives and approach:

- Formulate specific learning objectives for each prioritized training topic.
- Identify behavioural competencies and performance metrics to assess learning.
- Select an appropriate mix of training modalities based on learning preferences feasibility:
  - classroom-based workshops and seminars
  - on-the-job coaching and mentoring
  - e-learning courses and mobile applications
  - simulations, drills, and practice exercises
  - work shadowing and job rotation
- Decide whether to develop training in-house or outsource to external providers.
- Consider the need for multiple language tracks and visual/low-literacy tools.

Step 3: Develop training curriculum and materials:

- Break down each learning objective into key content areas and allot sufficient time.
- Incorporate case studies and practice scenarios relevant to the response context.
- Provide reference tools and job aids to reinforce skills post-training.
- Design participant evaluation methods appropriate to performance competencies.
- Produce lesson plans, facilitator guides, participant handbooks, visual aids.
- Field test curriculum with a sample of target learners and revise based on feedback.
- Consider open-source sharing of training materials to promote sector-wide capacity.

Step 4: Deliver training programmes:

- Select experienced trainers with both technical and facilitation skills.
- Brief trainers on participant backgrounds, learning needs, and expected training outputs.
- Arrange accessible, well-equipped venues conducive to participatory learning.
- Distribute training agendas, logistics information, and pre-reading in advance.
- Establish clear ground rules and norms for respectful interaction and confidentiality.

- Start with levelling exercises to surface participants' existing knowledge and attitudes.
- Use a mix of lectures, discussions, small group work, role plays, hands-on practice.
- Provide ample breaks and energizers to maintain focus and motivation.
- Administer daily feedback surveys to adapt facilitation and resolve logistical issues.

Step 5: Evaluate and follow up on training:

- Conduct post-training assessment to measure skills and knowledge acquisition.
- Reconvene participants after three to six months to assess training application and outcomes.
- Survey supervisors for observed behaviour changes and performance improvements.
- Provide follow-up support through on-the-job coaching, refresher training, peer exchanges.
- Designate training focal points at the field level to promote ongoing learning.
- Establish a community of practice to share successes, troubleshoot challenges, and generate innovations.
- Develop individual professional development plans linked to career progression.
- Evaluate the cost-effectiveness of training programmes to optimize investment of limited resources.

Illustrative WASH training topics:

- WASH coordination and humanitarian principles
- WASH needs assessment and response analysis
- WASH minimum standards and indicators
- WASH cluster tools and information management
- Water supply and quality management
- Excreta disposal and drainage
- Solid waste management and vector control
- Hygiene promotion and behaviour change
- WASH and protection mainstreaming
- WASH sector capacity strengthening
- WASH preparedness and contingency planning

Resources

UNHCR WASH Manual for Refugee Settings:

- UNHCR. 2020. *UNHCR WASH Manual: Practical Guidance for Refugee Settings*. Geneva: UNHCR. https://www.unhcr.org/us/media/unhcr-wash-practical-guidance-refugee-settings

UNICEF Cholera Toolkit:

- UNICEF. 2013. *UNICEF Cholera Toolkit*. UNICEF. https://www.washcluster.net/node/29581

4.3 Integrated outreach and campaign planning tools

Purpose: To provide guidance and templates for designing and managing integrated WASH campaigns that maximize synergies with health and nutrition.

When to use: When planning multi-channel outreach and mobilization campaigns around key public health priorities such as cholera prevention, hygiene promotion, and neglected tropical diseases.

Key components

Campaign objectives and indicators:

- State clear behaviour change and public health objectives of the campaign.
- Specify intended audience segments, geographic reach, and timeline.
- Identify synergies with health and nutrition campaigns on the ground.
- Select indicators to measure campaign exposure, retention, and effectiveness.

Formative research and message design:

- Review existing data on behavioural determinants, barriers, and motivators.
- Conduct focus groups to understand current knowledge, attitudes, and norms.
- Segment and prioritize key audiences based on risk profile and influence.
- Design core content of messaging based on formative research insights.
- Pretest and refine messages and materials with a diverse audience sample.

Multi-channel outreach strategy:

- Map trusted and accessible communication channels for priority audiences.
- Select an appropriate mix of interpersonal, print, audio-visual, and digital media.
- Define the frequency and intensity of campaign activities across each channel.
- Coordinate timing of outreach to reinforce core messages through repetition.
- Plan contingencies for physical distancing and movement restrictions.

Community mobilization and engagement:

- Recruit diverse mobilizers to reach marginalized groups and build local ownership.

- Train mobilizers on dialogue-based communication and conflict sensitivity.
- Adapt mobilization activities to community gathering spaces and events.
- Engage local media, drama groups, and influencers to amplify WASH messages.
- Provide visible WASH supplies and cues to action at mobilization sites.

Campaign management and coordination:

- Establish a cross-agency planning team with clear roles and accountability.
- Harmonize WASH content with health and nutrition information, education, and communication.
- Coordinate with logistics and supply teams to synchronize hardware and software.
- Monitor progress against work plans and quickly address implementation bottlenecks.
- Establish feedback mechanisms to gather community perceptions and reactions.

Monitoring and evaluation framework:

- Measure campaign reach through attendance logs, distribution records, and mass media ratings.
- Assess information retention and attitude shifts through post-exposure surveys.
- Observe adoption of promoted behaviours through household visits, transect walks, and spot checks.
- Analyse trends in disease surveillance and nutrition screening data in campaign areas.
- Document lessons learned and share human interest stories to sustain momentum.
- Evaluate the cost-effectiveness of different outreach channels to guide future campaigns.

Illustrative integrated campaign themes:

- Cholera prevention through water treatment and safe food handling
- Malaria control through environmental sanitation and bed net use
- Menstrual hygiene management and iron supplementation for adolescent girls
- Infant and young child feeding with emphasis on food hygiene and storage
- Neglected tropical disease prevention through face washing and vector control
- Promotion of oral rehydration solution and zinc to manage childhood diarrhea
- Handwashing with soap during antenatal and postnatal care visits
- Joint WASH and nutrition messaging for households with severe acute malnutrition

Campaign planning tools and templates:

- Audience insight-gathering tools (focus group guides, barrier analysis, journey mapping)
- Creative brief templates for message and material development
- Media mix and channel selection tools
- Activity planning and scheduling templates
- Team roles and responsibilities matrix
- Results chain and logical framework templates
- Budget and resource planning worksheets
- Real-time monitoring and community feedback tools
- Reporting and documentation guides

Tips for effective integrated campaigns

- Invest in formative research to understand audience segmentation and information ecosystems.
- Engage creative professionals to design compelling and culturally relevant content.
- Coordinate early and often with health and nutrition counterparts to identify mutual priorities.
- Tap into high-profile public events and media moments to launch and sustain campaigns.
- Decentralize campaign management to field teams who understand local contexts and languages.
- Use real-time monitoring data to adapt messaging and tactics based on community response.
- Set aside resources for refresher outreach and follow-up to prevent backsliding on behaviours.
- Document and disseminate results to demonstrate the value-added of integrated campaigns to donors.

4.4 WASH and nutrition behaviour change communication toolkit

Purpose: To provide a comprehensive set of tools and techniques for promoting integrated WASH and nutrition practices at household and community levels.

When to use: During community-level assessment, planning, and implementation of joint WASH and nutrition behaviour change strategies.

Tool 1: Barrier analysis and motivator mapping:

- Guide to conducting formative research on behavioural determinants:
  - Identify priority WASH and nutrition behaviours to focus on.
  - Select a small sample of 'doers' and 'non-doers' of each behaviour.
  - Conduct interviews to explore perceived consequences, social norms, access, and skills.

  - Analyse differences in reported barriers and motivators between doers and non-doers.
  - Use insights to design messages and strategies that minimize barriers and amplify motivators.
- Templates for:
  - designing formative research instruments (surveys, interview guides)
  - coding and analysing interview responses to identify behavioural determinants
  - summarizing key barriers and motivators by behaviour and audience segment
  - developing barrier reduction and motivator activation plans

Tool 2: Integrated WASH and nutrition counselling:

- Guide for integrating WASH messaging into nutrition counselling contacts:
  - Map key contact points along the continuum of care (antenatal, growth monitoring, community-based management of acute malnutrition, CMAM).
  - Identify age-appropriate WASH behaviours to promote at each contact (handwashing, safe disposal of feces, food hygiene).
  - Develop simple counselling aids (pictorial flip charts, reminder stickers).
  - Train outreach workers on behaviour change communication and negotiation skills.
  - Establish supervision and quality assurance mechanisms for counselling.
- Tools and job aids for:
  - contextualizing counselling content based on formative research
  - conducting interactive demonstrations and storytelling to promote behaviours
  - problem-solving common barriers with caregivers
  - making verbal commitments and household action plans
  - providing constructive feedback during follow-up visits

Tool 3: Participatory hygiene and sanitation transformation (PHAST):

- Step-by-step guide to implementing community-led total sanitation plus hygiene:
  - Train facilitators on the 7-step PHAST process and toolkit.
  - Conduct community mapping and transect walks to identify open defecation and waste sites.
  - Trigger disgust and desire for change through demonstrations and calculations.

  - Support community action planning for eliminating open defecation and improving hygiene.
  - Assist households in selecting and installing appropriate toilets and handwashing stations.
  - Verify and certify open defecation-free status through community monitoring.
  - Encourage communities to celebrate achievements and take responsibility for maintenance.
- Participatory tools for:
  - mapping water and sanitation conditions
  - analysing diarrheal disease transmission routes
  - calculating medical expenses and lost productivity due to poor sanitation
  - comparing improved sanitation options through cost-benefit analysis
  - developing community action plans and monitoring progress
  - certifying and celebrating open defecation-free status

Tool 4: Positive Deviance Hearth approach:

- Guide to identifying and promoting uncommon beneficial practices:
  - Conduct participatory wealth ranking and MUAC screening to identify positive deviant households.
  - Observe household WASH, feeding, and care practices to identify uncommon behaviours.
  - Interview mothers and grandmothers to understand enablers of positive practices.
  - Recruit positive deviant volunteers to demonstrate beneficial practices in their homes.
  - Conduct 12-day behaviour change sessions with underweight children and caregivers.
  - Facilitate participatory cooking to rehabilitate children and transfer skills to caregivers.
  - Reinforce new behaviours through home visits and community support structures.
- Tools and techniques for:
  - conducting positive deviance inquiry to discover successful practices
  - recruiting and training positive deviant volunteers as peer educators
  - designing and facilitating 12-day behaviour change sessions
  - engaging fathers and grandmothers to support the adoption of new practices
  - mobilizing community contributions to sustain and scale up the Positive Deviance/Hearth programme

Tool 5: School-based WASH promotion:

- Guide for using schools as platform for WASH behaviour change:
  - Assess school WASH conditions and improvement needs.

  - Establish WASH clubs to raise awareness and model good practices.
  - Train teachers to integrate hygiene lessons into the curriculum.
  - Engage parent-teacher associations to advocate for WASH-friendly policies.
  - Organize special events (handwashing day, toilet cleaning drive) to reinforce behaviours.
  - Support students to be agents of change in their households and communities.
- Resources and activity ideas for:
  - age-appropriate WASH games, songs, stories, and demonstrations
  - school WASH monitoring tools and checklists
  - lesson plans on personal hygiene, diarrhea prevention, and menstrual health
  - peer education and child-to-child methodologies
  - interschool WASH competitions and awards
  - outreach strategies to engage parents and surrounding communities

4.5 WASH in healthcare facility improvement planning template

| Facility name: ____________ | District: ________ | Date: ______ |

Improvement area	*Current gaps*	*Target*	*Activities*	*Responsibility*	*Timeline*	*Budget*	*Monitoring indicator*
Water supply							
Sanitation							
Handwashing							
Waste management							
Cleaning							
Staff capacity							
Policy/ procedures							

Key steps in improvement planning:

1. Form a team of facility management, staff, district officials, and partners.
2. Conduct WASH FIT or alternative facility assessment.
3. Convene a meeting to review assessment findings and identify gaps.
4. Prioritize and sequence activities based on impact and resources.
5. Assign clear responsibilities and a timeline for each activity.
6. Develop a budget and mobilize resources from the government and partners.
7. Monitor implementation and track improvements in WASH indicators.
8. Document and share lessons to inform ongoing sector improvement.

4.6 Integrated outreach strategy template

Objective	*Target behaviours*	*Target groups*	*Timeline*	*Delivery channels*	*Key messages*	*Responsible*	*Resources*

Refer to Annex 1 Section 4.4 for guidance on developing an integrated WASH and nutrition behaviour change strategy. Key considerations:

- Focus on a limited number of impactful behaviours from both sectors.
- Formative research to understand determinants, barriers, and enablers.
- Segment and prioritize key audiences based on their influence.
- Coordinate timing, locations, and delivery channels between sectors.
- Use harmonized messaging but tailored to each audience segment.
- Identify opportunities for cross-referrals and maximizing contacts.
- Jointly monitor and adapt approaches based on community feedback.

4.7 Integrated risk communication and community engagement plan

Refer to Annex 1 Section4.3 for guidance on developing and implementing integrated risk communication and community engagement strategies.

Objective	*Primary audience*	*Activities*	*Timeline*	*Channels*	*Responsible*	*Resources*	*Monitoring*
Promote handwashing at critical times	Caregivers of under fives						
Encourage use of household water treatment	Heads of household						
Dispel rumours and myths around hygiene and disease	Community leaders						
Engage schools in hygiene promotion	Students and teachers						

4.8 Community WASH and nutrition committee terms of reference (TOR) template

1. Purpose:
   a. Coordinate planning, implementation, and monitoring of integrated community WASH and nutrition activities.
   b. Provide a platform for joint problem-solving and mutual accountability.
   c. Advocate for community priorities in subnational coordination forums.
2. Membership:
   a. Representatives from village administration and council
   b. Community health and nutrition workers
   c. Hygiene and sanitation promotion volunteers
   d. Leaders of women's groups, youth groups and interest groups
   e. Representatives of vulnerable and minority populations
3. Roles and responsibilities:
   a. Conduct community assessments to identify WASH and nutrition risks and priorities.
   b. Develop community action plans and mobilize local resources.
   c. Monitor implementation of plans and track key indicators.
   d. Facilitate community feedback and complaints redressal.
   e. Organize community meetings and campaigns on WASH and nutrition.
4. Leadership:
   a. Committee chair and vice-chair elected by members
   b. Rotational terms of reference with clear selection criteria
   c. Secretariat function performed by community development officer
5. Meetings:
   a. Monthly meetings at agreed community venue
   b. Quorum of 50 per cent attendance required for decision-making
   c. Agenda circulated at least three days prior to meeting
   d. Minutes and action points documented and shared
6. Code of conduct:
   a. Members are expected to attend meetings regularly.
   b. Declare any conflicts of interest and adhere to humanitarian principles.
   c. Maintain confidentiality of sensitive community information.
   d. Consult constituents and provide feedback on committee decisions.

4.9 Community coordination timeline and task checklist

Month 1

- Stakeholder mapping and introductory meetings
- Establishment of WASH and Nutrition Committee

- Rapid assessment and problem analysis
- Community action planning workshop
- Selection and training of outreach workers

Month 2

- Launch of priority behaviour change activities
- Soap/hygiene kit distributions and demonstrations
- Food joint hygiene and safety sensitization
- Cooking demonstrations and recipe development
- Joint referrals for acutely malnourished children

Month 3

- Monitoring of planned activities and tracking of indicators
- Joint supportive supervision visits with health facility staff
- Review of community feedback data and complaints resolution
- Identification and documentation of human interest

Month 4

- Facilitation of model home competitions
- Recognition of positive deviants and community champions
- Refresher training for committee members and volunteers
- Development of sustainability and transition plan
- Dissemination of key successes and lessons learned

Month 5

- Support to community-led total sanitation campaigns
- Dialogue meetings with local authorities on institutionalization
- Formation and training of water user committees
- Repair and upgrade of WASH infrastructure through community contracting
- Exploration of local financing options for operation and maintenance

Month 6

- Endline assessment of key WASH and nutrition indicators
- Reflection meetings on lessons learned and recommendations
- Development of committee capacity building and transition plans
- Handover of responsibilities to permanent community structures
- Celebration and recognition of community achievements

Refer to Annex 1 Sections 3.3 and 4.4 for further guidance on community engagement approaches and WASH and nutrition behaviour change.

4.10 Outreach worker training package on WASH and nutrition

Module	Methodology	Duration	Facilitators	Materials
1. WASH–nutrition linkages and pathways	Presentations, small group work	1 day	WASH and nutrition specialists	Flipcharts, videos
2. Key WASH behaviours for nutrition outcomes	Demonstrations, role plays	1 day	Health promoters	Counselling cards
3. Negotiation and problem-solving skills	Practice sessions, feedback	1 day	Behaviour change trainers	Scenario cards
4. Screening and referral for acute malnutrition	Practical exercises	½ day	Nutrition focal points	MUAC tapes, referral forms
5. Facilitation of community conversations and campaigns	Mock sessions, action planning	1 day	Community development officers	Visuals, games
6. Monitoring, reporting, and feedback mechanisms	Presentations, group discussion	½ day	M&E specialists	Reporting templates

Note: M&E, monitoring and evaluation

Refer to Annex 1 Section 4.2 for more guidance on designing and delivering effective training programmes for outreach workers.

Section 5: Monitoring and feedback tools

5.1 Integrated monitoring framework

Purpose: To track and analyse the collective performance and outcomes of WASH interventions in humanitarian response, emphasizing integration with the health and nutrition sectors.

When to use: From the early weeks of response to establishing a common monitoring system, throughout the response and into protracted contexts and recovery.

Step 1: Define shared monitoring objectives:

- Clarify the aims and audiences for response monitoring data.
- Agree on priority WASH interventions and standards to monitor across agencies.
- Identify common indicators for WASH outputs, outcomes, and impacts.
- Determine how monitoring data will inform decision-making and course correction.

Step 2: Select appropriate indicators:

- Review Sphere standards and cluster guidance for core WASH indicators.

- Prioritize a few meaningful outcome indicators over many activity measures.
- Integrate key nutrition and health-sensitive indicators:
  - prevalence of diarrhea in children under five
  - percentage of health facilities with basic WASH services
  - proportion of WASH facilities accessible to people with limited mobility
  - percentage of households storing water safely in the home
  - percentage of caregivers with appropriate handwashing knowledge and practice
- Integrate with national health management information system (HMIS) for WASH-related disease and malnutrition data tracking and reporting.
- Ensure indicators are SMART (specific, measurable, achievable, relevant, time-bound).

Step 3: Harmonize methodologies and tools:

- Standardize operational definitions and calculation methods for key indicators.
- Agree on minimum quality standards and cleaning protocols for data.
- Design common formats for 4W (who, what, where, when), facility survey, and KAP (Knowledge, Attitude and Practice) survey tools.
- Develop data collection schedules and reporting templates across agencies.
- Pretest tools under field conditions and streamline to avoid survey fatigue.
- Train data collectors on ethics, sampling, interview skills, and data entry.

Step 4: Coordinate data management:

- Establish information sharing protocols, data security, and privacy safeguards.
- Agree on cleaning, validation, and analysis processes for each data stream.
- Develop simple dashboards that triangulate WASH, health, and nutrition trends.
- Present monitoring results in user-friendly formats for different audiences.
- Provide field teams with rapid feedback and guidance to improve data quality.
- Conduct joint analysis workshops to interpret trends and identify bottlenecks.

Step 5: Utilize monitoring for decision-making:

- Review monitoring data regularly to gauge progress against targets.
- Identify discrepancies between areas or partners to trigger quality checks.

- Interpret trends jointly with community feedback to understand the reasons behind the data.
- Adjust implementation tactics based on real-time output and outcome data.
- Advocate for resources to cover monitoring gaps and underserved areas.
- Document and share good practices to facilitate peer learning and adoption.

Step 6: Evaluate and evolve the system:

- Analyse costs and time required for each data stream against benefits for decisions.
- Phase out emergency indicators as appropriate, transition to recovery measures.
- Assess the capacity of local WASH actors to sustain critical monitoring activities.
- Institutionalize processes for routine data quality audits and utilization reviews.
- Contribute to sector-wide initiatives to streamline core WASH indicators.

Illustrative WASH monitoring indicators

Water supply:

- Percentage of households collecting at least 15 L safe water per person per day
- Percentage of water access points with <1 cfu *E. coli*/100 mL
- Average number of users per functioning water source
- Percentage of water user fees collected and spent on O&M

Sanitation:

- Percentage of households with access to private improved sanitation facility
- Percentage of communal latrines regularly maintained and cleaned
- Ratio of male to female toilets in public spaces (schools, markets, clinics)
- Percentage of villages certified as open defecation-free

Hygiene promotion:

- Percentage of households with soap and water at a handwashing facility
- Percentage of people citing at least three of five key handwashing times
- Ratio of hygiene promoters to the total population (target 1:500)
- Percentage of households with appropriate water treatment supplies

Environmental health:

- Percentage of solid waste safely disposed in designated sites
- Ratio of population to functioning bathing facilities (target 1:50)

- Percentage of communal latrines with functional lighting
- Number of community clean-up campaigns conducted per month

Cross-cutting issues:

- Percentage of WASH facilities meeting accessibility standards
- Percentage of women reporting feeling safe using WASH facilities
- Number of WASH committee members trained on protection principles
- Percentage of affected people satisfied with the adequacy of WASH services

Resources

Sphere WASH chapter and indicators:

- Sphere Association. 2018. *The Sphere Handbook: Humanitarian Charter and Minimum Standards in Humanitarian Response,* 4th edn. Geneva, Switzerland: Sphere Association. www.spherestandards.org/handbook

JMP Core Questions on Water, Sanitation and Hygiene for Household Surveys:

- WHO and UNICEF. 2018. 'Core Questions on Drinking Water, Sanitation and Hygiene for Household Surveys: 2018 Update'. United Nations Children's Fund (UNICEF) and World Health Organization (WHO).

UNHCR WASH Monitoring System:

- UNHCR. no date. 'Water, Sanitation and Hygiene'. UNHCR USA. Accessed 9 April 2025. https://www.unhcr.org/us/what-we-do/respond-emergencies/water-sanitation-and-hygiene

Oxfam MEAL minimum standards:

- Oxfam. 2013. *A Quick Guide to Monitoring, Evaluation, Accountability and Learning in Fragile Contexts.* Oxfam. https://policy-practice.oxfam.org/resources/a-quick-guide-to-monitoring-evaluation-accountability-and-learning-in-fragile-c-297134/

5.2 Outbreak investigation and response checklist

Purpose: To guide joint rapid investigation and control measures by WASH and health actors in the event of disease outbreaks with public health implications.

When to use: At first alert of a suspected outbreak based on established epidemic thresholds and risk assessment.

Step 1: Verify the alert and activate coordination mechanisms:

- Communicate with health facilities and community focal points to confirm the alert signal.

- Activate WASH and health outbreak coordination mechanisms at the relevant level.
- Assign a multi-disciplinary outbreak investigation and response team.
- Notify health and WASH authorities at all levels.

Step 2: Conduct rapid risk assessment:

- Review existing data on cases, deaths, and context.
- Develop case definitions (suspected, probable, and confirmed).
- Initiate active case finding and line listing.
- Map cases by location, time, and demographic characteristics.
- Identify potential transmission routes and risk factors.
- Assess local laboratory capacity for confirmation.
- Appraise local response capacity and available resources.

Step 3: Implement immediate control measures:

- Isolate and treat cases to reduce transmission.
- Trace and manage contacts according to protocol.
- Enhance disease surveillance and active case finding.
- Conduct health facility assessment using WASH FIT or similar tools.
- Assess and support WASH in affected communities.
- Promote safe hygiene behaviours and distribute soap/hygiene kits.
- Disinfect potentially contaminated water sources.

Step 4: Confirm outbreak and define scope:

- Collect and transport samples to the reference laboratory for confirmation.
- Classify suspected cases as probable and confirmed.
- Analyse person, place, and time characteristics of confirmed cases.
- Develop an epidemic curve to understand outbreak evolution.
- Determine the affected geographical area and population at risk.
- Generate hypotheses on transmission routes and risk factors.

Step 5: Conduct detailed field investigation:

- Review clinical records and interview cases and contacts.
- Conduct environmental assessments of implicated sources.
- Collect additional samples as necessary from cases, contacts, and environment.
- Construct a transmission chain to identify primary and secondary cases.
- Implement an analytical study to test hypotheses, as appropriate:
  - case-control study to identify risk factors and modes of transmission
  - cohort study to measure attack rates based on risk factor exposure

Step 6: Expand control and prevention measures:

- Conduct vector control and environmental clean-up campaigns.

- Expand access to safe water through temporary and permanent solutions.
- Improve sanitation conditions in public spaces and institutions.
- Engage community health workforce in risk communication and social mobilization.
- Distribute household water treatment and hygiene products.
- Prepare for possible temporary isolation and care facilities.
- Initiate planning for oral cholera vaccination, as appropriate.

Step 7: Communicate findings and mobilize resources:

- Synthesize investigation results into a preliminary outbreak report.
- Disseminate reports to national and international stakeholders.
- Engage media to communicate risk and prevention measures to the public.
- Activate the emergency operations centre if not already done.
- Mobilize surge support from national and international partners.
- Re-assess supply pipeline and logistics arrangements.
- Develop donor proposals and situational reports to mobilize resources.

Step 8: Enhance surveillance and monitoring:

- Renew efforts to enhance disease surveillance and active case finding.
- Monitor outbreak evolution through updated epidemic curves and maps.
- Produce regular situation reports tracking cases, deaths, and response actions.
- Evaluate response coverage, quality, and effectiveness.
- Document lessons learned for preparedness and future response.
- Declare the end of the outbreak based on epidemiological evidence.

Resources

Sphere WASH chapter and indicators:

- Sphere Association. 2018. *The Sphere Handbook: Humanitarian Charter and Minimum Standards in Humanitarian Response*, 4th edn. Geneva, Switzerland: Sphere Association. www.spherestandards.org/handbook

WHO Outbreak Investigation and Response Manual:

- WHO. no date. 'Outbreak Toolkit: Providing the Tools to Investigate Disease Outbreaks, Collect Data and Guide Response Activities'. Accessed 9 April 2025. https://www.who.int/emergencies/outbreak-toolkit

5.3 Community feedback mechanism checklist

Purpose: To establish accessible and responsive feedback loops with affected populations to inform continuous improvement of WASH services and accountability.

When to use: From the earliest phase of emergency response, with community engagement in design, and continuously adapted based on feedback received.

Step 1: Design the feedback system:

- Consult diverse community members on their preferred feedback channels.
- Assess pre-existing community structures for handling complaints.
- Determine the scope of issues to collect feedback on (e.g. targeting, quality, safety).
- Develop feedback classification and prioritization system.
- Map referral pathways for sensitive and programmatic feedback.
- Clarify roles and timelines for acknowledging and responding to feedback.
- Identify a system for documenting and tracking feedback resolution.

Step 2: Select appropriate channels:

- Ensure multiple communication channels are available, such as:
  - suggestion boxes
  - toll-free hotline
  - SMS shortcode
  - help desks
  - social media platforms
  - community meetings
  - focus group discussions
  - key informant interviews
  - participatory mapping
- Locate feedback interfaces at safe and accessible sites (e.g. water points, clinics, markets).
- Provide confidential and anonymous options for sensitive issues.
- Accommodate local languages, literacy levels, and technology access.

Step 3: Promote feedback mechanisms:

- Develop simple, visual, information, education, and communication materials for the purpose of feedback and process.
- Disseminate channels and usage through community meetings, radio, flyers, and posters.
- Emphasize confidentiality and non-retaliation for honest feedback.
- Train staff and partners on handling feedback appropriately.
- Explain to the community how their feedback will be used to make improvements.
- Manage expectations on what is feasible to address and by when.

Step 4: Collect and acknowledge feedback:

- Monitor each feedback channel at regular intervals (e.g. daily, weekly).
- Record all feedback in a central logbook or database.

- Categorize feedback by sector, issue, severity, and sensitivity.
- Assign a tracking number to each actionable feedback.
- Acknowledge receipt to the individual or community, where possible.

Step 5: Process and respond to feedback:

- Prioritize feedback based on severity, frequency, and sector.
- Refer sensitive issues immediately to designated focal points.
- Forward remaining feedback to relevant managers for follow-up.
- Investigate and verify issues as needed through community consultation.
- Implement actions to address issues where feasible.
- Document actions taken and rationale for actions not taken.
- Respond to individual complaints if contact information is provided.

Step 6: Record and analyse feedback data:

- Develop a spreadsheet or simple database to track feedback cases.
- Record key data fields for each feedback:
  - date received
  - feedback category and description
  - referral date and focal point
  - investigation notes
  - resolution status and date
  - communication back to the complainant
- Analyse feedback data to identify trends by location, population group, and time period.
- Assess feedback system utilization and satisfaction rates.
- Present analysis in dashboard format for decision-making.

Step 7: Close the feedback loop:

- Validate analysis and recommendations with community representatives.
- Discuss systemic changes based on feedback trends with sector leadership.
- Adapt interventions and retarget resources in line with feedback.
- Communicate back to communities how their feedback informed changes.
- Close resolved complaints in the tracking system with outcome notes.
- Publicize aggregated feedback data and trends (e.g. 'You Said, We Did' boards).
- Support community-led monitoring and evaluation of feedback actions.

Step 8: Learn and improve the system:

- Review the effectiveness and utilization of each feedback channel.
- Identify barriers and enablers to providing and responding to feedback.
- Assess feedback incorporation into management decisions and course corrections.

- Revise feedback categories, prioritization, and referral protocols as needed.
- Close feedback channels that are ineffective or risky.
- Expand feedback channels that are well-utilized and trusted.
- Document and share learning on feedback handling with other sectors and agencies.

Resources

CHS Alliance PSEAH Implementation Quick Reference Handbook:

- CHS Alliance. 2020. *PSEAH Implementation Quick Reference Handbook*. CHS Alliance. https://www.chsalliance.org/get-support/resource/pseah-implementation-quick-reference-handbook/

IFRC Community Engagement and Accountability (CEA) Toolkit:

- IFRC. 2021. *Community Engagement and Accountability (CEA) Toolkit*. IFRC. 16 August 2021. https://www.ifrc.org/document/cea-toolkit

5.4 Supportive supervision checklist

Purpose: To provide a structured tool for conducting joint supportive supervision visits to WASH programme sites, with an emphasis on identifying strengths, gaps, and improvement actions.

When to use: Quarterly or biannually, as part of routine programme quality assurance and continuous improvement processes.

Step 1: Prepare for the visit:

- Review past supervision reports and action items.
- Analyse trends in routine WASH monitoring data for the site.
- Coordinate multi-agency team with technical, community engagement, and protection expertise.
- Inform site personnel of objectives, expectations, and agenda for the visit.
- Print copies of the supervision checklist and other tools.

Step 2: Conduct document review:

- Review plans, budgets, procurement, and distribution records.
- Check WASH committee meeting minutes and activity logs.
- Verify up-to-date stock cards and financial documents are in place.
- Crosscheck project tracking sheet against 4W reporting data.
- Note any discrepancies or questions for follow-up during the visit.

Step 3: Inspect WASH facilities:

- Observe water points, toilets, and waste management sites against quality standards.

- Check functionality, cleanliness, privacy, safety, and accessibility of facilities.
- Look for signs of overuse, disrepair, or poor maintenance.
- Assess the availability of spare parts, supplies, and tools for O&M.
- Ask users about their experience and satisfaction with the facilities.

Step 4: Interview personnel and volunteers:

- Engage staff/volunteers in discussions on successes, challenges, and suggestions.
- Assess the level of training, supervision, and adherence to safety protocols.
- Inquire about coordination with other sectors and local authorities.
- Probe on feedback and accountability mechanisms for affected populations.
- Observe interpersonal skills and record any concerns about conduct.

Step 5: Conduct focus group discussions:

- Meet with WASH committee and other community representatives.
- Gather perspectives on the relevance, quality, and reliability of WASH services.
- Explore any unintended consequences or protection risks from interventions.
- Discuss community role in design, monitoring, and maintenance of facilities.
- Probe how WASH services can be more inclusive of marginalized groups.

Step 6: Synthesize findings and give feedback:

- Convene supervision team to review findings against each section of checklist.
- Identify strengths to recognize and critical weaknesses to address.
- Prioritize gaps and develop time-bound improvement actions.
- Meet with site personnel to share key findings and recommendations.
- Remind staff that supervision aims to support, not punish performance.
- Agree on action items, timelines, and responsibilities for follow-up.

Step 7: Document and follow up:

- Summarize key findings and actions in the supervision report.
- Share report with WASH programme leadership and coordination platforms.
- Enter any systemic issues into the risk and issue log for resolution.
- Monitor completion of action items and document improvements.
- Analyse trends across supervision rounds to identify persistent gaps.
- Adjust the supervision approach and checklist based on feedback and priorities.

Supervision areas and illustrative questions

Area	*Sample questions*
Service delivery	Are services achieving sufficient quality, quantity, and coverage per standards? How reliable are water supply and sanitation services over time? Are there adequate systems for O&M of infrastructure? Do services reflect user preferences and protection considerations?
Behaviour change	Are hygiene promotion activities well targeted and technically sound? Is there observable improvement in key hygiene behaviours at household level? How engaged are community members in promoting hygiene? Are there sufficient hygiene supplies and cues to action in public spaces?
Community engagement	Did communities substantively participate in service design and siting? Are there representative WASH committees with clear roles? What is the level of community financial or in-kind contribution? Are there functional feedback mechanisms for quality, safety, accessibility?
Inclusion and protection	Are facilities safely accessible to women, children, people with disabilities? Is there adequate gender segregation and privacy for toilets and bathing? Do siting and lighting of facilities mitigate GBV risk? Are there dignified solutions for incontinence and menstrual hygiene?
Monitoring and reporting	Are output and quality indicators consistently tracked and reported? Is monitoring data used to inform decisions and course corrections? Are there mechanisms to validate service quality and user satisfaction? Is there two-way information flow between communities and project teams?
Coordination and collaboration	Are WASH interventions coordinated with health, nutrition, shelter, protection? Is there active participation in subnational WASH coordination forums? Are referral protocols in place between sectors for integrated issues? How are local authorities engaged in planning, monitoring, and handover?
Staffing and capacity	Do field teams have an appropriate mix of technical and soft skills? Is there a staff training and development plan based on performance gaps? How are national staff being mentored to take on greater responsibility? Are there duty of care policies and psychosocial support for frontline workers?
Resource management	Is delivery of services and supplies timely against work plan targets? Are budgets spent according to donor and agency rules? Is there adequate logistical support to enable efficient service delivery? What cost-effectiveness measures are in place to optimize resources?

Note: GBV, gender-based violence

Tips for effective supportive supervision:

- Approach supervision as an opportunity for mutual learning and relationship building.
- Communicate the why, what, who, and how of supervision visits well in advance.

- Deploy multi-disciplinary teams to model integrated working and cross-learning.
- Spend more time listening and observing than instructing or presenting.
- Engage staff and communities as active partners in analysing root causes and solutions.
- Demonstrate respect and cultural sensitivity in all interactions with stakeholders.
- Prioritize a few key high-impact actions rather than overwhelming teams with feedback.
- Recognize positive practices and innovations, not just gaps to be filled.
- Be solutions-focused and provide specific, actionable recommendations.
- Follow up relentlessly on supervision findings to reinforce accountability and learning.

5.5 Performance review and learning tools

Purpose: To provide a set of participatory methods and tools for analysing WASH programme performance, capturing lessons learned, and identifying corrective actions.

When to use: During the implementation and transition phases of the response, as part of quarterly and annual programme review and planning cycles.

Tool 1: After action review (AAR):

- Structured debrief process to reflect on a completed project phase or critical event.
- Key steps:
  - Reconfirm the original objectives and intended outcomes.
  - Reconstruct the key events and decision points as a shared team narrative.
  - Identify strengths and weaknesses in the response across four questions:
    - What was expected to happen?
    - What actually occurred?
    - What went well and why?
    - What could have gone better, and how?
  - Analyse root causes and contributing factors behind performance gaps.
  - Recommend a few key corrective actions to sustain strengths and address weaknesses.
  - Document, share, and monitor the implementation of the AAR action plan.
- Tips for effective AARs:
  - Create an atmosphere of openness, trust, and shared accountability.
  - Focus on systems and processes, not on placing blame on individuals.
  - Celebrate successful practices and innovations, not just finding faults.
  - Engage an external facilitator for high-stakes or sensitive reviews.
  - Distil lessons into short briefs or videos for wider dissemination.

Tool 2: Participatory impact assessment:

- Beneficiary-led evaluation to understand community perceptions of project results.
- Key steps:
  - Train a diverse team of data collectors in participatory methods and tools.
  - Develop context-specific questions for assessing relevance, effectiveness, and sustainability.
  - Conduct transect walks, social mapping, and focus groups to gather community feedback.
  - Facilitate community scoring of project performance against locally defined indicators.
  - Probe for unexpected outcomes, negative consequences, and equity issues.
  - Support communities to develop their own recommendations for future programming.
  - Validate findings with other stakeholders and communicate back to communities.
- Tips for meaningful participation:
  - Partner with local civil society organizations, youth, and women's groups to lead the process.
  - Ensure a balance of genders, ages, and diversity in the data collection teams.
  - Use visual, interactive tools suitable for low-literacy participants.
  - Triangulate qualitative feedback with quantitative outcome indicators.
  - Manage power dynamics and expectations carefully in group discussions.
  - Budget sufficient time and resources for translation, transport, and refreshments.

Tool 3: Collaborative quality improvement (CQI):

- Team-based problem-solving methodology to test and scale up service delivery changes.
- Five phases of CQI:
  - Define a specific service delivery problem backed by data.
  - Analyse root causes and potential solutions using quality improvement tools.
  - Develop change ideas and implement Plan-Do-Study-Act (PDSA) cycles to test them.
  - Monitor process and outcome measures to determine if changes are working.
  - Standardize and spread effective changes to other delivery sites and partners.
- Illustrative WASH applications:
  - Reduce time spent queuing for water collection by redesigning tap stands.

  - Increase adherence to handwashing in cholera treatment centres through cues and nudges.
  - Improve satisfaction with shared toilet cleanliness using cleaning schedules and inspections.
  - Boost household water treatment through integration with antenatal care visits.
- Key CQI enablers:
  - Leadership buy-in and championship of CQI from senior management.
  - Dedicated time and resources for facility-level teams to pursue CQI.
  - Regular coaching visits and learning sessions to support quality improvement.
  - Simple, real-time monitoring systems to track a few key process indicators.
  - Rewards and recognition for teams that achieve meaningful CQI gains.

Tool 4: Learning review and reflection:

- Facilitated discussion to extract key lessons from a project and inform future design.
- Guiding questions:
  - What were the most significant successes and factors behind them?
  - What were the biggest challenges faced, and how were they overcome?
  - Were there any negative unintended consequences on people or the environment?
  - What would you do differently next time to enhance equity and sustainability?
  - If the project was to be replicated elsewhere, what advice would you give?
  - What are the key advocacy messages that should inform policy and practice?
- Practical steps:
  - Decide on the focus and scope of the review based on key learning priorities.
  - Gather diverse perspectives from project cycle (proposal to evaluation).
  - Compile evidence of success and failure from monitoring data and reports.
  - Conduct a learning review workshop with implementing teams and partners.
  - Synthesize lessons and recommendations into a concise learning summary.
  - Socialize findings internally and with relevant coordination platforms.
  - Integrate key lessons into the next project cycle and disseminate case studies.
- Tips to nurture a learning culture:
  - Encourage open sharing of mistakes and failures as learning opportunities.
  - Make time and space for regular reflection as individuals and teams.

- Expose staff to different approaches through exchange visits and secondments.
- Capture and communicate inductive insights from implementation, not just donor-driven lessons.
- Translate lessons into practical decision support tools for preparedness and response.
- Advocate for flexible and adaptive programming that enables course correction.

Resources

Quality Improvement Essentials Toolkit:

- Institute for Healthcare (IHI). 2017. *Quality Improvement Essentials Toolkit.* IHI. https://www.ihi.org/resources/tools/quality-improvement-essentials-toolkit

5.6 Monthly reporting format for community committees

Refer to Annex 1 Section 5.1 for further guidance on designing and implementing integrated WASH and nutrition monitoring systems.

Section	*Key information*
1. Participants	Number of active committee members
	Representation of different groups
2. Activities implemented	List of WASH-nutrition activities conducted
	Number of participants reached
	Status of completion against plan
3. Monitoring data	Values for key WASH-nutrition indicators
	Trends compared to previous months
	Disaggregation by vulnerability where relevant
4. Community feedback	Number and type of feedback received
	Actions taken to respond to feedback
	Satisfaction rate with complaint resolution
5. Challenges and support needs	Implementation challenges faced
	Support required from subnational level
6. Lessons and innovations	Successful approaches and lessons learned
	Innovations and adaptations made
7. Next month priorities	Priority activities and targets for coming month
	Requests for specific guidance or inputs

Annexes to include:

- minutes of committee meetings held
- photos and human interest stories
- copies of monitoring data collection tools

ANNEX 2

Addressing conflict, COVID-19, and climate change

A multisectoral approach to integrated WASH programming

Humanitarian crises are growing in length and complexity due to external destabilizing pressures, including conflict, COVID-19, and climate change, with the average length of refugee situations now exceeding 20 years. Until now, there has been no specific WASH publication of this kind that reflects on these fundamental external factors that will play a vital role in the delivery of WASH services over the humanitarian–development divide within the context of fundamental sub-sectors. In their second insightful book on this important topic, Marïelle Snel and Nik Sorensen call for humanitarian and development WASH professionals to work together in a more coordinated manner to develop more effective humanitarian WASH programming that keeps long-term development goals in mind.

In this book, the authors bring together experts from across the humanitarian/development fields, with a focus on the humanitarian–development–peace nexus and a multisectoral response to connecting humanitarian and development sectors as an innovative answer to bridging these challenges. Contributors reference case studies to look more closely at ways each sub-field could better integrate with WASH programming. There is no one-size-fits-all solution to an integrated humanitarian–development response. However, the authors and contributors in this book provide deeper insights into the 'how' question underlying integrated WASH programming.

This work will be of interest not only to professionals working in the humanitarian and development WASH sector but also to others across the humanitarian, development, and peace sectors, ranging from government officials to managers working directly or indirectly around WASH.

Resource

Snel, Marïelle, and Nikolas Sorensen, eds. 2023. *Addressing Conflict, COVID-19, and Climate Change: A Multisectoral Approach to Integrated WASH Programming*. Rugby: Practical Action Publishing Ltd.

ANNEX 3

Sources consulted in the creation of the guidelines

These guidelines were created with the generous help of WASH, health, and nutrition professionals from various government, NGO, and UN organizations. In addition to their input, the following sources were also referenced in the creation of these guidelines.

Action Against Hunger (ACF). 2015. *Link NCA Guidelines: A Participatory and Response Oriented Method for Conducting a Nutrition Causal Analysis*. ACF. https://docpdf.linknca.com/159/159/supports/25097/catDoc246/nca_guidelines_en_web.pdf?CFID=38659475&CFTOKEN=619e16de6bc726ff-AC762210-03D6-B80C-B23C38E72C31DBCF

ACF. 2017a. *A Practical Package for Stunting Reduction: Contribution to Malnutrition Reduction Through a Multi-Sector Approach*. ACF. https://accioncontraelhambre.org/sites/default/files/documents/2017_babywash_en_0.pdf

ACF. 2017b. *WASH Nutrition: A Practical Guidebook on Increasing Nutritional Impact through Integration of WASH and Nutrition Programmes*. Paris: Action Against Hunger.

ACF and SMART. 2014. 'Guidelines: Rapid SMART Surveys for Emergencies'. SMART. https://smartmethodology.org/survey-planning-tools/smart-methodology/rapid-smart-methodology/

CHS Alliance. 2020. *PSEAH Implementation Quick Reference Handbook*. CHS Alliance. https://www.chsalliance.org/get-support/resource/pseah-implementation-quick-reference-handbook/

FHI 360. 2024. *IYCF-E Assessment Guide*. Durham, NC: FHI 360. https://www.nutritioncluster.net/sites/nutritioncluster.com/files/2024-12/IYCF-E-Assessment-Guide-v6.pdf

Global WASH Cluster (GWC). 2023. *Competency Framework for Cluster Coordination*. GWC. https://www.washcluster.net/file-download/download/public/52856

GWC. 2024. 'Coordination Resources'. GWC. Retrieved 18 February 2025. https://www.washcluster.net/coordination-resources

GWC. no date. 'GWC Coordination Tool Kit (CTK) – Confluence.' Accessed 9 April 2025. https://washcluster.atlassian.net/wiki/spaces/CTK/overview

GWC. 2025. "GWC Inter Cluster Collaboration-Coordination Matrix-Guidance Note." Global WASH Cluster. https://www.washcluster.net/node/32296.

Institute for Healthcare (IHI). 2017. *Quality Improvement Essentials Toolkit*. IHI. https://www.ihi.org/resources/tools/quality-improvement-essentials-toolkit

Inter-Agency Standing Committee (IASC). 2015. *Multi-Sector Initial Rapid Assessment (MIRA) Tool*. IASC. https://interagencystandingcommittee.org/sites/default/files/migrated/2019-02/mira_manual_2015.pdf

International Federation of Red Cross and Red Crescent Societies (IFRC). 2017. *WASH Guidelines for Hygiene Promotion in Emergency Operations*. Geneva: IFRC.

IFRC. 2021. *Community Engagement and Accountability (CEA) Toolkit*. IFRC. 16 August 2021. https://www.ifrc.org/document/cea-toolkit

Lopez, Jason, Sergio Tumax Sierra, Ana María Rodas Cardona, and Stephen Sara. 2020. 'Implementing the Clean Clinic Approach Improves Water, Sanitation, and Hygiene Quality in Health Facilities in the Western Highlands of Guatemala'. *Global Health: Science and Practice* 8 (2): 256–69. https://doi.org/10.9745/GHSP-D-19-00413

Médecins Sans Frontières (MSF). 2018. *Management of a Cholera Epidemic: Practical guide for doctors, nurses, laboratory technicians, medical auxiliaries, water and sanitation specialists and logisticians*. Médecins Sans Frontières. https://medicalguidelines.msf.org/en/viewport/CHOL/english/management-of-a-cholera-epidemic-23444438.html?language_content_entity=en

Organisation for Economic Co-operation and Development (OECD). 2018. *Implementing the OECD Principles on Water Governance: Indicator Framework and Evolving Practices*. Paris: OECD Publishing. https://doi.org/10.1787/9789264292659-en

Oxfam. 2013. *A Quick Guide to Monitoring, Evaluation, Accountability and Learning in Fragile Contexts*. Oxfam. https://policy-practice.oxfam.org/resources/a-quick-guide-to-monitoring-evaluation-accountability-and-learning-in-fragile-c-297134/

Oxfam. 2016. *Guide to Community Engagement in WaSH: A Practitioners' Guide, Based on Lessons from Ebola*. Oxfam. https://policy-practice.oxfam.org/resources/guide-to-community-engagement-in-wash-a-practitioners-guide-based-on-lessons-fr-620139/

SMART. 2017. 'Measuring Mortality, Nutritional Status, and Food Security in Crisis Situations: SMART Methodology.' SMART. https://smartmethodology.org/survey-planning-tools/smart-methodology/

Sphere Association. 2018. *The Sphere Handbook: Humanitarian Charter and Minimum Standards in Humanitarian Response*, 4th edn. Geneva, Switzerland: Sphere Association. www.spherestandards.org/handbook

Stockholm International Water Institute (SIWI) and UNICEF. 2020. *WASH Accountability in Fragile Contexts*. Stockholm and New York: UNICEF-UNDP-SIWI Accountability for Sustainability Partnership. https://siwi.org/publications/wash-accountability-in-fragile-contexts/

UNICEF. 2013. *UNICEF Cholera Toolkit*. UNICEF. https://www.washcluster.net/node/29581

UNICEF. 2016. *Nutrition-WASH Toolkits: Guide for Practical Joint Actions Nutrition-Water, Sanitation and Hygiene (WASH)*. https://www.unicef.org/eap/reports/nutrition-wash-toolkit-guide-practical-joint-actions

UNICEF. 2017. *Sustainability Checks: Guidance to Design and Implement Sustainability Monitoring in WASH*. New York and Stockholm: UNICEF and UNDP-SIWI.

UNICEF. no date. 'Water, Sanitation and Hygiene.' UNHCR USA. Accessed 9 April 2025. https://www.unhcr.org/us/what-we-do/respond-emergencies/water-sanitation-and-hygiene

UNICEF and Global Water Partnership (GWP). 2022. 'Strategic Framework for WASH Climate Resilient Development.' United Nations Children's Fund and Global Water Partnership.

UNICEF and SIWI. 2023. *WASH Bottleneck Analysis Tool: Country Implementation Guide*. New York: United Nations Children's Fund.

United Nations High Commissioner for Refugees (UNHCR). 2019. 'Uganda - WASH KAP Survey Palabek Settlement (Refugees & Host Community), October 2019'. https://microdata.unhcr.org/index.php/catalog/253/study-description

UNHCR. 2020. *UNHCR WASH Manual: Practical Guidance for Refugee Settings*. Geneva: UNHCR. https://www.unhcr.org/us/media/unhcr-wash-practical-guidance-refugee-settings

WASH in HCF. no date. 'WASH in HCF Evaluation and Reporting Tools'. WASH in Health Care Facilities. Accessed 9 April 2025. https://washinhcf.org/resource/wash-in-hcf-evaluation-and-reporting-tools/

World Health Organization (WHO). 2018. *Guidelines on Sanitation and Health*. Geneva: World Health Organization. https://www.who.int/publications/i/item/9789241514705

WHO. 2020. *Health Cluster Guide: A Practical Handbook*. WHO. https://healthcluster.who.int/publications/i/item/9789240004726

WHO. 2021. *Strengthening Infection Prevention and Control in Primary Care: A Collection of Existing Standards, Measurement and Implementation Resources*. Geneva: World Health Organization.

WHO. n.d. 'Outbreak Toolkit: Providing the Tools to Investigate Disease Outbreaks, Collect Data and Guide Response Activities'. Accessed 9 April 2025. https://www.who.int/emergencies/outbreak-toolkit

WHO and UNICEF. 2018. 'Core Questions on Drinking Water, Sanitation and Hygiene for Household Surveys: 2018 Update'. United Nations Children's Fund and World Health Organization.

WHO and UNICEF. 2020. *Operational Framework for Primary Health Care: Transforming Vision into Action*. Geneva: World Health Organization and United Nations Children's Fund.

WHO and UNICEF. 2022. *Water and Sanitation for Health Facility Improvement Tool (WASH FIT): A Practical Guide for Improving Quality of Care through Water, Sanitation and Hygiene in Health Care Facilities*, 2nd edn. Geneva: World Health Organization.

ANNEX 4
Case study references

Al-Basha, Farah. 2024. 'Implementation of Sustainable Groundwater Management in the Humanitarian Response in Yemen'. In *Climate Change and Water Scarcity in the Middle East: A Transitional Approach*, by Marïelle Snel, Nikolas Sorensen, and Reed Power, 1st edn, 119–21. London: Routledge. https://doi.org/10.4324/9781003436706

Al-Khateeb, Ali. 2024. 'Greening in Schools and Health Care Facilities in Iraq'. In *Climate Change and Water Scarcity in the Middle East: A Transitional Approach*, by Marïelle Snel, Nikolas Sorensen, and Reed Power, 1st edn, 122–23. London: Routledge. https://doi.org/10.4324/9781003436706

Bishara, Umar. 2021. 'Nigeria: Integrated WASH Programming'. In *Bridging the WASH Humanitarian-Development Divide: Building a Sustainable Reality*, by Marïelle Snel and Nikolas Sorensen, 27–28. Rugby UK: Practical Action Publishing Ltd. https://practicalactionpublishing.com/book/2577/bridging-the-wash-humanitariandevelopment-divide

Corwith, Anne, and Erin Sorensen. 2023. 'Integrated WASH and Education'. In *Addressing Conflict, COVID-19, and Climate Change: A Multisectoral Approach to Integrated WASH Programming*, edited by Marïelle Snel and Nikolas Sorensen. Rugby UK: Practical Action Publishing Ltd.

Dodos, Jovana, and Bram Riems. 2023. 'WASH-Nutrition Integration: For Vulnerable Populations Affected by Conflict, Climate Change and the COVID-19 Pandemic'. In *Addressing Conflict, COVID-19, and Climate Change: A Multisectoral Approach to Integrated WASH Programming*, edited by Marïelle Snel and Nikolas Sorensen, 85–108. Rugby UK: Practical Action Publishing.

Enwiya, Omeed. 2021. 'Iraq: WASH in Schools, Behavior Change Through Students, and Youth as Change Agents in Zakho District'. In *Bridging the WASH Humanitarian-Development Divide: Building a Sustainable Reality*, by Marïelle Snel and Nikolas Sorensen, 42–43. Rugby UK: Practical Action Publishing Ltd. https://practicalactionpublishing.com/book/2577/bridging-the-wash-humanitariandevelopment-divide

Jansen, Bert. 2024. 'BluElephant – Wastewater Treatment System'. In *Climate Change and Water Scarcity in the Middle East: A Transitional Approach*, by Marïelle Snel, Nikolas Sorensen, and Reed Power, 1st edn, 124–25. London: Routledge. https://doi.org/10.4324/9781003436706

Jeffery, Allison. 2023. 'Child Protection and WASH Integration'. In *Addressing Conflict, COVID-19, and Climate Change: A Multisectoral Approach to Integrated WASH Programming*, edited by Marïelle Snel and Nikolas Sorensen, 153–74. Rugby UK: Practical Action Publishing.

Keam, Rosanna. 2021. 'Afghanistan: Combined Humanitarian, Development, and Disaster Risk Reduction Projects'. In *Bridging the WASH Humanitarian-Development Divide: Building a Sustainable Reality*, by Mariëlle Snel and Nikolas Sorensen, 28–30. Rugby UK: Practical Action Publishing Ltd. https://practicalactionpublishing.com/book/2577/bridging-the-wash-humanitariandevelopment-divide

Kocharyan, Hasmik. 2021. 'Jordan: Environmentally Sustainable Solid Waste Management Project in Azraq Camp'. In *Bridging the WASH Humanitarian-Development Divide: Building a Sustainable Reality*, by Mariëlle Snel and Nikolas Sorensen, 30–31. Rugby UK: Practical Action Publishing Ltd. https://practicalactionpublishing.com/book/2577/bridging-the-wash-humanitariandevelopment-divide

Nyamoko, Peter. 2021. 'Yemen: Rehabilitating Water Systems for Conflict-Affected Populations'. In *Bridging the WASH Humanitarian-Development Divide: Building a Sustainable Reality*, by Mariëlle Snel and Nikolas Sorensen, 32–33. Rugby UK: Practical Action Publishing Ltd. https://practicalactionpublishing.com/book/2577/bridging-the-wash-humanitariandevelopment-divide

Sorensen, Nikolas, and Mariëlle Snel. 2023. 'Integrating WASH with Health in Humanitarian Settings'. In *Addressing Conflict, COVID-19, and Climate Change: A Multisectoral Approach to Integrated WASH Programming*, edited by Mariëlle Snel and Nikolas Sorensen. Rugby UK: Practical Action Publishing Ltd.

Thaw Si Htin Zaw. 2021. 'Myanmar: Multisectoral Approach to WASH in Emergencies'. In *Bridging the WASH Humanitarian-Development Divide: Building a Sustainable Reality*, by Mariëlle Snel and Nikolas Sorensen, 47–49. Rugby UK: Practical Action Publishing Ltd. https://practicalactionpublishing.com/book/2577/bridging-the-wash-humanitariandevelopment-divide

Webb, Susannah. 2023. 'Integrated WASH and Shelter'. In *Addressing Conflict, COVID-19, and Climate Change: A Multisectoral Approach to Integrated WASH Programming*, edited by Mariëlle Snel and Nikolas Sorensen, 109–34. Rugby UK: Practical Action Publishing.

Index

Accountability mechanisms xix, xxi, 12–13, 16, 48, 51, 66–67, 72, 77, 87, 90, 92, 118, 217
Action Against Hunger (ACF) 71
Action plans (integrated) xxxi, 54, 73, 77, 79, 82, 87, 90–91, 93, 99, 108, 111, 116, 122, 137–138, 143, 146, 172
Afghanistan 41–42
After action review (AAR) xv, 55, 189, 219,
Aid Fund for Northern Syria (AFNS) 150–151
Artificial intelligence (AI) 147, 151–152
Assessment checklists 4
Assessment tools 13, 40, 94, 121, 128, 146, 157, 159, 173, 191
Azraq refugee camp 137

Bangladesh 16–17
Baseline assessments 92
Behaviour change communication 43, 61, 69, 117, 160, 201–202
Blended finance arrangements 14, 16
BluElephant wastewater treatment 104

Capacity assessment tools 191
Capacity building plans 106, 133, 193–194
CCP pressures (climate, conflict, and pandemics) ix, xv, xxiv, xxvi, 4, 6–10, 12–14, 18–20, 145
Central Emergency Response Fund (CERF) 184
Checklists (various) 4, 29–31, 40, 54, 59–61, 77, 79, 83, 85, 96, 110, 115, 117, 123, 127, 146, 159–160, 163, 172, 177–179, 181–182, 185, 204, 206, 211, 213, 216–217
Child protection 9, 12
Clean clinic teams 20, 93
Climate adaptation xxi, 1, 152
Climate change xvii, 1, 4, 6, 8, 17–18, 42, 48, 95, 107, 149, 152, 223
Collaborative quality improvement (CQI) xv, 220–221
Community committees xxx–xxxi, 85, 96, 117, 127, 146, 160, 222
Community dialogues 71, 87, 98, 118, 123
Community engagement xx, 8, 13, 18, 31, 33, 39, 41, 43, 45, 47–48, 61–62, 71, 73, 83, 85, 94, 96, 115, 117, 127, 152, 160, 172, 183, 188–190, 192, 205, 207, 214, 216, 218
Community level xv, xviii, 43, 45, 48, 59, 69, 70, 72–73, 76, 79, 81, 83–85, 87, 96, 104, 108, 113–118, 125, 127–128, 134, 139–140, 146, 160, 165, 177, 194, 201
Community mapping (participatory) 58, 79, 85, 96, 117–118, 120–121, 188, 214
Community scorecards xxxi, 51, 77, 87, 109–110, 118, 142, 189
Community-based management of acute malnutrition (CMAM) 202
Community-led total sanitation (CLTS) xv, 129, 190, 202, 207
Complaint mechanisms 76, 176, 189
Conflict-sensitive programming xv, 8
Coordination committee terms of reference (TOR) templates 60, 85, 117, 159, 163, 206
Coordination mechanisms xvi, xxi, xxvii, xxxiii, 1–2, 6, 12, 32, 35, 38, 44, 57, 60, 62, 64–65, 67, 72, 87, 103, 112, 118, 123, 125–126, 131, 134, 140, 146, 161, 194, 211–212

Coordination performance scorecards 30, 60, 67, 159, 171
Coordination platforms xx, 29–30, 59, 64, 67, 83, 115, 133, 139, 141, 143, 145, 157–159, 163–164, 181, 183, 191–192, 217, 221
Coordination timelines, 37, 51, 53, 91–92, 122, 183, 186, 214, 217
Cox's Bazar 17

Data collection xxx, 14, 37, 50–51, 54, 65, 76–77, 80, 83, 92, 108, 111, 120, 127–128, 138, 140–141, 143, 158, 177–178, 189, 193, 195, 209, 220, 222
Data science 152
Data sharing protocols 18, 37, 77, 91
Decision-making frameworks 19
Digital technologies 147
Disease surveillance 28, 33, 37, 40, 44, 54, 94, 98, 101, 141, 200, 212–213

Emergency actions (0–14 days) 29, 39, 59, 68, 83, 96, 115, 127
Emergency response protocols 147
Environmental enteropathy xvi–xvii, 186
European Civil Protection and Humanitarian Aid Operations (ECHO) 184
Exit strategies 125–126

Facility-based WASH improvement 82, 87, 92–93, 102
Feedback mechanisms xx, 28, 39, 67, 77, 85, 91, 98, 123, 135, 141, 166, 200, 208, 214, 218
Focus group discussions 51, 79, 97, 120, 142, 188, 190, 214, 217
Food and Agriculture Organization (FAO) of the United Nations 162
Foundational principles xix
Framework pillars 29, 59, 83, 115

Gaza 8, 13
Gender-based violence (GBV) 42, 130, 218
Geographic information systems (GIS) 152
Global acute malnutrition (GAM) 71, 184
Global Alliance for Vaccines and Immunization (GAVI) 184
Global WASH Cluster (GWC) 148, 185, 190–191
Ground Truth Solutions (GTS) 5, 150

Health facilities xxxii, 28, 41, 43, 45, 53, 55, 80–84, 87, 92–93, 97, 101–103, 105, 109–110, 135, 171–172, 176, 178–179, 186, 209, 211
Health management information system (HMIS) 37, 54, 67, 209
Health system capacity mapping 31, 40, 160, 193
Household surveys 51, 54, 79, 110, 120, 142, 177, 211
Humanitarian–development–peace nexus xvi, 6–7, 10, 223
Humanitarian response xvi–xvii, 1, 3, 7, 10, 12–13, 17–18, 62, 104, 148, 171, 208, 211, 213
Hygiene promotion xxx, 8, 13, 17, 28, 38, 43, 47, 63, 70, 82, 86, 90, 96, 98, 100–101, 158, 161, 172, 180, 184, 190, 192, 198–199, 205, 210, 218

IDP camps 8, 12–13
Impact bonds 16
Implementation tools 146, 158, 160, 194
Infant and young child feeding (IYCF) 13, 68, 71, 79, 128, 139, 178, 184, 200
Infection prevention and control (IPC) 20, 31, 33, 40–41, 53–54, 85, 94, 99, 110, 153, 159, 161, 169, 172, 180, 182, 193, 208
Information management 3, 30, 32–33, 51, 62, 65, 67, 77, 91–92, 108, 140, 170, 195, 198
Innovative financing 10, 14–16, 95, 148, 153
Integrated action plan xxxi

Integrated phase classification (IPC) for WASH 15
Integrated programming xvi, 4, 15–16, 20, 53, 71, 76, 121–123, 126–127, 130, 171, 194
Inter-Cluster Coordination Group (ICCG) 162, 164
International Federation of Red Cross and Red Crescent Societies (IFRC) 190, 216
International Organization for Migration (IOM) 46, 52
Internet of Things (IoT) 152
Intersectoral coordination (ISC) xvi, 1, 9, 12–14, 16, 18
Iraq 106–107, 132

Joint Monitoring Programme (JMP) 14–15, 41, 51, 108, 177, 211
Joint workplan 31, 61, 85, 117, 160, 194
Jordan 136–137

Knowledge, Attitudes and Practices (KAP) 71, 79, 110, 128, 177, 209

Learning and adaptation 94, 105, 125, 137
Learning exchanges 77, 95, 105, 111, 126, 141, 190, 192
Localization xvi, xxiii, 5, 13–14, 132, 145, 148–149, 151, 153, 158–159

Malnutrition xvi–xvii, xix, xxv, xxviii, 9, 59, 66, 68, 70–71, 100–101, 122, 131, 135, 138–139, 177–178, 184, 186, 200, 202, 208–209
Mapping tools (stakeholder) 30, 34, 60–61, 65–66, 74, 85, 117, 159, 166, 206
Menstrual hygiene management (MHM) 129, 176, 183, 200
Mid-upper arm circumference (MUAC) 128, 176, 184, 203, 208
Ministry of Health (MOH) 33, 37, 63, 93, 129–130, 169, 184, 194
Monitoring and evaluation (M&E) xvi, xxiv, xxxi–xxxii, 4, 9, 14–15, 17, 20, 35, 46–47, 49, 77, 80, 91, 164, 179, 183, 200, 208, 215
Monitoring, evaluation, accountability and learning (MEAL) 211
Monitoring frameworks (integrated) 4, 51, 55, 77, 80, 91, 108, 140
Monthly reporting 55, 85, 96, 117, 127, 160, 222
Multi-stakeholder platforms 72
Myanmar 8, 12–13, 17

National level xvii, xxiii, xxvii, xxxii, 27, 29–31, 35, 50, 54, 57, 59–62, 64, 76, 80, 83–84, 108, 115–116, 140–141, 145–146, 157, 163, 194, 222
Network analysis (social) 85, 117, 122, 159, 167
Nigeria 12, 14, 18, 70–71, 73, 100, 147
Non-governmental organizations (NGOs) xvi–xvii, 18, 29, 32, 34, 62, 64–65, 90, 148–149, 151, 161, 170, 194
Nutrition-sensitive WASH xvii, 9, 58–61, 69, 72–73, 114, 117, 122, 127, 137–139, 146, 159–160, 170, 177, 185, 187
Nutrition-sensitive WASH risk 61, 117, 159, 177, 185

Operation and maintenance (O&M) 42, 75, 100, 104, 106, 170, 180, 189, 193, 207, 210, 217–218
Oral rehydration therapy (ORT) 101
Outbreak management 153
Outreach strategies 123, 204

Pandemics xv, xvii, xix, xxiv, xxvi, 1, 4, 8, 17–18, 145
Participatory assessment 50, 84, 139, 146, 165
Participatory community mapping 58, 79, 85, 96, 117–118, 120–121, 188, 214

Participatory hygiene and sanitation transformation (PHAST) xvii, 190, 202
Participatory impact assessment 220
Participatory monitoring xx, 5, 49, 72–73, 77, 87, 107–108, 118, 134, 138
Performance review 31, 40, 61, 80, 85, 117, 143, 160, 219
Plan-Do-Study-Act (PDSA) xv, 20, 220
Planning frameworks 16
Pooled funding mechanisms 15, 149
Pregnant and lactating women (PLW) 70–71, 139, 142, 184, 186
Private sector partnerships xvii, 147
Protection from sexual exploitation, abuse, and harassment (PSEAH) 216
Public–private partnerships 47, 104, 150, 152

Quality improvement xv, xvii, 15, 20, 78, 83, 109, 135, 220–222

Refugee settlements 16–17
Reporting templates 208–209
Resilience actions (14–90 days) 29, 39, 46, 59, 72, 84, 102, 116, 132
Risk communication 31, 85, 160, 205, 213
Roles and responsibilities 30, 33–34, 36, 45, 54, 60, 63, 66, 79, 84–85, 88–90, 93, 102, 105–106, 111, 116–117, 143, 159, 164–165, 169, 172, 181, 183, 192, 201, 206

Save the Children 8, 12–14, 18, 75, 86, 90, 100, 132, 149
Scorecard xxxi, 30, 51, 54, 60, 67, 72, 77, 80, 87, 108–110, 112, 118, 140–142, 144, 159, 171–172, 189
Social accountability xvii, xx, 87, 109, 118
Social network analysis 85, 117, 122, 159, 167
Solar-powered 74–75, 106–107, 137
Stakeholder analysis 30, 60, 85, 117, 159, 166
Stakeholder coordination xxiv, 4, 9, 20, 30–31, 33, 60–61, 63–64, 84, 86, 116, 118, 153, 169–170
Stakeholder identification 30–31, 40, 60–61, 85, 117, 159, 160, 163
Stakeholder mapping 30, 34, 61, 65–66, 74, 206
Standardized Monitoring and Assessment of Relief and Transitions (SMART) 67, 128, 158, 179, 184, 195, 209
Strategic Advisory Group (SAG) 64
Strategy development 58, 60–61, 69, 114, 117, 122, 138, 160, 185, 193
Strengths-based approach xvii, 4–6, 145
Supportive supervision 31, 85, 94, 96, 117, 126, 143, 160, 173, 194, 207, 216, 218
Sustainability planning 28, 45, 48, 82, 149
Sustainable Development Goals (SDGs) xxviii, 77, 108
SuSanA's Monitoring and Evaluation Toolkit 15
Syria 86–87, 90, 129–130, 137, 150

Templates (various) 4, 10, 20, 27, 29–30, 54, 59–60, 83–84, 115–116, 121, 146, 157–158, 165, 185, 199, 201–202, 208–209
Terms of reference (TOR) 30, 33, 60, 63, 85, 87–88, 92–93, 117, 119, 127, 159–160, 163, 165, 181, 206
Transition planning 28, 126, 133, 193

United Nations (UN) xvii, xxvi, 17, 27, 31–32, 34–35, 57, 60–62, 64–65, 85, 90, 117, 162, 167, 170, 177, 211
United Nations Children's Fund (UNICEF) 14–15, 17, 20, 28, 32–34, 41, 51, 62–63, 67, 107–108, 149, 162, 170, 177,

181–182, 184–185, 187, 194, 199, 211
United Nations Development Programme (UNDP) 170
United Nations High Commissioner for Refugees (UNHCR) 162, 170, 177, 198, 211
United Nations Office for the Coordination of Humanitarian Affairs (OCHA) 63, 67, 137, 162
User-centred approaches 16–17, 158

Vulnerability 4, 44, 51, 59, 108, 174, 177, 182, 222

WASH AI platforms 151
Wastewater treatment 104
Water and Sanitation for Health Facility Improvement Tool (WASH FIT) 14–15, 54, 79, 170, 181, 189–190, 204, 212
Water quality monitoring 100, 104, 152
Water trucking 41, 52, 70, 98
West Bank 104
Workplan 31, 61, 85, 117, 122, 160, 194
World Food Programme (WFP) 63, 162, 170
World Health Organization (WHO) 14–15, 28, 32–34, 41, 51, 107–108, 162, 170, 177, 181–182, 184–185, 187, 211, 213
World Vision International 42

Yemen 8, 46, 52, 74–75

www.ingramcontent.com/pod-product-compliance
Lightning Source LLC
LaVergne TN
LVHW021132160826
845679LV00016B/1724
* 9 7 8 1 7 8 8 5 3 4 7 0 3 *